Maggie O'Farrell

Contemporary Critical Perspectives

Series Editors: Jeannette Baxter, Peter Childs, Sebastian Groes and
Sean Matthews

Guides in the *Contemporary Critical Perspectives* series provide companions
to reading and studying major contemporary authors. They include new
critical essays combining textual readings, cultural analysis and discussion of
key critical and theoretical issues in a clear, accessible style. Each guide also
includes a preface by a major contemporary writer, a new interview with the
author, discussion of film and TV adaptation and guidance on further reading.

Titles in the series include:

J. G. Ballard edited by Jeannette Baxter
Ian McEwan edited by Sebastian Groes
Kazuo Ishiguro edited by Sean Matthews and Sebastian Groes
Julian Barnes edited by Sebastian Groes and Peter Childs
Sarah Waters edited by Kaye Mitchell
Salman Rushdie edited by Robert Eaglestone and Martin McQuillan
Andrea Levy edited by Jeannette Baxter and David James
Ali Smith edited by Monica Germanà and Emily Horton
Hanif Kureishi edited by Susan Alice Fischer
Don DeLillo edited by Katherine Da Cunha Lewin and Kiron Ward
Hilary Mantel edited by Eileen Pollard and Ginette Carpenter
John Burnside edited by Ben Davies
David Mitchell edited by Wendy Knepper and Courtney Hopf

Upcoming Titles

Rachel Cusk edited by Roberta Garrett and Liam Harrison

Maggie O'Farrell

Contemporary Critical Perspectives

Edited by
Elaine Canning

BLOOMSBURY ACADEMIC
LONDON • NEW YORK • OXFORD • NEW DELHI • SYDNEY

BLOOMSBURY ACADEMIC
Bloomsbury Publishing Plc
50 Bedford Square, London, WC1B 3DP, UK
1385 Broadway, New York, NY 10018, USA
29 Earlsfort Terrace, Dublin 2, Ireland

BLOOMSBURY, BLOOMSBURY ACADEMIC and the Diana logo are trademarks
of Bloomsbury Publishing Plc

First published in Great Britain 2024

For legal purposes the Acknowledgements on p. viii constitute an extension
of this copyright page.

Cover Design: Eleanor Rose
Cover image © Yumeee/ Shutterstock

A catalogue record for this book is available from the British Library.

Library of Congress Cataloging-in-Publication Data
Names: Canning, Elaine M., 1973- author.
Title: Maggie O'Farrell : contemporary critical perspectives / edited by Elaine Canning.
Description: London ; New York : Bloomsbury Academic, 2023. | Series: Contemporary critical
perspectives | Includes bibliographical references and index.
Identifiers: LCCN 2023020473 (print) | LCCN 2023020474 (ebook) | ISBN 9781350325005
(hardback) | ISBN 9781350325043 (paperback) | ISBN 9781350325012 (pdf) | ISBN
9781350325029 (epub)
Subjects: LCSH: O'Farrell, Maggie, 1972–Criticism and interpretation. | English literature–
Northern Irish authors–History and criticism.
Classification: LCC PR6065.F36 Z63 2023 (print) | LCC PR6065.F36 (ebook) | DDC 823/.914–dc23/
eng/20230628
LC record available at https://lccn.loc.gov/2023020473
LC ebook record available at https://lccn.loc.gov/2023020474

ISBN: HB: 978-1-3503-2500-5
ePDF: 978-1-3503-2501-2
eBook: 978-1-3503-2502-9

Typeset by Deanta Global Publishing Services, Chennai, India

Series: Contemporary Critical Perspectives

To find out more about our authors and books visit www.bloomsbury.com
and sign up for our newsletters.

Contents

Series Editors' Preface   vii

Acknowledgements   viii

List of Contributors   ix

Chronology of Maggie O'Farrell's Life and Works   xii

Introduction: In Search of Maggie O'Farrell

Elaine Canning   1

1   'The Space Between': Maggie O'Farrell's *The Vanishing Act of Esme Lennox*

     Susan Alice Fischer   9

2   Love, Loss and (Be)longing in *After You'd Gone* and *The Distance Between Us*

     Elaine Canning   22

3   'The Women We Become after Children': Palimpsests of the City and the Self in Maggie O'Farrell's *The Hand that First Held Mine*

     Ruth Gilligan   31

4   Vantage Points: How Maggie O'Farrell Dissects a Marriage by Shifting Points of View in *This Must Be the Place*

     Edward Matthews   46

5   Lost in Translation: The Dis-located Structures of Maggie O'Farrell's *My Lover's Lover*

     Sarah Gamble   60

6   'A Small Victory for Love over Death': The Haunted Narratives of *I Am, I Am, I Am, Instructions for a Heatwave* and *The Hand that First Held Mine*

     Tasha Alden   75

7   The Taming Shrew: Agnes in Maggie O'Farrell's *Hamnet* as (Early) Modern Husbander

     Nicholas Taylor-Collins   89

8   Filling Historical and Emotional Voids: *Hamnet*
     Laurie Maguire   106

9   Remaking the Duchess: Underpainting and Overpainting in *The
     Marriage Portrait*
     Elaine Canning   121

'Post-it Baby': An Interview with Maggie O'Farrell
Elaine Canning   129

Bibliography   145
Further Reading   154
Index   159

Series Editors' Preface

The readership for contemporary fiction has never been greater. The explosion of reading groups and literary blogs, of university courses and school curricula, and even the apparent rude health of the literary marketplace indicate an ever-growing appetite for new work, for writing which responds to the complex, changing and challenging times in which we live. At the same time, readers seem ever more eager to engage in conversations about their reading, to devour the review pages, to pack the sessions at literary festivals and author events. Reading is an increasingly social activity, as we seek to share and refine our experience of the book, to clarify and extend our understanding. It is this tremendous enthusiasm for contemporary fiction to which the Contemporary Critical Perspectives series responds. Our ambition is to offer readers of current fiction a comprehensive critical account of each author's work, presenting original, specially commissioned analyses of all aspects of their career, from a variety of different angles and approaches, as well as directions towards further reading and research. Our brief to the contributors is to be scholarly, to draw on the latest thinking about narrative, or philosophy, or psychology, indeed whatever seemed to them most significant in drawing out the meanings and force of the texts in question, but also to focus closely on the words on the page, the stories and scenarios and forms which all of us meet first when we open a book. We insisted that these essays be accessible to that mythical beast, the Common Reader, who might just as readily be spotted at the Lowdham Book Festival as in a college seminar. In this way, we hope to have presented critical assessments of our writers in such a way as to contribute something to both of those environments, and also to have done something to bring together the most important qualities of each of them.

Jeannette Baxter, Peter Childs, Sebastian Groes and Sean Matthews.

Acknowledgements

First of all, I would like to express my heartfelt thanks to Maggie O'Farrell herself who gave her time so generously in June 2022 to spend a few hours in conversation with me. Huge thanks also to Maggie for her wonderful novels, memoir and picture books which have of course inspired this critical guide and made the writing of it possible. The composition of this collection of essays has allowed me to enjoy Maggie's novels all over again, as well as to engage with her latest new novel and children's books.

Special thanks also to the brilliant and incomparable Mary-Anne Harrington, Maggie's editor, who received my email queries with so much kindness and enthusiasm and supported in every way she could. You are a star, Mary-Anne!

Many thanks to all the fantastic, expert contributors from the UK and US who have made this volume what it is. Thanks for bearing with my messages and notes, for always responding so warmly and professionally, and for sharing your scholarship with me and everyone who may read this book.

Thank you to the series editors – Jeannette Baxter, Peter Childs, Sebastian Groes and Sean Matthews – for commissioning this volume. And huge gratitude to Lucy Brown and Aanchal Vij at Bloomsbury Publishing for their endless support and advice.

Finally, thanks to my family, for everything.

Contributors

Tasha Alden is Senior Lecturer in Contemporary Fiction at Aberystwyth University. Her monograph *Reading Behind the Lines: Postmemory, History, Story* (2014) explored the uses of the past in a selection of recent historical novels, focusing on postmemory as a lens through which to understand innovation in historical fiction representing the World Wars. She has also written on Sarah Waters, Pat Barker, David Jones, Adam Thorpe, Ian McEwan and Emma Donoghue, and is currently working on the uses of the past in contemporary queer writing, on form and grace in the works of Marilynne Robinson and Iris Murdoch, and on language and metaphor in reproductive immunology. Her research interests include memory, ethics and empathy, the historical novel and queer writing.

Elaine Canning is a writer, editor and public engagement specialist living in Swansea, South Wales, and a Fellow of the Learned Society of Wales. Originally from Belfast, she holds an MA and PhD in Hispanic Studies from Queen's University, Belfast, and an MA in Creative Writing from Swansea University. She is currently Head of Special Projects at Swansea University, which include the Rhys Davies National Short Story Competition and the International Dylan Thomas Prize. She has authored a monograph and papers on Spanish Golden-Age drama, and her short stories have appeared in *Nation.Cymru* and *The Lonely Crowd*. She is editor of *Take a Bite: The Rhys Davies Short Story Award Anthology* (2021), *New World, New Beginnings: Resilience and Connectivity through Poetry* (2021) and *Cree: The Rhys Davies Short Story Award Anthology* (2022). Her debut novel, *The Sandstone City*, was published by Aderyn Press in 2022 and featured on Wales Arts Review's 2022 list of top ten long-form fiction titles.

Susan Alice Fischer is Professor and Chair of the English Department at Medgar Evers College of The City University of New York. She has published on women's London narratives and migration literature, and is a co-editor of *Changing English: Studies in Culture and Education*. Her edited volume on Hanif Kureishi appeared in the series 'Contemporary Critical Perspectives'.

Sarah Gamble is Associate Professor of English with Gender at Swansea University, Wales, where she specializes in women's writing and the contemporary

Gothic. She is the author of *Angela Carter: Writing from the Front Line* (1997) and *Angela Carter: A Literary Life* (2004) and the editor of *The Fiction of Angela Carter* (2001). She has also published articles on a range of contemporary women writers, such as Sarah Waters, Pat Barker and Maggie O'Farrell. She is currently researching the influence of art on Carter's work and writing a book on gender and tattooing.

Ruth Gilligan is an Irish novelist and academic now based in the UK, where she works as Professor of Creative Writing at the University of Birmingham. She has published five novels to date and was the youngest person ever to top the Irish bestsellers' list. Her most recent novel, *The Butchers* (2020), won the 2021 Royal Society of Literature Prize, awarded to the book that best encapsulates the 'spirit of a place'. Gilligan is an ambassador for the global storytelling charity Narrative 4, which runs 'story exchange' projects between diverse young people around the world in the hope of breaking down barriers and fostering empathy. She also contributes regular literary reviews to publications such as the *Times Literary Supplement*, *Irish Independent* and the *Guardian*.

Laurie Maguire is Professor of English Emerita at Oxford University and Fellow of Magdalen College. She is the author or co-author of ten books on Shakespeare and Renaissance Drama, with research interests in performance history, classical reception, textual studies and medical humanities. Her most recent book, based on her 2018 British Library Panizzi lectures, is *The Rhetoric of the Page* (2020). She is currently writing a biography of Judith Shakespeare.

Edward Matthews received his PhD in Creative Writing from Swansea University in 2020. His publications include *Journal of Borderlands Studies*, *Reed Magazine*, *Construction Literary Magazine*, *STORGY* and *Zero Hours on the Boulevard*, a Brexit short story collection. He has worked as an editor and marketing officer at the Welsh independent publisher *Parthian Books*, where he edited *Ironopolis*, a novel that was nominated for the Orwell Prize for Political Fiction and the Portico Prize. He has also interviewed winners of the Dylan Thomas Prize for Swansea University, creating a podcast out of conversations with writers such as Max Porter and Joshua Ferris. His debut novel, *Border Memories*, was published in 2022. He currently works as a researcher for community colleges in San Diego, California, USA.

Nicholas Taylor-Collins is Senior Lecturer in English at Cardiff Metropolitan University. He has previously taught at Swansea University and the University of

Warwick. Taylor-Collins has published extensively on the Shakespeare–modern Irish literature connection, notably in his monograph *Shakespeare, Memory, and Modern Irish Literature* (2022), and his co-edited *Shakespeare and Contemporary Irish literature* (2018). He has also published articles in *Modern Language Review, Cahiers Elisabéthains, Irish Studies Review, The Yearbook of English Studies* and *Notes and Queries*. Separately, he is the author of *Judge for Yourself* (2020), a book designed to help undergraduates and book-club members read, evaluate and judge brand-new ('hyper-contemporary') writing with confidence. He is now researching his next monograph, *Guardian of Death: John Banville's Affirmation of Life*.

Chronology of Maggie O'Farrell's Life and Works

1972   Maggie O'Farrell was born in Coleraine, Northern Ireland, on 27 May. Her family moved to Britain in 1974 but she continued to spend childhood summers in Ireland. She grew up in Scotland and Wales, attending Brynteg Comprehensive School (Bridgend, Wales) and North Berwick High School (East Lothian, Scotland).

1980   Hospitalized with encephalitis (account featured in 'Cerebellum, 1980' in O'Farrell's memoir *I Am, I Am, I Am* (2017)). Immobilized for a year; it took another year for Maggie to learn to walk again. During the long stint in hospital, she was an avid reader for as long as she was able to hold a book; when she couldn't, she listened to audiobooks.

1990s   Read English Literature at New Hall, Cambridge University (now Murray Edwards College). She met her future husband, novelist William Sutcliffe, while studying at Cambridge. She went on to become a journalist based in Hong Kong and London, including working as deputy literary editor at the *Independent*. While undertaking her role at the *Independent*, she began writing her debut novel, *After You'd Gone*.

2000   *After You'd Gone* published by Headline Review to international acclaim. According to *Kirkus Reviews*, 'O'Farrell is an astute observer of little behaviors, the telling fidgets and habits of everyday existence, and she's at her best when piecing these together to create a sense of a real life experienced through fiction. The complex structure works beautifully, communicating the shared and interlocking sufferings of the Raikes women through its carefully worked-out layering of narrative lines.'

2001   *After You'd Gone* wins a Betty Trask Award for a first novel by an author under the age of thirty-five.

2002   Publishes *My Lover's Lover* (Headline Review).

2004   *The Distance Between Us* published by Headline Review. Wins the
         Society of Authors' Somerset Maugham Award in 2005.

2006   Publishes *The Vanishing Act of Esme Lennox* (Headline Review).
         'The prose is spare, yet the Edwardian world it describes crosses two
         continents and is rich and clear as stained glass', writes Jane Gardam
         in the *Guardian*.

2010   *The Hand that First Held Mine* published by Headline Review.
         Winner of the 2010 Costa Novel Award. Moves to Edinburgh.

2013   Publishes *Instructions for a Heatwave* (Tinder Press, Headline).
         Shortlisted for the 2013 Costa Novel Award.

2016   *This Must Be the Place* publishes with Tinder Press, Headline.
         Shortlisted for the 2016 Costa Novel Award.

2017   Publishes memoir *I Am, I Am, I Am: Seventeen Brushes with Death*
         (Tinder Press, Headline). A *Sunday Times* No. 1 Bestseller. Shortlisted
         for the PEN Ackerley Prize for a literary autobiography of excellence
         (2018) and longlisted for the Wellcome Book Prize 2018.

2020   Twenty years after the publication of her first novel, *After You'd
         Gone*, Tinder Press (Headline) publishes Maggie's multi-award-
         winning eighth novel, *Hamnet*, a re-imagining of Shakespeare's
         young son, Hamnet, with his mother, Agnes, centre-stage. A *Sunday
         Times* Bestseller. Winner of the 2020 Women's Prize for Fiction;
         the 2020 Waterstones Book of the Year Award; the National Book
         Critics Circle Prize for Fiction in 2021; Fiction Book of the Year at
         the 2021 British Book Awards; and best novel at the Dalkey Literary
         Awards (2021). Shortlisted for the Walter Scott Prize and longlisted
         for the Andrew Carnegie Medal for Excellence in Fiction (both 2021).
         2020 also marks the year when Maggie releases her first children's
         book, *Where Snow Angels Go*, published by Walker Books with
         illustrations by Daniela Jaglenka Terrazzini.

2021   Elected a fellow of the Royal Society of Literature.

2022   *The Marriage Portrait* published by Tinder Press, Headline. A *New
         York Times* Bestseller; Reese Witherspoon's Book Club December
         2022 pick; '100 Must Read Books of 2022' (*TIME*).
         Releases her second book for children, *The Boy Who Lost His Spark*,
         published by Walker Books with illustrations by Daniela Jaglenka
         Terrazzini.

2023   1 April–17 June: Royal Shakespeare Company's dramatization of *Hamnet* at the Swan Theatre, Stratford-upon-Avon; 30 September 2023–6 January 2024: RSC's dramatization at the Garrick Theatre, London.

A film adaptation of *Hamnet* is also underway with Amblin Partners, Hera Pictures and Neal Street Productions: Chloé Zhao to direct and co-adapt script with Maggie herself.

Maggie lives in Edinburgh with her husband, William Sutcliffe, and their three children.

Introduction

In Search of Maggie O'Farrell

Elaine Canning

A critically acclaimed and award-winning author, including the recipient of the prestigious Women's Prize for Fiction (2020), Maggie O'Farrell is one of Britain's most successful contemporary fiction writers. Her debut novel *After You'd Gone* was released in 2000 to international acclaim; it set the bar for a further eight novels over a twenty-year period, culminating in her latest novel, *The Marriage Portrait*, in 2022, a bold re-imagining of the dynastic society of Renaissance Italy and a young woman's perilous place within it. A novelist first and foremost, O'Farrell's novels 'appeal to a broad audience, but they're also smart and provocative. Over and over, they try to work out who people really are, how ordinary lives can conceal extraordinary stories' (D'Erasmo 2013). Her penchant for a non-chronological, non-sequential narrative style is one which she continues to develop in her *Sunday Times* bestselling memoir *I Am, I Am, I Am: Seventeen Brushes with Death*. O'Farrell asserts: 'I've never been an adherent to chronology and I don't particularly like using it as a narrative structure. To me, stories are not linear, they don't go very neatly in a line from A to B' (see 'Post-it Baby': 129). O'Farrell's work masterfully navigates time and narrative perspective to create complex worlds where identities are blurred, doubled, haunted, fragmented and re-incarnated.

Awards and Accolades

Since the publication of her debut novel, O'Farrell's work has received numerous awards and accolades. The first came in 2001 when *After You'd Gone* won a Betty Trask award for a first novel by an author under the age of thirty-five; this was followed by the Society of Authors' Somerset Maugham Award in 2005 for *The Distance Between Us*. On *The Vanishing Act of Esme Lennox* (2006), Strehle writes: 'While this novel did not win prizes, it sold well, earned O'Farrell good reviews on both sides of the Atlantic, and was highly praised' (Strehle 2017: 66). In 2007, Waterstones included O'Farrell in their '25 Authors for the Future' list, while nominations for the Costa Novel Award followed for her next three novels: she won the award in 2010 for *The Hand that First Held Mine* and was shortlisted in 2013 and 2016 respectively for *Instructions for a Heatwave* and *This Must Be the Place*.

According to Strehle, 'O'Farrell's record of positive reviews, literary prizes and healthy sales suggests that twenty-first-century readers remain interested in realist human narratives' (2017: 61). It was three years after this assertion that O'Farrell's international profile peaked with the publication of *Hamnet*, a sixteenth-century Shakespeare-inspired story with the Bard's son and wife centre-stage. The recipient of rave reviews, together with an array of some of the world's most distinguished literary prizes, including the 2020 Women's Prize for Fiction and the 2021 National Book Critics Circle Prize for Fiction, *Hamnet*, I would argue, significantly broadened O'Farrell's standing within cross-cultural, transatlantic dialogues on contemporary fiction. Moreover, the staging of *Hamnet* by the Royal Shakespeare Company in the summer of 2023, along with future plans for a film adaptation of the work, are certain to introduce O'Farrell to a more varied, diverse readership. Her most recent novel – *The Marriage Portrait* – set in sixteenth-century Italy continues to draw US attention as a *New York Times* bestseller and one of '100 Must Read Books of 2022' (*TIME*).

Despite having enjoyed much commercial success and recognition by industry leads, including booksellers, journalists, literary awards and festivals, the number of critical essays dedicated to O'Farrell's work remains extremely limited. It is therefore the aim of this guide to redress the balance, to elucidate the multi-textured, multi-perspectival, multi-temporal nature of O'Farrell's work within the contemporary literary landscape.

The Novels

Two months before the US publication of *After You'd Gone*, *Kirkus Reviews* described O'Farrell as 'an astute observer of little behaviors, the telling fidgets and habits of everyday existence, and she's at her best when piecing these together to create a sense of a real life experienced through fiction'. On her debut itself, they continued: 'The complex structure works beautifully, communicating the shared and interlocking sufferings of the Raikes women through its carefully worked-out layering of narrative lines' ('*After You'd Gone*' 2001). For O'Farrell, there's a need to reinvent method every time to avoid writing the same book. With each book, she tries to do something different, learn something different (see 'Post-it Baby': 130). Her nine novels are set within a range of time frames with varying focal characters and narrative points of view, but there is an ongoing preoccupation with narrative layering and non-chronological storytelling in a style which is uniquely O'Farrell's. While she explores different characters affected by circumstance, miscommunication, absences and disappearances, her novels pivot around recurring complex human stories about love, loss and grief and are overshadowed by spectres and secrets. On writing about *The Hand that First Held Mine*, Day asserts: 'Maggie O'Farrell's particular talent is for hinting at the disquiet that lurks beneath our relationships. Her four previous novels have each been shaped by the psychological unravelling of characters who stumble across hidden truths and past distortions' (Day 2010). Female characters abound in all her novels, including women in the margins, with complicated histories, motivations and concerns; but there are, too, male characters which are sensitively drawn and granted a substantial degree of psychological depth.

Take John Friedmann, for example, in *After You'd Gone*, the love of Alice Raikes's life whose own life is tragically cut short when he becomes a victim of a London bombing. He is dead at the point where the story begins but nevertheless is frequently present through Alice's musings and memories, through the temporal shifts which move from his and Alice's first encounter to the development and affirmation of their relationship. A man pressurized by filial duty to the father who will only welcome a daughter-in-law of Jewish descent, John disregards his father's wishes and chooses Alice as his wife, simultaneously selecting the burden of estranged son.

Daniel, in *This Must Be the Place*, is also deeply complex; he is a man with his own pressures, both externally and internally imposed. As Matthews demonstrates in this volume, Daniel is presented through multiple narrative voices which expose his multifaceted personality.

What unifies many of the reviews of O'Farrell's novels is a focus on her delineation of relationships and the gaps in between. In her review of *Instructions for a Heatwave*, D'Erasmo contends that: 'In her previous novels, Maggie O'Farrell has often measured the distance between intimates, and the unexpected intimacy of distance – geographical, temporal, cultural' (D'Erasmo 2013). Characterization, too, has drawn reviewers' attention, particularly the emotional charge of characters, or, as Day puts it, 'the texture of human emotion' which 'O'Farrell has a remarkable ability to convey with precision' (Day 2010).

Others have focused on narrative structure, such as Showalter, who states that 'O'Farrell fans will be drawn in by the excitement of [this] criss-crossed narrative beginning' of *The Distance Between Us* (Showalter 2004). Groskop, on the other hand, points out the 'four separate narrative threads' of *Instructions for a Heatwave* which 'never become confused' (Groskop 2013).

With the publication of *Hamnet* and *The Marriage Portrait*, reviewers collectively and repetitively extol O'Farrell's eloquent evocation of the past, alongside the visual and rhythmic nature of her writing and her mastery of the fluidity and dissolution of time. Writing on *Hamnet* for *The Literary Review*, Sherratt-Bado describes O'Farrell as 'a spellbinding word-weaver, conjuring up a vivid historical milieu that is at once familiar and surreal in its immediacy' (Sherratt-Bado 2020). For Charles, she is 'always a master of timing and rhythm' (Charles 2020). In her review of *The Marriage Portrait*, Smith contends that the latest novel 'is every bit as evocative and spellbinding' as *Hamnet* and O'Farrell's writing 'is so vivid it melts away the time and space between now and sixteenth-century Italy' (Smith 2022).

Writing the Self: *I Am, I Am, I Am*

In 2017, seventeen years after the publication of her first novel, the release of O'Farrell's memoir *I Am, I Am, I Am: Seventeen Brushes with Death* represents a temporary departure from fiction writing. Hailed by reviewers and her peers – 'exceptionally accomplished and emotionally sophisticated' (*The Scotsman*); 'spectacularly moving, funny, impeccably controlled, artful and sincere' (Max Porter); 'extraordinary' (Kate Mosse); 'life-affirming' (*Irish Independent*) – it retains all the hallmarks of her previously published novels with its focus on non-chronological storytelling, its playfulness with time and the emotional pulse of the main character: this time, Maggie herself (with the final chapter dedicated to her daughter). Fifteen of the seventeen sections of the book are named after parts of the body, such as 'Neck', 'Lungs', 'Bloodstream' and 'Circulatory System', while the remaining two sections, 'Cause Unknown' and 'Daughter', follow the same thematic trajectory of an instance of a brushing with death. This is a memoir which is unconventional in structure and tone and which illuminates fragility and resilience. Moreover, it sings with the voice of O'Farrell that is instantly recognizable. 'As well as making sense of the extraordinary, O'Farrell's expertise lies in finding significance in the ordinary, making connections and finding clarity where most might find fog' (Sturges 2017).

Writing for Children

In her first two books for children, *Where Snow Angels Go* (2020) and *The Boy Who Lost His Spark* (2022), the extraordinary and the magical percolate through the lives of a young girl and boy when they need it most, helping them to heal and reconnect with others. For Sylvie in *Where Snow Angels Go*, it is the appearance of the snow angel himself which makes her ponder why he is there, why she needs protection and why not all are blessed with their own snow angel. From his first appearance at the end of her bed, Sylvie welcomes the confused, vulnerable snow angel with his blue-tinged skin, celestial robes and huge snow-white feathery wings. But the snow angel worries that he has got his first mission wrong, for Sylvie should not be able to see him or remember him. Such is Sylvie's faith and trust that she never forgets him: she accepts that he will be her saviour despite her unawareness of the illness ravaging her body which will afflict her for several seasons. 'The snow angel had been wrong about one thing. Sylvie did not forget about his visit: it was burned into her memory as if it had just happened. She could remember every detail about him, every single word he had said' (O'Farrell 2020b: 25). Sylvie makes several futile attempts to make him reappear and is finally reunited with him to enlist his help so that those she loves may create their own snow angels.

Unlike Sylvie, Jem in *The Boy Who Lost His Spark* is initially a non-believer: he refuses to lend any credence to the old folktale about the mischievous black fur-ball creature with emerald eyes – the *nouka* – when he first moves to the cottage on the side of a steep hill with his sister and mother. Indeed, it is Jem's sister, aptly named Verity, and the old lady who relates the *nouka* tale to Verity's class who believe in the *noukas* from the beginning of O'Farrell's second picture book for children. And unlike Sylvie, who doesn't know of her illness until the snow angel arrives, Jem is conscious of the odd feelings stirring inside him which he is bottling up, made worse because he misses their city flat:

> Not so long ago, Jem would have picked up a spade and joined [Verity] but lately he hadn't felt like it; it was as if someone had put misted-up glasses on his face and he could no longer see the fun or the magic in Verity's games. He missed their flat, he missed the city – its yellow pools of streetlights, the trams that used to rattle past at night. He felt so low and listless, sitting there, as if his insides had been stuffed with damp rags. (O'Farrell 2022b: 8)

Strange goings-on at home, such as conkers stuffed inside shoes, a cheese grater in the laundry and a woollen web across the stairs (O'Farrell 2022b: 6) aren't enough to make Jem believe in the *noukas*. In the end, Jem's unhappiness will send a *nouka* to seek him out; the little creature will engage in mischief-making, including plotting inky dots on Jem's volcano diagram homework, until the boy finally accepts both its existence and his new home.

From a thematic, structural and aesthetic perspective, O'Farrell's two picture books are strongly interconnected. Both have principal characters who experience solitary moments due to physical illness or emotional turmoil; both books explore unconventional friendships with otherworldly creatures and highlight how an individual and a whole community can benefit from a little sprinkle of magic dust. These are stories about protection and comfort; they are occasionally dark, positing important questions about what it feels like to be out of place or different sometimes. Both books open with a question that sets the tone for entry into a strange world: 'Have you ever woken suddenly, in the middle of the night, without knowing why?' (O'Farrell 2020b: 5); 'Has anything strange ever happened in your house?' (O'Farrell 2022b: 5). They are beautifully made, with O'Farrell's words and illustrations by Daniela Jaglenka Terrazzini in a sensitive, moving symbiosis. Ultimately, they champion individuality, family and the curious, unusual aspects of life. As the old lady tells Jem in *The Boy Who Lost His Spark*: 'Now isn't that [. . .] just exactly what makes life interesting – the things that don't make sense? Wouldn't life be dull if we understood everything about it?' (O'Farrell 2022b: 70–1).

An Overview of the Collection

This volume of essays seeks to offer new critical readings of O'Farrell's texts through a variety of thematic and methodological frameworks and cross-literary references. The contributions are organized thematically rather than chronologically in order to create a fluidity between content that mirrors the non-sequential structure characteristic of O'Farrell's work.

In the opening chapter, Susan Alice Fischer considers 'the space between' in *The Vanishing Act of Esme Lennox* with a focus on the themes of institutionalization and deinstitutionalization of women bound by patriarchal conventions. Through an analysis of O'Farrell's cross-generational, multi-perspective, time-shifting narrative, Fischer explores how the author reconfigures the place of the marginalized, excluded female within history and society.

Focusing on representations of non-place and place as posited, respectively, by Augé ([1995] 2008) and Tuan (1975), along with a consideration of in-between spaces and white space on the page, my chapter interrogates how O'Farrell problematizes the complex emotional pull of love, loss and (be)longing in her first and third novels, *After You'd Gone* and *The Distance Between Us*. In doing so, the chapter compares O'Farrell's treatment of place/space governed by time, memories and responsibility with David Park's *Travelling in a Strange Land* and Kit de Waal's *The Trick to Time*.

Assessing the concept of the palimpsest in relation to the city and the self in *The Hand That First Held Mine*, Ruth Gilligan deploys Sarah Dillon's theory of 'palimpsestuousness' to uncover the ambitious multi-layered narrative deployed by O'Farrell. She interrogates how the author treats core themes intrinsic to the novel, such as motherhood and female identities, and the relationship between O'Farrell's creation of a palimpsestic work and that of Virginia Woolf.

An examination of multiple narrative perspectives to reveal the complexities and nuances of a marriage is the subject matter of the subsequent chapter by Edward Matthews on *This Must Be the Place*. Matthews focuses on variations in responses to and reflections on shared experiences by husband and wife, Daniel and Claudette, through a discussion of points of view. Moreover, he also emphasizes how O'Farrell's varied multi-perspectival approach is linked to escalation of plot. Adopting George Saunders's axiom of storytelling, Matthews considers O'Farrell's narrative strategy in relation to Colum McCann's *Let the Great World Spin* and Zadie Smith's *NW*.

Boundaries between time and characters are developed through the domestic gothic and hauntology in the chapters that follow by Sarah Gamble and Tasha Alden. In her analysis of *My Lover's Lover*, Gamble explores the themes of translation, reinterpretation, dislocation and estrangement and their centrality to the plot, characters and language of O'Farrell's second novel. She argues that the novel is 'an intricately constructed narrative' and highlights the many changing identities, landscapes, voices and time frames within it.

Alden explores the past's refusal to remain in the past as a recurring motif in O'Farrell's fifth and sixth novels *The Hand that First Held Mine* and *Instructions for a Heatwave*, as well as in her memoir *I Am, I Am, I Am* (2017). Deploying trauma theory with a focus on mourning rather than melancholia (Forter 2007, 2011), Alden discusses O'Farrell's manipulation of time, as well as her use of fragmentation, dream states and multiple viewpoints and their relationship with assimilation of past traumas.

The following two chapters focus on O'Farrell's award-winning *Hamnet* with multiple considerations of intertextuality and adaptation. In a novel which foregrounds Agnes Hathaway, Nicholas Taylor-Collins assesses the relationship between *Hamnet*'s Agnes and *The Taming of the Shrew*'s Katherina, before turning to Maria from John Fletcher's *Shrew* sequel, *The Woman's Prize* (?1609–11). It is Taylor-Collins's contention that both these women offer interesting 'staging posts' for O'Farrell's Agnes as he interrogates the extent to which womanhood becomes 'gentlemanly' in *Hamnet* and the ways in which Agnes husbands her unnamed spouse.

Laurie Maguire assesses how O'Farrell shapes a story about a family where legal and historical data is lacking in 'Filling Historical and Emotional Voids'. She considers the notions of defamiliarization and inversion, the attribution of agency to Agnes and the manner in which the novel is layered with twins, pairs and doubles. She concludes with an analysis of the Elizabethan world created by O'Farrell.

The final chapter reflects upon O'Farrell's most recently published novel, *The Marriage Portrait*, and explores how the concepts of 'underpainting' and 'overpainting' inform both plot and characterization. With chapter titles styled in the manner of a Renaissance painting or *tavola*, along with temporal shifts and a narratological layering effect characteristic of O'Farrell's other novels, the identities of both husband and wife, Alfonso and Lucrezia, are problematized as they are simultaneously overlaid and stripped back. Moreover, I examine the extent to which Lucrezia de' Medici is afforded agency within the narrative as she struggles within the confines of a fateful marriage.

Complementing this collection of critical essays is an exclusive interview with Maggie O'Farrell conducted in June 2022. In it, she discusses, among other topics: her approach to narrative structure and storytelling; how she has to shield from self-consciousness when writing; at what point she feels a book has its own pulse; the joy of 'making' a children's book; the terrible occasion when one of her novels became reduced to an irretrievable crumpled ball of Post-it notes (and became a better book because of it); and why a writer might need someone to wrestle a book out of their hands.

As the first full-length critical study of O'Farrell's texts, I hope that the essays contained herein make a significant contribution to current scholarship on contemporary fiction and invite further critical engagement with O'Farrell's work.

1

'The Space Between'

Maggie O'Farrell's *The Vanishing Act of Esme Lennox*

Susan Alice Fischer

Introduction

Maggie O'Farrell has noted that, at public readings of *The Vanishing Act of Esme Lennox* (2006b), typically two or three people would approach to tell her that they, too, had a relative like the eponymous protagonist who had been locked up in a psychiatric 'asylum', a fact they had sometimes discovered only decades later (O'Farrell 2006a; 'Maggie O'Farrell – The Vanishing Act of Esme Lennox' 2016).[1] While legislation enacting 'community care' has long since closed such places, O'Farrell's novel seeks to uncover the 'subterranean existence' (2006b: 10) of these hidden lives which reverberate across generations, making descendants understand their lives in entirely new ways.

The idea that such lives have been hiding in plain sight runs throughout the novel, bringing to light what should have been perceived long ago. Yet it takes time for Iris, Esme's much younger relative, to tune in, 'like reception to a radio frequency' (2006b: 107), and pick up pieces from the past. She shoves a letter from the hospital informing her of Esme's existence into a drawer, she assumes that a caller from that institution has dialled the wrong number, and she stares at a photograph of Esme for years without seeing her. The aptly named Iris will

---

[1] Had I been at one of O'Farrell's readings, I too would likely have approached to speak of my two aunts about whose existence I learned only in my early thirties. Because of the shame associated with 'madness', my generation knew nothing about the two additional sisters in my father's large family who had disappeared into psychiatric institutions until long after our aunts had died and we were adults. For more on the secrecy surrounding 'madness' and institutionalization, particularly in the context of Eastern European Jewish immigration, see my 2001 essay on Rachel Lichtenstein and Iain Sinclair's *Rodinsky's Room*. The authors highlight the gap that remained after Rodinsky inexplicably vanished from his East End room in the 1960s. Lichtenstein discovered he had been institutionalized – a far more plausible and commonplace explanation than the spectral urban mythology that grew around Rodinsky.

eventually allow the light to seep in, and her vision of Esme, her family and herself will be transformed.

The novel details the erasure of inconvenient women, such as Esme, through institutionalization that separates them from 'decent' society. At the same time, uncovering Esme's hidden life reveals the centrality of such stories. The stylistic choices the author makes dissolve the boundaries between the 'normal' and the 'abnormal', revealing them as constructs that produce devastating consequences.

The Gendered Construction of Madness

The historical impetus for the novel is the deinstitutionalization of psychiatric hospitals during the latter part of the twentieth century – to be replaced by 'community care' – and the concomitant exploration of why people – particularly women – were kept in them in the first place. The history of psychiatric asylums reveals that one could be confined to them indefinitely for a host of reasons that often blurred the line between mental illness and mere nonconformity. As in Esme's case, punishing women for not adhering to gender roles was often a factor. In *The Female Malady: Women, Madness, and English Culture, 1830–1980* – a source O'Farrell acknowledges at the end of her novel – Elaine Showalter traces the history of the institution from the Victorian era, noting that the 1845 Lunatics Act produced 'an unprecedented period of asylum construction' ([1985] 1987: 17). She adds that 'by the 1850s women were the majority of the inmate population, and that the asylum rather than the attic was identified as the madwoman's appropriate space' ([1985] 1987: 17). Busfield (1999) adds that by 1900, 55 per cent of those in 'County and Borough asylums' were female (1999: 62), not a large numerical difference. Yet, women's confinement was often based on gendered diagnoses, such as 'hysteria' (1999: 62).

Discussing her research for the novel in an article published in the *Guardian* in 2006, O'Farrell elaborates upon the types of women who had been institutionalized, and she underlines the social control to which they had been subjected. Often, they were deemed 'immoral'. They were too sexual, or not sexual enough, or, one assumes, not heterosexual. Some were pregnant. As she delved into the records, she found that 'Sometimes they had been put away for almost no reason at all' (O'Farrell 2006a). She wondered,

> what would have happened to many of us had we been born into a different time. A time when a man could commit a wife or daughter to an asylum with just a signature from a GP. A time when it was considered a sign of insanity to refuse

to cut your hair. Or to be found trying on your mother's clothes. Or to turn down offers of marriage. Or to show reluctance to sit on your relatives' knees. Or to not wash your kitchen floor for a week. Or to feel sad and weary after having given birth. These were all written in asylum records in the early half of the last century. (2006a)

While the asylums were often far from benign treatment centres for the mentally ill, the contradictory forces that brought about deinstitutionalization ran the spectrum from the hopeful to the cynical (Taylor 2011: 198). Barbara Taylor (2011) notes that a progressive trend pushed against the asylum's carceral formation and advocated for care in the community, believing it would provide a better option than shutting people away indefinitely (Taylor 2011: 195–6). Yet, because of the ways it was implemented, deinstitutionalization is also seen as part of the erosion of the Welfare State in Britain and other Western countries during the second half of the twentieth century (Barham 2020: 11; Taylor 2011: 198). Indeed, asylum closures were motivated more by cost-cutting measures than by 'any deep commitment to community care on the part of the government' (Campbell 2020: 1). Taylor (2011) notes that Conservative MP Enoch Powell 'announced' the government's 'intention to close the hospitals' in his 1961 'Water Tower Speech', and by the mid-1980s, 'the hospital population had declined by two-thirds', a feat she calls 'a truly astonishing rate of reduction when one realises that it was achieved, as Peter Sedgwick wrote at the time, "through the creation of a rhetoric of 'community care facilities' . . . [which] do not, in the actual world, exist"' (Taylor 2011: 194, 210). Often community care merely meant 'not the asylum' (Busfield 1999: 59). Unsurprisingly, the biggest push for deinstitutionalization came during the Thatcher years, with its assault on the Welfare State, placing the onus of care on the individual.[2]

Maggie O'Farrell's protagonist, Esme Lennox, is released from Cauldstone, 'in the mid-90s, when the aftershocks of Thatcher's care in the community scheme were still being felt. The large Victorian-built asylums had been closed down and as many as 20,000 people were sent out into the "community"' (O'Farrell 2006a). Patients were often released without full assessment of their needs, much less provision of adequate housing and care, as seen in Esme's case. At the time of her release, Esme has been locked away since the 1930s, when she

---

[2] In practice, this often meant a further burden for women caring for those falling through the enlarging holes in the welfare state's safety net, as Cherrill Hicks (1988) makes clear in *Who Cares: Looking After People at Home*. In the novel, it is the nearest relation, Iris, who is contacted and who, when she sees the dire 'community' options open to Esme, brings her to her own home, which turns out to have been Esme's (O'Farrell 2006b: 84–7).

was sixteen. She is now about to be discharged after more than sixty-one years in Cauldstone, 'a unit specialising in psychiatry' (O'Farrell 2006b: 32), as Peter Lasdun, in charge of tracking down family to whom she might be released, calls the former 'asylum'. Until he contacts Iris, Esme has been completely 'airbrushed from her family history' (O'Farrell 2006a).

The Vanishing Act of Esme Lennox focuses on women's acceptable roles and what happens to those, like Esme, who refuse to conform to them, and how far others, such as her sister Kitty, will go to fulfil them. At the heart of the novel is the fact that non-conformist women could so easily be removed from society and deemed mad – or even driven mad by their treatment. The novel's various mentions of witches reference one part of this long and cruel history of eradicating such women (O'Farrell 2006b: 11, 134–6). The novel also alludes to previous literary instances of 'mad' women. Maintaining that the 'difference that the asylum silenced and confined is also the feminine', Showalter points out that 'the fictional character of the deranged woman who haunts the margins of nineteenth-century women's texts [can be interpreted as] the symbolic representation of the female author's anger against the rigidities of patriarchal tradition' ([1985] 1987: 6, 4). This anger can be seen in Charlotte Perkins Gilman's story 'The Yellow Wallpaper', first published in *The New England Magazine* in 1892, which O'Farrell mentions as influential ('Maggie O'Farrell – The Vanishing Act of Esme Lennox' 2016). The story shows that women can be driven to madness through official medical treatment, something that O'Farrell's novel also addresses.

The protagonist-narrator of 'The Yellow Wallpaper' has recently given birth and appears to be suffering from a 'nervous' malady. She is a creative woman forced into domestic life and forbidden to write. Her physician husband brings her to a house he has leased, reminiscent of an English country home – or asylum – replete with 'hedges and walls and gates that lock' (Gilman [1892] n.d.: 648). She is confined to a room that resembles a nursery and a locked ward, with its bed nailed to the floor, the windows barred, suggesting both infantilization and institutionalization. During her enforced 'rest cure', her repressed creativity is projected onto the room's wallpaper where she comes to see bars holding back scores of women who are, like her, trying to break free. In 'Why I Wrote the Yellow Wallpaper' (1913), Gilman explains that she had suffered from 'melancholia' for some time when she was sent to a respected physician who prescribed domesticity with no more than 'two hours' intellectual life a day' in which she 'was never to touch pen, brush or pencil' again. This brought her 'so near the borderline of utter mental ruin' that she cast aside the doctor's orders and wrote her story 'to save people from being driven crazy' (Gilman [1913] 2011). In so doing, the author critiques 'the patriarchal version of insanity and disempowers its authority' (Battisti and Fiorato 2012: 198).

The Vanishing Act of Esme Lennox shows that for women, patriarchal psychiatry can be a catalyst, rather than a cure, for 'madness'. Developing this theme, O'Farrell's stylistic choices also echo the abrupt shifts, breaks in perspective and fragmentary quality of Gilman's narrative, indicative of her protagonist-narrator's medically induced mental state. The narrative characteristics expose and counter the ways society has cordoned off women who step outside the norm. The novel is narrated through three main different points of view: those of Esme, related in third-person omniscient; Iris, her young relative, also in third-person omniscient; and Kitty, Esme's older sister, a first-person narration, more disconnected than the others.

This multi-perspectival narration runs together, and the novel has no chapters. Rather, episodes merge one into the other, often without transition, or interrupt each other, to reconnect juxtaposed realities – connections that, like Esme's photograph, are hidden in plain sight and disrupt the official story. This lack of separation in the narrative erases arbitrary and punitive boundaries – the sort that define and confine 'mad' women to 'asylums' – as it rewrites Esme back into the record.

Just as the different perspectives and episodes cut into one another, there is a fluid sense of time: the past runs into the present and back again, thus stressing that the present cannot be understood without the past, and that women's individual lives are related to their collective history. In her continual scanning back and forth, Esme attempts to make sense of where '[i]t begins' (O'Farrell 2006b: 1): that is, what led to her spending over sixty-one years in Cauldstone. She is caught in a 'zoetrope inside her head' – constantly 'whir[ring]' images replaying segments of her life – 'and she doesn't like to be caught out when it stops' in painful places (2). The reader is thus called upon to piece together the fragments of Esme's and Iris's pasts, and to tune into those of Esme's sister, Kitty, who is suffering from Alzheimer's and whose own 'radio frequency' is constantly breaking up. Fragmentation and interruption thus reflect Esme's brutally ruptured life, as well as her sister's unravelling. They also represent the fragments that Iris and the reader grapple with to uncover Esme's reality as a new picture coalesces at the end of the novel. Merging past and present, voices and perspectives not only makes clear that the past always exerts its influence on the present but also that the 'sane' and 'insane' worlds are not so different and that the boundaries and separations between them are arbitrary. In juxtaposing

Esme's past to Iris's life, and to women across generations, the novel also suggests that 'the space between' them is '[n]ot that distant' (51, 52).

The Othering of Esme Lennox

Through Esme's recollections, as well as Kitty's broken narrative, the reader is able to reconstruct Esme's childhood and the events leading to her incarceration. As Jane Garden (2006) and Nadine Muller (2009) both note, the novel alludes to Frances Hodgson Burnett's *The Secret Garden* (1911), which introduces young Mary Lennox. Growing up in colonial India, the only child of unloving parents, Mary is found alone days after a cholera outbreak kills them and her ayah, and she is shipped back to a relative in Britain. A morose and imperious child at the beginning of the novel, Mary refers to her former Indian servants in racist terms. Sharing a last name and a childhood in colonial India with Mary Lennox, Euphemia Lennox – who prefers the name Esme – is, on the other hand, a lively and curious child with a capacity for love for her baby brother, Hugo, and for Jamila, her ayah, both of whom die during a typhoid outbreak. Esme's childhood in India comes to an end, and she travels back to Britain with her parents and Kitty. Yet her story 'takes a sinister turn', reversing Mary Lennox's, in which the earlier protagonist eventually 'flourishes under love and education', both ultimately denied to Esme (Muller 2009: para. 19).

Esme is also the counterpart to her older sister, Kitty, who is favoured by their depressed mother and aloof father. Deprived of both affection and understanding from an early age in India, Esme is seen as 'impossible, disobedient, unteachable, a liar' (O'Farrell 2006b: 26), and she is excessively punished: for walking barefoot, skipping out of lessons and running off to play with Hugo. After typhoid kills Jamila and Hugo while her parents and Kitty are away at a house party, Esme is discovered days later, holding Hugo's corpse, which has to be forcibly prised from her arms, foreshadowing the violent separation from her infant son who will be ripped away from her in the asylum.

Esme is a creative, intelligent and sensitive child – 'ridiculously oversensitive', Kitty will say – who has the misfortune to be born into an unimaginative and emotionally remote family, though she is close to her sister (127). From her earliest years in India, Esme perceives reality differently from the rest of her family. Her favourite place is 'the space under the table' where she can observe what others cannot (6), similar to Iris who as a child also prefers this oblique vantage point (101). Elsewhere, she 'narrows her eyes until her parents blur into two hazy shapes, her mother a triangle and her father a line' (3), reminiscent of Lily Briscoe's vision prefiguring the canvas she will come to paint at the end of Virginia Woolf's *To the Lighthouse* ([1927] 1981: 85, 201, 209). While Lily's artistic vision is actualized, Esme's creativity will be destroyed. This and other early memories, of being 'tethered to her chair' and 'forgotten' (O'Farrell 2006b: 7) with 'a binding across her middle' because she 'must learn to behave' (6) or of 'shriek[ing]' at an insect on her ear (5), foreshadow Esme's difference and incarceration as a teenager, as well as the restraints placed upon her in the asylum where she is committed after uncontrollable screaming following her rape (169).

During her childhood in India, Esme's highly developed sensorium enables her to hear 'the slow weeping, of rubber trees leaking their fluid' (38). In addition to listening 'to the sound of trees crying', Esme 'look[s] at the sunlight splintering and re-forming on the ground [and] at the spiral gashes in the trunks around her' (38). While her parents and Kitty are away at the house party, just before the typhoid outbreak, she experiences 'the glee . . . of having the run of the house'. She caresses the velvet curtains, examines the 'threads of coloured silk' in 'her mother's workbox' and tries on her mother's jewellery and make-up (38–9). This heightened sensitivity also connects with Esme's changing body and emerging sexuality. While alone, she flops down onto her parents' bed and feels something new: 'A soreness, a tenderness in two points on her chest, a strange, exquisite kind of pain' that leaves her 'flushed and shocked' (39). It is significant that just after this thrilling moment, the first major trauma in Esme's life takes place: Hugo's death. This foreshadows and is juxtaposed with the time when Esme at sixteen – again experiencing her body in a new way – goes to her parents' bedroom to try on her mother's silky négligé. This time, her parents return home earlier than expected and her father slaps her, demanding she remove the garment. They punish her by making her attend a party with a view to 'marry[ing] her off to the Dalziel boy' who will 'break [her] spirit' (163). Any manifestation of female sexuality must be punished and contained.

Repressing Esme's difference and sexuality continues upon the family's return to the frigid climate of Edinburgh, where the rules of comportment are enforced by her rigid Victorian grandmother. The novel highlights the arbitrary nature of separation: between sane and insane, most obviously, but also with other capricious constructions of 'normal' or 'acceptable' behaviour. Esme's failure to wear a hat or gloves is unacceptable, her desire for a crimson dress scandalous. As their grandmother remarks, the girls are 'colonials', and thus not used to the 'nicer' distinctions they must learn if they are to marry into the right sort of family. Conventional Kitty is eager for the role of wife and mother that she has been raised for and Esme, younger by six years, is expected to follow suit. Aware of how hard she must try to make a good match, Kitty knows what to do and follows the rules, foregoing her desire to take a secretarial course. Esme is simply uninterested in marriage. Instead, when she reaches sixteen, Esme wants to continue at school with a scholarship and perhaps go on to university. But, after snatching the book she has been reading away from her, just as 'the people on the page and the room they were in were holding her fast', her father says, '[t]here would be no profit in it'; he does not want his daughters to 'work for a living' (142, 143). While still at home under these social strictures, Esme feels 'there would be no escape, no relief from these walls, from this room, from this family until she married, and the thought of that was as bad, if not worse' (143–4). Esme's creative and intellectual bent is deemed disobedience and thus subject to ever more ferocious punishment.

Despite her intelligence, Esme does not understand her difference, and she is ostracized and labelled 'the Oddbod' by her contemporaries (140). She tells the girls at her school in Scotland about her perceptions of India, 'describ[ing] . . . the yellow mimosa dust, the iridescent wings of the dragonflies' (130), thinking they are sincere in their interest, only to realize she is being mocked. The location of Esme's early childhood in India others her: the girls at school laugh at her, asking if her hair is 'naturally' curly and if her mother 'wears a sari' (130), thus symbolically extending Esme's 'difference' to other forms of othering. The trick they play upon her – though no one gives her credence – in sewing her name tag into a too-small school jacket prefigures both the straight-jacket of the asylum, as well as the naming and labelling of her as mad. When she displays her anger at the girls, Esme is likened to 'a wildcat' who 'put a curse on' one of the girls, and thus she is by implication a witch (134). Esme is larger – both taller and with a more expansive vision of life – but society allots her too small a space (134; cfr. Muller 2009: 8).

It is Esme's difference – and her indifference to him – that unfortunately attracts Kitty's 'suitor' James Dalziel. He sees her 'a challenge', someone who 'could match a man, stroke for stroke', and he crushes her accordingly (150, 156). Accosting her one foggy evening, as she is returning from school (147–8), he 'catch[es] her wrist' startling her with 'the insistence, the power of his grip' (151). When her family visits his for tea, with his 'hand on her waist', he pulls her towards him and 'press[es] his lips to her skin, at the place where her blouse ended and her neck began' (157). Trying to understand where one thing ends and another begins, Esme nonetheless finds it 'electrifying' and 'the most intimate thing anyone had ever done to her' (157). Later she will be forced to attend the New Year's party at his family home, where James will rape her, which will lead to her incarceration. Passing the Dalziel home in Iris's car, following her release from Cauldstone, Esme feels she 'should have heard the tightening of the strings. What if, she always thinks. She has spent her life half strangled by what-ifs' (164).

Like many who are perceived as different and othered, Esme is intent upon deciphering the lines of separation between 'normal' and 'other'. Yet, she cannot read the world as others do, as a system of binary opposites, with clear demarcations, sharply separating one from the other. At its central point, the novel returns to the beginning, clarifying the 'it': 'It begins here. Or perhaps not' (1). As the novel recalls the opening lines, 'two girls at a dance' (1, 165) close to midnight on New Year's Eve, the ensuing rape is the immediate event leading to Esme's sectioning, but so much has already conspired to other and separate her from the world of the 'normal'. Esme wonders, 'Where does the hand become the wrist? Where does the shoulder become the neck? She will often think that this was the moment that tipped it' (166). Her attempt to understand where something begins, what distinguishes sanity from insanity, becomes more acute once she is incarcerated and she attempts to locate the moment that tipped the balance against her.

During the rape, she dissociates, physically and mentally 'splitting' from the pain, thinking of cutting her hair, 'the sound of the rubber trees' and a collection of film programmes (168). After, she cannot stop screaming (169). When her parents call a doctor, Kitty overhears the words 'hysteria' and '*treatment* and *place* and *learn to behave*' (173), and Esme is committed to Cauldstone, diagnosed with 'dementia praecox', a label later updated to 'schizophrenia' and 'bi-polar' (174, 99). She 'shouts' that it 'is all a mistake' until the nurses restrain her 'with wide leather belts', strapping her to the bed (176–7). Esme tries to prove to Dr Naysmith that she is 'better' by acting 'like a good girl' (194, 197), but her attempts at conformity do not free her. Instead, in an act of defensive separation, she 'disappears'. As Nancy C. Andreasen (2007) notes, Esme's 'vanishing act' is both the erasure 'from the real world of "sane people"' and also 'her primary coping mechanism to retain her sanity, one that is used almost universally by people who are able to survive hopeless situations: vanish from the here and now and use your memory and imagination to place yourself in a better place' (Andreasen 2007: 634).

Repression of female sexuality is at the heart of Esme's punishment and of the many silences that envelop the Lennox family: Esme's pregnancy following her rape, Kitty taking and passing off Esme's son as her own because she lives in unconsummated and loveless marriage with Duncan Lockhart. Even in her distress, Kitty cannot ask her mother about sex: 'we just didn't have that kind of conversation' (O'Farrell 2006b: 219). She is enraged because Esme 'had done that with [James]. And in me rose an anger. How had she known and not me? She was younger than me, she wasn't as pretty as me. . . . And I did want a baby so badly' (219). Briefly reconsidering whether to keep the child who 'smelt of' Esme (218), Kitty justifies her actions upon viewing Esme 'through this small hole in a door with iron locks [where she] saw a creature . . . creeping, its shoulder pressed into the softened wall, mumbling to itself' (225). This moment, recalling Gilman's protagonist 'creeping' against the wallpaper, decides Kitty. She adopts Esme's son, who will become Iris's father, hides the secret and tells herself she did not intend to keep her sister locked away forever. When Kitty is institutionalized in a nursing home for Alzheimer's, the memory that returns most insistently and that she cannot help voicing is that 'Esme wouldn't let go of the baby' (207). As Kitty's narrative – the official story – unravels, this truth resurfaces.

In juxtaposing Esme's and Iris's lives, the novel underlines the similarities of these two unconventional women whose truths are rooted in the repression of female sexuality. Iris's longing for a scarlet dress echoes Esme's yearning for a crimson dress in her youth (13, 72). Esme is amazed by Iris's independent life, which she had wished for herself: wearing what she wants, having affairs without having to marry, working and living alone (108–13). Iris lives in part of the family home, where Esme once lived, and uses flatware that Esme remembers was purchased on Princes Street (111). Now Esme stays in the guest room in the attic, which had been a baby's room, alluding to the madwoman in the attic of earlier generations (182–7). Their proximity is underlined, as Esme proves to be Iris's grandmother, and Iris comes to realize that, had she been born in Esme's time, she, too, could have suffered Esme's fate.

In Iris's relationships with Alex and Luke, different aspects of her similarities to Esme emerge. Luke recalls James with his first sexual encounter when he was seventeen at a New Year's party (64), his possessive attitude, his fingers on her waist (21), the way he 'barks out in his new, authoritative voice' (121). She recognizes that it is 'time . . . to excise Luke from her life' (152). When she meets Luke's wife, Gina, Iris's 'eyes veer away' (233). Yet Iris 'makes herself look' at 'the woman she is betraying' (234), recalling Kitty's betrayal of Esme. As Iris thinks about her relationship with her step-brother Alex, she wonders when 'it begins': 'How would she begin' to tell that story (99)? She remembers the 'time Kitty caught them . . . their arms sliding and twining round each other, trying to find a hold that satisfied' (227, 228). Like Esme, who tries to stop herself thinking about 'the hard thing' (37), Iris 'had buried this so effectively, stopped herself thinking about this so efficiently for such a long time, it's as if it never happened. She has managed to rewrite her own history, almost' (227). Ultimately, as she sees missing pieces of Esme's life, Iris will begin to understand her own history, connecting her more to Esme than to Kitty. On the last day of the novel, as secrets resurface and Iris realizes she is Esme's granddaughter, she 'is dressed – in something green' (230), recalling the missing piece of cloth that was Esme's only tangible tie to her son (78). As Esme sees her mother in Iris, and Iris sees her father in Esme, past and present connect across generations.

Writing Secrets

Given how many realized, particularly in the aftermath of deinstitutionalization, that they had family members who had been locked away, it is unsurprising to find an author drawing upon his own family history by writing about such a relative. Speaking of his 2008 novel, *The Secret Scripture*, Sebastian Barry states, 'I didn't know anything about the woman who became Roseanne McNulty in *Secret Scripture*. . . . All I knew was that she was in my great-uncle's band, and that she was sectioned for some reason. And she lived the rest of her life in an institution, and he married again' (qtd in Clark 2020).

Like O'Farrell, Barry rewrites the history of an elderly protagonist – here Roseanne McNulty – who had a child taken from her and who was institutionalized, and is now being considered for release, as the psychiatric hospital in which she has been living since 1957 is about to close. The senior psychiatrist at Roscommon Mental Hospital, Dr Grene, is assessing whether she can re-enter society with community care – 'whatever that is, O Lord', he remarks (Barry 2008: 15). Like O'Farrell, Barry critiques both the cruel institutionalization of women who step outside the bounds of societal norms, as well as the economic, rather than therapeutic, reasons for community care.

Here, too, the secrets leading to incarceration are pieced together through multiple voices. The patient writes 'Roseanne's Testimony of Herself' in secret, hiding her papers under the loose floorboards of her hospital room, while 'Dr Grene's Commonplace Book' contains his attempts to understand her history, as well as reflections on his own life. As he assesses Roseanne, he tries to escape from the pain of having lost his wife, whom he betrayed and who spent 'a whole decade' in 'the old maid's room at the top of the house' (114). That Grene has his own madwoman in the attic and bears some responsibility for driving her there, raises the question of how reliable a narrator he is. Until now, he had spent little time trying to help Roseanne, whom he sees a 'fixture' who 'not only represents the institution, but also, in a curious way, my own history, my own life' (16). He comes to Roseanne's room as much to find comfort after his wife's death, as to assist Roseanne, and 'finds himself in a paradoxical reversal with his baffling patient, speaking to her of his own losses and hurts' (O'Connor 2008). As he writes following one such visit: 'Assess her. It suddenly seemed so absurd I laughed out loud. The only person's sanity in doubt in that room was my own' (Barry 2008: 169).

Like O'Farrell's, Barry's novel questions the misogyny and fear of women's sexuality that often led to institutionalization, this time in Ireland. In uncovering Roseanne's story – long before he reads Roseanne's hidden sheath of papers that is left by the novel's 'guardian angel' on his desk – Grene believes that she was 'sectioned for social rather than medical reasons' (16). He uncovers an 'official' narrative of Roseanne's life: 'Fr Gaunt's account of Roseanne's life . . . serves as the official documentation condemning her to live out her life in various asylums' (Harney-Mahajan 2012: 55–6). The priest condemns Roseanne for not converting from Presbyterianism when she marries her Catholic husband, he labels her a fallen woman for being seen with another man, he orchestrates the annulment of her marriage on spurious grounds of 'nymphomania', and he writes the report that consigns her to the asylum. As he reads Fr Gaunt's narrative, Grene condemns the damage it has wrought: 'It is like a forest fire, burning away all traces of her, traversing her narrative and turning everything to ashes and cinders. A tiny, obscure, forgotten Hiroshima' (Barry 2008: 230). This is particularly true of Fr Gaunt's 'clinical . . . anatomizing of Roseanne's sexuality. . . . He betrays at every stroke an intense hatred if not of women, then of the sexuality of women, or sexuality in general' (230).

As Roseanne's life is revealed, the stories of two people belonging to different generations prove to be much more intertwined than either initially realizes. Ultimately, much like Iris, who re-evaluates her own history after she learns of Esme's existence, Grene, who has been adopted, will learn that the woman he has been 'assessing' is his own mother and that he was the new-born torn from her at birth and later placed in an English orphanage. He feels 'fated to record the dismaying bleakness of institutions' (286). Given the policing of women's sexuality and reproduction, the intertwining histories of these two institutions – orphanages and asylums – are unsurprising.

As a young girl, Roseanne did not realize, as she says in the opening to her narrative, that she could 'be the author' of herself (4). In writing her story, without knowing it, she also leaves a history to 'the family following' her (11).

Grene is pleased 'she has helped herself' by writing her life (298; see McCarthy 2017: 40), and on behalf of the institution that incarcerated her, he apologizes to the woman he now knows as his mother. As Tara Harney-Mahajan (2012) observes, his apology and her forgiveness 'sits uncomfortably' (69), as does the fact that he has not told her he is her son. He promises that 'I will tell her. Just as soon as I can find the words. Just as soon as we reach that part of the story' (Barry 2008: 297). He also fails to tell her that he has pieced her story together using the fragments he has collected from her and Fr Gaunt. Within the boundaries of the narrative, Dr Grene does not reveal their relationship to her, and thus he maintains control of Roseanne's narrative. Apparently, women's full authorial control of their lives and stories still has a long way to go.

Official Stories/Counter-Narratives

Maggie O'Farrell, Charlotte Perkins Gilman and Sebastian Barry focus on rewriting 'official stories' of women's 'insanity'. In Gilman's 'The Yellow Wallpaper', the physician husband tells the protagonist's official medicalized story. Although her written testimony remains, having no other recourse, she projects her story onto the paper of the walls that are her prison and is driven 'mad'. Sebastian Barry's Roseanne's telling of her story counters Fr Gaunt's official narrative, yet at the same time, she is denied full resolution.

O'Farrell's Kitty represents the remnants of the 'official story' that defined Esme as 'mad', but significantly this story is breaking up. Esme's and Iris's points of view return Esme to visibility and offer a counter-narrative. This is also suggested by the two versions of Esme's name. Euphemia, deriving from the same root as euphemism, suggests her silencing and her concealment. Esme – the name she prefers – is pronounced 'Izme, Is Me' (O'Farrell 2006b: 40), thus underlining Esme's determination to be and speak for herself.

The novel ends with the beginning: 'Two women in a room. One seated, one standing' (240). After Esme smothers her sister, Alex remains with Iris and Iris refuses to let go of Esme's hand as the authorities take her. At the end, Iris 'will follow it, through the white, through the crowd, out of the room, into the corridor and beyond' (245). Esme's story comes together, Kitty's disintegrates and Iris's is re-envisioned, as she comes to terms with her own history with her family and with Alex. The secrets are visible, the lies of 'normality' exposed. While Esme has had her say, and thus a resolution of sorts, her terrible final act shows no restitution can be made.

2

Love, Loss and (Be)longing in *After You'd Gone* and *The Distance Between Us*

Elaine Canning

Introduction

At the opening of O'Farrell's first and third novels, we encounter a principal character in the same physical space: the bed/bedroom. In *After You'd Gone* (2000), it's Alice, preoccupied with something we don't yet understand but which has been keeping her awake at night. Folded on her side, we're told: 'The day she would try to kill herself, she realised winter was coming again' (O'Farrell 2000: 3). Jake, on the other hand, in *The Distance Between Us* (2004) is 'splayed like a starfish across the bed', concerned about something which has 'his mind running at full tilt', while a fan spills cool air into the room (O'Farrell 2004: 3). Both Alice and Jake will soon vacate their rooms and enter the street, their movement between time and space assuming very different trajectories.

After You'd Gone is the story of Alice Raikes, a young, tormented widow who has already lost the love of her life, John Friedmann, at the point where the novel begins. But it is not John's death that is the trigger point at which she attempts to take her own life: it is the witnessing of something in a restroom in Edinburgh station which prompts her hasty departure from the city and subsequent stepping into the road in London. A keen traveller who has seen various parts of the world and is planning a couple's break in Andalusia before John is killed in a London bomb attack, Alice becomes confined to the restrictions of a hospital bed and coma.

In contrast, Stella and Jake in *The Distance Between Us* are unknown to each other at the beginning of the novel, physical and culturally distanced in separate parts of the world. The sight of a red-haired man on a bridge in London who seems all too familiar sends Stella packing to a remote part of the Scottish Highlands. It is there that she will encounter Jake, recently married and on his first trip to the UK from Hong Kong, fleeing from his own troubled circumstances. While Stella and Jake move across countries and continents, Alice remains fixed in a London hospital with family by her bedside.

What interconnects both novels, along with other works by contemporary novelists such as Park and De Waal, is the relationship between place/space and time, memory and responsibility. Indeed, this is also reflected in the novels' titles. 'The distance' referenced in O'Farrell's third novel not only accentuates the physical and emotional proximity or detachment experienced by Stella and Jake but serves to underline Alice's removal from John and the world in *After You'd Gone*. Moreover, Stella and Jake, like Alice, are also forced to consider what happens 'after' each other's departures.

The concept of place/space itself can be considered in a variety of ways in relation to the core themes of both novels. In his analysis of place and non-place, Augé contends that: 'If a place can be defined as relational, historical and concerned with identity, then a space which cannot be defined as relational, or historical, or concerned with identity will be a non-place' (Augé [1995] 2008: 63). He defines non-places as: 'aircraft, trains and road vehicles [. . .] airports and railway stations, hotel chains, leisure parks, large retail outlets' (Augé [1995] 2008: 64). Tuan, on the other hand, describes place as '[. . .] a center of meaning constructed by experience. [. . .] To know a place fully means both to understand it in an abstract way and to know it as one person knows another' (Tuan 1975: 152).

In this chapter, I consider the extent to which Augé's definition of 'non-place' may be applied to O'Farrell's *After You'd Gone* and Park's *Travelling in a Strange Land* as characters struggle with the impact of grief and responsibility. Moreover, I discuss whether the protagonists' contrasting states of confinement occur in what might be described as in-between spaces, rather than a place or non-place. Second, I explore the physicality of place in *The Distance Between Us* and De Waal's *The Trick to Time* and the impact of connection with/disconnection from place as defined by Tuan. In both analyses, the significance of 'textual space' – white space on the page, changes in narrative perspective – will also be considered to determine how O'Farrell problematizes the core themes of love, loss and (be)longing in these works.

Non-place and In-between Spaces: *After You'd Gone* and *Travelling in a Strange Land*

Writing on *After You'd Gone*, Casey states: 'O'Farrell's meticulous narrative – which offers, in addition to Alice's voice, varying perspectives of the friends and family at her bedside – dips in and out of different time periods, reflecting the fluid nature of memory' (Casey 2001). In fact, while much of Alice's present hinges around an in-between space, the cause of which is an incident in a non-place, the novel's multiple shifts in perspective also engender movement between physical spaces of the past. We learn, for example, from Alice's mother, Ann: 'When Alice was still young enough to seem like a child to Ann, she left to travel the world. She waved goodbye from a train window' (O'Farrell 2000: 59). Ann herself studied biology at Edinburgh University; what she liked about the city was 'the dual personality of the city's main street' (24), a foreshadowing of her own double existence as wife and mistress. Responses to place are also linked to relationships and personalities: thus, Alice's paternal grandmother, Elspeth, a sensible, grounded woman from North Berwick, has a very different view of Edinburgh compared to her daughter-in-law, Ann: 'Edinburgh was steeped in a coagulating damp and mist' (51). It's a place which Elspeth associates with ill-health, rather than well-being. Elspeth's love of North Berwick, the place where she belongs and to which Alice returns her ashes, is not shared by Ann, who sees it as 'a godforsaken windswept village in the middle of nowhere' (54). And while Alice lives in London, her father, Ben, will never understand why she moved there: it perturbs and confuses him, and the tube is 'a fearsome thing: a horrible machine into which you get sucked, dragged down by crowds and escalators' (78–9).

Prior to the terrible incident which leaves Alice in a coma, she is already presented as unrooted and absent due to the weight of grief. As she passes through the streets, head down, with no predetermined end point, she is oblivious to what is going on around her: 'She passed shops with drawn-down, padlocked shutters, street-cleaning lorries scrubbing the kerbs with great circular black brushes, a group of bus drivers smoking and chatting on a corner, their hands curled around polystyrene cups of steaming tea. They stared as she passed, but she saw none of this' (4). She ends up at King's Cross Station, one of Augé's non-places, and finds herself on a train to Edinburgh to see her family. According to Augé:

> a person entering the space of non-place is relieved of his usual determinants. He becomes no more than what he does or experiences in the role of passenger, customer or driver. Perhaps he is still weighed down by the previous day's worries, the next day's concerns; but he is distanced from them temporarily by the environment of the moment. (Augé [1995] 2008: 83)

This is true of Alice's journey – she sleeps on the train, temporarily shutting out the rest of the world. She validates Augé's sentiments on the traveller's space: 'The traveller's space may [. . .] be the archetype of non-place' (Augé [1995] 2008: 70). However, the concept of the non-place is problematized by O'Farrell on two separate occasions in the novel. The first occurs when Alice visits the restroom in Edinburgh; she sees 'something so odd and unexpected and sickening that it was as if she'd glanced in the mirror to discover that her face was not the one she thought she had' (O'Farrell 2000: 6). We later learn through temporal shifts and changes in perspectives what the history behind this sighting was: Alice realizes that her father, Ben, is not her father. The restroom, therefore, is not a place devoid of history or identity; in fact, it is the catalyst for Alice stepping into the road, for her overturning her own life and that of those around her. What she sees there redefines her past and impacts her future. Subsequently, though chronologically earlier in terms of the actual sequence of events, a crematorium restroom becomes the site of interrogation and discovery. It is the day of Elspeth's funeral and Ann pushes Alice to reveal if John is Jewish. It is in the same place – this non-place – where Alice reveals that John's mother is dead. Although the second reconfiguration of the non-place does not carry the same weight of the first in relation to plot, it serves to highlight that the non-place does not always protect from the 'usual determinants' as articulated by Augé.

This categorization of the non-place is also called into question in Park's *Travelling in a Strange Land* (2018). The entire novel is set within a car journey: three days before Christmas, Tom has to drive from Belfast to Sunderland to bring his sick son Luke home. He undertakes a journey through a strange land of ice and snow, though the real journey is the emotional and psychological one he imposes upon himself. The strange land he is travelling through is that of fatherhood, and the lengthy car journey only serves to highlight his frustrations, failings, grief and loss. Rather than being protected within the shell of the car, Tom is confronted with memories and recollections of the past, as well as his dead son Daniel's voice, with a satnav as his only tracker. There is an initial feeling of safety, a shutting out of the world, when his wife Lorna joins him in the passenger seat before he sets off on the journey himself: 'Lorna gets in the passenger seat and we sit in the iced car as if in an igloo, blind to the world, and for just a second it feels safe, as if we are protected from everything that lies outside' (Park 2018: 3). But once on the road, there is no self-imposed blindness or escape from his thoughts.

In both *After You'd Gone* and *Travelling in a Strange Land*, O'Farrell and Park overturn the concept of the non-place – the restroom, the car. Furthermore, although Alice and Tom end up in very different places, they inhabit in-between spaces. Through temporal shifts, both spaces are infused with stories relating to their pasts and their loved ones, metamorphosing them into sites related to history and identity. Alice, in a comatose state, rests between the real world and a more dreamlike one, while Tom's non-place morphs into a space filled with music, family voices and family narratives. He moves through the world with very little contact with others – there is the young girl on the boat, the woman in the garage, Agnes to whom he offers a lift with her shopping, and Rosemary, a middle-aged woman who has an accident en route. When he steps outside the car or, in Agnes's case, welcomes her in, he tells them all what his purpose is: to bring his son home. Having already lost one son, Daniel, Tom is determined not to let Luke down. The journey is a self-imposed confinement which he must complete in his quest for a sense of belonging to his family again.

Alice's comatose state calls into question her desire for belonging in the outside world. If she purposefully stepped into the road after her discovery in the restroom, then her actions suggest that she has no desirable sense of identity or place. She is assaulted by a myriad of voices as she lies in the hospital bed:

> Is this my voice I can hear? It is as if I'm living in a radio, floating up and down on airwaves, each with their different voices – some I recognise and some I don't. I can't choose the bandwidth.
>
> This place feels clean. The smell of antiseptic crackles in my nostrils. Some voices I can distinguish as outside myself, those that sound farther off, as if through water. And then there are those within – all kinds of spectres. (O'Farrell 2000: 26)

The many voices Alice hears, both internal and external to her, underline the complexity of the vignettes and narrative perspectives woven between Alice's bouts of semi-consciousness. Indeed, several of the changes in narrative are presented in the first person, suggesting that they are Alice's own reminiscences or dreams. In them, Alice recalls her piano lessons with Mrs Beeson and how she practised hard; a beach scene with the callous Mario in which he holds her under the water; how much she loved John and how she would think about her love for him in Augé's non-places – on tube trains, on crowded buses and at work (187). She also questions what you're supposed to do with the love you have for somebody if that person is no longer there (298).

It is primarily through these first-person musings and remembrances, placed before and after the white space on the page, that Alice begins to heal; so too does Tom. Alice's discovery that her father is not her biological father is what threatens her recovery: 'I've been hearing my father's voice. I know I'm not imagining it. [. . .] I cannot bear it. It makes me miserable. It makes me want to turn, sink, let the waters close over my head' (276). But our discovery that her father, Ben, knew the circumstances all along and always saw her as his own offers hope which will be translated into the final pages.

Before considering Alice's final state within her in-between space, let's return to Tom. The story ends before he gets to Luke, but we are certain he will bring his son home. The final pages focus on Tom's tentative steps towards self-healing: his visit to the Angel; the deletion of the photograph of his dead son, a burden he has been carrying alone; and the presentation of a final gift to others. He starts to lift the wigwam he has placed next to the Angel, but 'something tells me I have to leave it, that this is where it belongs, and I hope that Lilly will somehow come to understand, understand that her father left it here for the homeless, for every soul in need of shelter and, as the sun finally sets over this snow-covered world, for every fellow traveller, lost like him in a strange land' (Park 2018: 165).

Like Tom, Alice's healing is only just at the start: she receives a visit from John Friedmann's father, the man who would not accept her for being non-Jewish, who now asks for forgiveness. There is an ambivalence in Alice's words: 'I am being carried forwards, or up, and I'm not sure if this is what I want [. . .] but it seems there's nothing I can do, my head rushing rushing towards some surface I didn't know was there or that I'd forgotten was there' (O'Farrell 2000: 372). In a similar vein to Tom, Alice has stepped (or swum) into another in-between place, one that takes her closer to belonging once more.

Finding One's Place: *The Distance Between Us* and *The Trick to Time*

> Calling him after a place would, she decided, tether him to the world and not to people, would free him for ever from the stranglehold of family. (O'Farrell 2004: 45)

So says Caroline, the mother of Jake Kildoune, a free spirit who left Wales in a campervan and travelled the world before a brief encounter with a Scottish man who would become Jake's dad.

In both *The Distance Between Us* and De Waal's *The Trick to Time*, the physicality of place is prominent in worlds where characters feel varying degrees of connection and disconnection. Indeed, the length of time spent in a place does not always determine one's affinity towards it. Tuan asserts that: 'To live in a place is to experience it, to be aware of it in the bones as well as with the head. Place, at all scales from the armchair to the nation, is a construct of experience; it is sustained not only by timber, concrete, and highways, but also by the quality of human awareness' (Tuan 1975: 165). Without this degree of experience, as manifested in *The Distance Between Us* and *The Trick to Time*, several protagonists exist, but never fully settle.

Take Stella, for example, in *The Distance Between Us*. Half-Scottish, half-Italian, we are told that she 'doesn't like staying in one place' (O'Farrell 2004: 6). When her sister Nina doesn't know where she is, Nina's husband responds: 'It's an integral part of the . . . the Stella package. [. . .] The vanishing act' (21). Unlike Esme Lennox, to whom the intertextual reference relates, a young woman institutionalized against her will with no free movement, Stella is constantly moving from one city to the next. Despite making a pact with Nina to study at Edinburgh University, Stella changes her first choice to London at the last minute; and when Nina is finalizing plans for her wedding, Stella leaves for Italy to visit her maternal grandfather's village. What alienates her from a particular place, from a city, is fear and trauma, something she has carried from childhood after a violent encounter. Upon seeing the red-haired man on a bridge in London, a reminder of the past from which she has fled, Stella questions whether anything in her flat belongs to her (24) and loses her sense of time and place: 'The building and, indeed, the whole city seem to have disappeared, dissolved around her, receded into the night' (27). The shock propels her back to Scotland, into the Highlands, away from her job and life and into temporary work at Kildoune Lodge. The owner, Irene, does not question her: 'Sometimes, she knows, people just have to exit their lives' (77).

Jake exits his life for a different reason – a marriage he rushed into and no longer wishes to be part of – and eventually finds himself in the same remote spot of Scotland as Stella. Born in Hong Kong to a Welsh mother and the son of a Scottish father he does not know, he has a British passport but has never visited the UK. In fact, unlike Stella, his roots are firmly placed where he was born and grew up: Hong Kong. Hence, when his wife, Mel, insists they return to Norfolk for her to recuperate after a terrible street surge and crush during Chinese New Year, Jake does so with a heavy heart. At Mel's parents' house, he views the village 'indistinct with mist as if dissolving into air' and the windmill with 'immense sails stuck into a giant black X, as if warning him away' (40). Here, in England, he is displaced. Indeed, in a scene reminiscent of the opening of *After You'd Gone* where Alice does not see anything around her, at the beginning of *The Distance Between Us*, Jake similarly does not notice the bustle of his district, Wanchai. However, while Alice's blindness comes from a closing off from the world due to grief and loss, Jake seems to take nothing in due to overfamiliarity, his rushed pace, or both.

> Jake sidesteps [. . .] and heads south, past the basketball courts, a small red kerbside shrine with a bouquet of spent joss sticks, past men sitting in a *yum chai* shop, mah-jong tiles clicking on the tables between them, past serried rows of draped motorbikes, intricate webs of bamboo scaffolding, past restaurant tanks where doomed fish are stretching out their gills, searching for oxygen in the cloudy water. But Jake doesn't see any of this. (O'Farrell 2004: 5)

Hong Kong is home and the place to which he will return, despite finding some connection at Kildoune with the father he has never met. And in the knowledge that he will only ever remain temporarily in Scotland, 'He wants to imprint himself with this place, with this dilapidated house, so he can remember it, keep a reserve of it, for a time when he's no longer here' (242).

The theme of displacement is one which is also prevalent in De Waal's *The Trick to Time*. Mona, a sixty-year-old dollmaker from Ireland, lives in a seaside town in England far from her family and her previous life. She has no roots in the town, despite being a shop owner and living out her day-to-day life there. The natural world brings her comfort, especially the sea, which is the reason why she takes the long way down to the seafront to visit the carpenter who makes her wooden dolls. Through a series of flashbacks to childhood memories, we glimpse Mona's initial love for the sea advocated by her father. As they stand on Kilmore Shore, Mona's father explains the trick to time: 'You can make it expand or you can make it contract. Make it shorter or make it longer. [. . .] By the sea all life's worries wash away' (De Waal [2018] 2019: 21). But not all life's worries have gone – Mona still misses her William, the man he once was, and who comes alive through a series of temporal shifts. Place, for Mona, has caused much pain – the hospital where her baby girl, Beatrice, died; the hospital where William was locked inside. Home is Ireland, not where she has found herself.

In the end, Stella, Jake and Mona traverse space and time in order to situate themselves in places where some connection is viable. After Stella leaves Kildoune, Jake travels to London and Scotland in pursuit of her forgiveness and love. As Lee-Potter contends, 'The alchemical trick is for him to be transformed from a Cantonese-speaking Welshman with the wrong girl into an English-speaking Scotsman with the right girl' (Lee-Potter 2004). He returns to Hong Kong without her, despite extending an invitation to his home, his city. Stella will follow later, unannounced, on her own terms and establish her own sense of self and connection via a job at a radio station. Mona, on the other hand, will pack up in readiness for a return home to Kilmore Quay. 'Some people will have moved on', she thinks, 'but it's not a tourist town and there are generations of people who will have had the sense to stay where they were. She will be remembered. There's a little catch in her throat but she doesn't cry' (De Waal [2018] 2019: 257). But Mona's real dream is to return with Beatrice and William, and this is what she has to imagine – the three of them settled in Ireland will only ever exist in her mind.

Ultimately, through an analysis of the function of in-between spaces in *After You'd Gone* and Park's *Travelling in a Strange Land*, along with the impact of place (urban, rural, coastal) upon the individual in *The Distance Between Us* and De Waal's *The Trick to Time*, it is evident that varying degrees of connection and alienation permeate the texts, which in turn condition an individual's sense of belonging. The distance between the start and end point of the physical and/or emotional trajectories of the main protagonists in all four works has shifted, just as the stylistic and narrative choices of O'Farrell, Park and De Waal have been approximated.

3

'The Women We Become after Children'

Palimpsests of the City and the Self in Maggie O'Farrell's *The Hand that First Held Mine*

Ruth Gilligan

Introduction

The opening scene of Maggie O'Farrell's fifth novel *The Hand that First Held Mine* takes place in a garden, where the soil – the omniscient narrator warns us – is 'soaked [. . .] with the blood of Celts, Anglo-Saxons, Romans' and 'filled out with the rubble of their bones' (2010b: 3). Having delineated the layers of violent history underfoot, the narrator turns our attention to the young woman who has just appeared across the grass. Her name is Alexandra, though her mother calls her Sandra, and she is about to meet the man who will change her life and change her name forever, this time to Lexie. However, rather than these new incarnations eradicating their predecessors altogether, we are later told she is in fact 'made up of myriad Lexies and Alexandras, all sheathed inside one another, like Russian dolls' (O'Farrell 2010b: 70).

To explore this stratification of soil and self, this chapter will focus on the concept of the 'palimpsest'. Originally a term for a piece of manuscript from which the text has been erased so that new writing can be set down instead, 'palimpsest' has since been appropriated by multiple fields – from psychoanalysis and archaeology to neuroscience and literary studies. Taking each of these into account, I will argue that there are versions of the palimpsest at work in most of O'Farrell's early novels as characters try to dig up or gain access to erased memories; as Susan Strehle summarizes, O'Farrell's protagonists are typically 'struggling against the obscure residue of a repressed past' (2017: 61). However, by applying Sarah Dillon's recent distinction between 'traditional palimpsest reading' and an engagement with what she instead terms 'palimpsestuousness', this chapter will reveal how *The Hand that First Held Mine* adopts a more complex strategy than its predecessors as a means to interrogate questions of motherhood and female identity. It will also demonstrate how O'Farrell uses the novel's form to embody – and, ultimately, foreground – this advanced approach.

Excavating Woolf and Freud

Shortly after the scene in the garden, Lexie moves to London where she secures a job as an elevator assistant, memorizes the department store's topography and spends her days ascending through its various strata. Her nights, by contrast, she spends traversing the streets of Soho, observing the myriad buildings and people, drinking in 'every detail, with a feeling between panic and euphoria: this is perfect, this is all perfect, it couldn't be more perfect, but what if she can't remember it all, what if even the tiniest element were to slip from her?' (O'Farrell 2010b: 77). These lengthy descriptive passages – the freewheeling prose of the wandering flaneuse occasionally lapsing into free indirect discourse; the teeming multiplicity of London set alongside the 'blackened craters' left behind by the war (O'Farrell 2010b: 111) – all of this explicitly calls to mind Virginia Woolf's *Mrs Dalloway*. O'Farrell has confirmed she was indeed immersed in Woolf's novel at the time of writing her own: 'I've been poring over *Mrs Dalloway* in the last few months, trying to unpick the prose and the structure, in an attempt to work out how Woolf does it. It's almost impossible, as it's so brilliantly and tightly written' (O'Farrell 2010a).

As well as its brilliant structure and prose, Woolf's work draws numerous parallels between the city and the self, given both are haunted by what has gone before. The post-War streets of *Mrs Dalloway* are riddled with monuments to – and devastating scars of – history, while the novel's characters likewise find themselves marked by the past, constantly slipping between the present moment and their memories. Some of these reminiscences are voluntary, called forth willingly and laced with nostalgia; some characters even look to the future when all of *this* will be but a distant memory and 'those hurrying along the pavement this Wednesday morning are but bones with a few wedding rings mixed up in their dust and the gold stoppings of innumerable decayed teeth' (Woolf 1996: 13). More often, however, buried traumas are jolted, unbidden, to the fore as a result of sensory triggers such as 'the violent explosion' of a car engine (Woolf 1996: 11) or the 'extraordinary vigour' of Big Ben's chimes (Woolf 1996: 35).

The sense of the past still being an active, not dormant presence coincides with Woolf's view of memory as expressed more thoroughly in her 1939 essay

'A Sketch of the Past'. Here she argues that 'things we have felt with great intensity [. . .] are in fact still in existence' and also 'that we are sealed vessels afloat on what it is convenient to call reality; and at some moments, the sealing matter cracks; in floods reality; that is, these [memory] scenes' (Woolf 1985: 142). Given this, many critics have drawn parallels between Woolf and Sigmund Freud, particularly his early model of memory wherein he posits that the past is not over it still exists, it is just buried many layers below the surface. In his seminal 'Studies on Hysteria', for example, Freud compares the subconscious to an archaeological site, likening the process of psychoanalysis to 'excavating a buried city' (2004: 143).

O'Farrell's Buried Cities

In O'Farrell's earlier books, we encounter numerous protagonists who have memories – and secrets – buried many layers deep, and who thus spend their time desperately trying to access their subconscious and piece together fragments of the past. In her debut *After You'd Gone* (2000), for example, Alice is suspended in a coma for most of the book, while in *The Distance Between Us* (2004), Nina is plagued by severe memory loss. Elsewhere, in *The Vanishing Act of Esme Lennox* (2006c), Kitty suffers from Alzheimer's Disease while Esme has endured a lifetime of trauma in an institution – in both instances, snippets of memory slowly emerge over the course of the novel as Kitty's granddaughter struggles to compile the two women's histories and thus, the truth of who they really are.

For all her many layers and incarnations, in *The Hand that First Held Mine* Lexie is not the character with the suppressed or damaged memory; instead, in the novel's other narrative strand we encounter Elina and Ted, a young couple who have just become parents for the first time. Elina – a half-Finnish, half-Swedish artist now living in London – recently gave birth, but has absolutely no recollection of that formative moment: 'She can recall being pregnant. She can see the baby here, lying in her lap. But how it got there is a mystery' (O'Farrell 2010b: 21). The reader discovers the truth before she does, as the omniscient narrator – this time adopting Ted's point of view – recounts the horrific scene in the maternity hospital where Elina almost died from extensive blood loss. The memory soon returns to Elina, though, triggered by the image of a bright red scarf erupting from her wardrobe: 'She thinks that it somehow reminds her of something she has seen recently. And then she recalls what it is. Jets of blood. Beautiful, in their way. The pure, garnet brightness of them in the scrubbed white of the room' (O'Farrell 2010b: 52).

While Elina's traumatic past is uncovered in the book's early chapters, for her partner Ted – a film editor, born and raised in London – it is not so straightforward. In fact, we are told that 'his memory has always been bad', and that while he has heard plenty of stories from his upbringing, 'they don't seem in any way connected to him' (O'Farrell 2010b: 41–2). This disconnect has been a lifelong affliction, but the arrival of his son has only served to exacerbate the problem – a tension which O'Farrell has revealed was central to the novel's inspiration:

> I was interested in the way having children makes you remember and reassess your own childhood, in micro detail: things I'd never thought about or remembered before would suddenly rear their head. And this made me wonder what it would be like if the memories that resurfaced were of places and people you didn't recognise, if your own life suddenly seemed strange to you. (2010c)

Her choice of language here is key, the idea of remembrances 'rearing their head' once again calling to mind the traumatic eruptions of Woolf and Freud; sure enough, as the novel unfolds, we watch as more and more details from Ted's childhood come to him unbidden. When pushing his son's pram around Parliament Hill, for example, he is suddenly struck by the image of him as a boy, standing at a window, looking down on a man he doesn't recognize. He describes the moment as 'one of the visual disturbances he used to suffer from as a child. A "bizzy" his mother used to call them'; he also says he 'knows it will pass, that it means nothing, a neurological blip, a momentary confusion of pathways' (O'Farrell 2010b: 89). However, just as Ted struggles to find the precise language to articulate these occurrences, so too does he struggle to make sense of the alternative version of events these remembered fragments seem to gesture towards.

Palimpsest

In 2005, Sarah Dillon published the article 'Re-inscribing De Quincey's Palimpsest: The Significance of the Palimpsest in Contemporary Literary and Cultural Studies'. Here she traces the history of palimpsests which, 'until 1845 were palaeographic oddities of concern only to those researching and publishing ancient manuscripts' (Dillon 2005: 243). She also describes the technical process that was involved in creating such 'oddities' – that is, using chemicals to erase the original text from a manuscript's vellum so that a new text could be written on top – but how this was often imperfectly done such that in time, the text's 'ghostly trace then reappeared' (Dillon 2005: 244). Later, Dillon explains, this process of reappearance was actively encouraged via the use of chemical reagents and, moving to the twentieth and twenty-first centuries, imaging technologies. Conducted by manuscript and art restorationists alike, Dillon defines this kind of work as 'traditional palimpsest reading', which 'has as its sole aim and objective the resurrection of the underlying script', while, by contrast, 'the overlying one is irrelevant' (Dillon 2005: 253). Dillon goes on to draw a comparison between this resurrection process and Foucault's description of History as 'the making visible of what was previously unseen' (Foucault 1980: 50).

Turning to literature, for Dillon the most obvious example of such 'traditional palimpsest reading' appears in the genre of 'classical detective fiction', where the protagonist – and, in turn, the reader – is charged with spotting clues or hidden traces that will ultimately reveal the 'not dead, but sleeping' truth. Inevitably she mentions Sherlock Holmes, however she chooses to focus on one story in particular, 'The Adventure of the Golden Pince-Nez'. The story begins with Holmes 'engaged with a powerful lens deciphering the remains of the original inscription upon a palimpsest', a process which Watson describes as 'most conducive to a display of those peculiar powers for which my friend was famous' (Doyle 2001: 607). This parallel between Holmes's detective work and the act of palimpsest reading is later reinforced by Holmes himself – he tries to examine some evidence that has been washed away by the rain and complains: 'It will be harder to read now than that palimpsest' (Doyle 2001: 611). Such links are summed up by Dillon as follows:

> The palimpsest references in 'The Golden Pince-Nez' – part of the tale's self-reflexivity about the practice of reading that its protagonist employs – suggest that the classical detective plot is structured as a layered palimpsest, and that the detective reading exhibited in that plot is equivalent in its aims and methodology to the reading practice of palimpsest editors from the nineteenth century to the present day. (2007: 65)

Returning to *The Hand that First Held Mine*, Ted now finds himself in the role of detective, scouting for 'the underlying script' of his own life. The reader is likewise eager to piece the clues together – both to solve the mystery of Ted's origin story but also to figure out the connection between Ted and Lexie, given both their narratives play out side by side but separately for the duration of the book. However, where *The Hand that First Held Mine* begins to differ from

O'Farrell's previous use of memory loss and interweaving narrative structures is in its self-reflexivity. Much like Doyle, O'Farrell starts to place literal and metaphorical palimpsests side by side, inferring a parallel between the two. For example, just as the concept of the palimpsest originated in the world of manuscripts and art restoration, so too does the art world play a key role in the novel. Ted's partner Elina is an artist, while Lexie's partner Innes – the man who appeared in the garden to change her life and change her name – is both an art dealer and the editor of the Soho-based art journal, *Elsewhere*. It feels especially pertinent, then, that Ted's 'bizzies' increasingly take the form of images or 'visual disturbances', mostly figures who are framed like portraits in a window. Later, Ted and Elina actually attend an exhibition in London's National Portrait Gallery of John Deakin's photographs, which were taken around the streets of Soho. Though Ted has no idea why, one photo in particular strikes a chord – it is a black and white shot of a couple slouching side by side and, crucially, 'The sign on the wall behind them reads "elsewher", the end of the word obliterated by the man's head' (O'Farrell 2010b: 190). This is a literal 'ghostly trace' – an actual piece of 'underlying script' – but it is also a metaphorical one, a narrative clue for the reader to spot (we assume, correctly as it turns out, that the photo is of Lexie and Innes). Although Ted doesn't yet understand the image's relevance, he is still markedly struck by it, such that in the gallery café afterwards he has a kind of epiphany:

> He is sitting at the table, drinking coffee, talking with his friend and his girlfriend and, without warning, something rears its head. The recollection of himself as a child on a woman's knee [. . .] This keeps happening, Ted finds, and more since Jonah was born. Flashes of something else, somewhere else [. . .] A hint, a glimpse, a blurred image, like a poster seen from the window of a speeding train. (O'Farrell 2010b: 191)

Not only does O'Farrell's exact phrase 'rears its head' feature here, the phrases 'a blurred image' and 'a poster' once again link back to the various forms of visual culture that populate Ted's life. Meanwhile, 'something else, somewhere else' gestures towards the magazine's title – a title with which Ted isn't yet directly familiar, but which has already subsumed itself into his inner language via the 'ghostly trace' in the photograph. After this latest 'bizzy', Ted slinks away to the gift shop to purchase a postcard of the image, only to produce it again later in the novel, just as the truth of his past is finally becoming clear. The postcard has been buried away – 'it is bent and creased from being folded inside Ted's wallet' – but now, finally, it has been unearthed (O'Farrell 2010b: 349).

At another point towards the novel's climax, Elina accidentally spots a stack of paintings poking out from where they have been hidden down a side panel in Ted's parents' bathroom. This 'ghostly trace' – not a mark on a canvas but, ironically, a set of *actual* canvases – is one of the final clues in the puzzle, given the reader instantly recognizes these as the paintings that once belonged to Lexie (who in turn inherited them from Innes – they have been passed down and down and down through generations). Sure enough, one paragraph later, Ted's mother utters her Christian name for the first time, revealing to the reader that she is in fact Innes's stepdaughter, Margot. So again, moments of literal and metaphorical palimpsest discovery have been placed side by side, O'Farrell's self-reflexivity once more rearing its head.

On top of these artistic links, Ted's search for hidden traces also resonates with his own job as a film editor. Elina describes what he does as 'removing and splicing the bad bits from films, making sure it all appears smooth and faultless, as if it was never any other way' (O'Farrell 2010b: 48). Later in the novel, as the 'bizzies' get worse and the half-remembered clues grow more frequent (Ted tries to write them all out, making a list of jumbled words – a scrap of text which Elina finds buried down the side of the sofa [O'Farrell 2010b: 219]), we watch Ted at work:

Ted moves the mouse again and the images scroll forward, then back, at inching speed. Forward, back.

There! He has it! He knew it! A black flicker across the camera. A piece of equipment, a dangling wire, a dinger-end, who knows? But he's found it and, with a swift few clicks of the mouse, eliminated it. [...]

For no reason at all, he suddenly thinks of his father. Pulling him down a street as a child. (O'Farrell 2010b: 184)

Here we observe Ted, the 'traditional palimpsest reader', hunting for – and ultimately finding – a *literal* trace or 'underlying script' on the film footage. We then witness how the process triggers the emergence of a metaphorical trace – a piece of 'underlying script' from his own repressed past.

Palimpsestic Forms and the Palimpsestic City

It is undeniable, then, that there is self-reflexive playfulness at work in *The Hand that First Held Mine*, as O'Farrell takes the metaphorical concept of the palimpsest and places it alongside – or sometimes literally *within* – works of art, thus foregrounding the term's origins. She also draws parallels between Ted's editorial work and his personal quest for the traces which might finally provide narrative clarity to his life. However, even beyond these inclusions, O'Farrell also uses the novel's form to take these parallels further. Not only are the characters haunted by more and more ghostly traces, the narrator actually goes on to break the fourth wall, excavating London entirely and pointing out the 'underlying scripts' that lurk below the surface:

> Innes's flat today is no longer a flat. At first glance, it is unrecognisable, fifty years on. But [. . .] the raised grain of his wallpaper is just discernible under the awful lilac paint that has been daubed on the walls. There is still the loose board on the landing, which always tripped people up, now covered with beige carpet, and no one who lives here now knows that under there, still, is a spare key for the *Elsewhere* offices. [. . .] Under the carpet by the door there is a stain on the floorboards, which appeared during a party they held that same year. (O'Farrell 2010b: 125)

Like the stratification of the garden soil in the novel's opening scene, here we have an urban equivalent, the narrator-as-archaeologist digging back through time and tenancies and tarnished flooring. Surfaces are destabilized such that – like a restorationist using imaging technology – the reader is invited to see what lies beneath. Later, in an even more loaded example, the narrator's camera tracks the progress of an unnamed girl strolling the Soho streets and directs our attention towards the numerous pertinent palimpsests she passes on her way:

> She crosses and recrosses the paving slab where Innes first embraced Lexie in 1957; [. . .] she leans for a moment against the piece of wall against which Lexie and Innes posed for John Deakin on an overcast Wednesday in 1959. And right where the girl from upstairs is grinding out her cigarette is where, in wet weather, it is possible to see the ghost-outline of letters spelling 'e l s e w h e r e', and probably no one notices this and if they did they wouldn't know why. (O'Farrell 2010b: 319)

Again, we are being invited to witness the layering of time – the result of different moments from the protagonists' lives having been written onto the surface of the city. The narrator even uses the phrase 'ghost-outline' when referring to the former *Elsewhere* sign – something, we are told, nobody would notice or understand – but of course, having been trained as detectives or 'traditional palimpsest readers' ourselves, we notice, we understand. And as palimpsest readers, we recognize an additional link, for while we might have assumed that

Lexie and Innes were the couple in the crucial photograph in the John Deakin exhibition, now our suspicions have officially been confirmed.

In the culmination of this approach, O'Farrell brings the novel's two timelines together – not only via a photograph, but by physically layering them one over the other and foregrounding the overlap:

> The *Elsewhere* offices are currently a café. Or a bar. It's uncertain which. It says 'The Lagoon Café Bar' above the door so you can take your pick.
>
> What was Innes's back room, where he kept paintings and his sofa and assorted junk, is now a kitchen. They grill panini, mix hummus and lay out olives in little bowls there – the Lagoon's cuisine is unspecified Mediterranean, and served by a mix of Bosnians, Poles and Australians.
>
> [. . .]
>
> And sitting at the table where Lexie's desk used to be is Ted. (O'Farrell 2010b: 178)

This is the first time in the novel that a literal palimpsest has been used to link the two main characters, as both occupy the exact same spot decades apart. And, as we eventually discover, the spatial overlap foreshadows the factual connection, since Ted ultimately discovers that Lexie – not Margot – was his mother.

The description of The Lagoon Café Bar and the multiplicity of nationalities who work there also gestures towards another way in which many critics have argued the city embodies the concept of the palimpsest – not only in terms of time, but also in terms of diversity, as a variety of cultural experiences and everyday realities intersect and overlap. In her book *The Intelligible Metropolis*, for example, Nora Plesske describes how the idea of the palimpsest 'helps to focus on the consciousness of historical marginality and cultural alterity hidden beneath or within the strata of the dominant cultural text. Palimpsestic reading as a procedure of textual archaeology brings to light invisible everyday practices' (Plesske 2014: 304). Attending in particular to London, Plesske encourages us to see beyond – or indeed, beneath – a city's dominant culture and discourse, and to read instead for the other (or indeed, Other) lived realities. That being said, Plesske does also write about 'Historical Layering' – that is, the particular coexistence of London's past and present – and how the capital 'conflates various historical layers and obliterates temporal boundaries' (2014: 305). She describes the 'interweaving stratifications of past, present, and future in the urban texture' and how this creates 'a palimpsest in which London's contradictory historical narratives find expression' (Plesske 2014: 305). I have already mentioned how this takes place in *Mrs Dalloway* where, as Kate Flint has it, 'Woolf uses the continual eruption of memory to destabilise the locations of the present. In palimpsestic fashion, characters remember the London of their childhood and write it onto the contemporary topography' (2017: 50). However, as we have seen, in O'Farrell's London this process is taken even further, such that it is not only the characters but the narrative form itself which 'writes' the London of the past 'onto the contemporary topography' and ensures the reader notices when exactly this takes place.

Palimpsestuousness

For all its resurfacing and remembering of things past, *Mrs Dalloway* is still set over the course of a single day – that is, the contemporary still dominates the narrative focus. In *The Hand that First Held Mine*, by contrast, the novel alternates between Lexie's story and that of Elina and Ted, with both strands written in the present tense. By adopting this structure – and by pointing out the moments at which the two strands (at least spatially at first) overlap, there is a sense of both stories existing simultaneously; to borrow Plesske terms, O'Farrell 'obliterates temporal boundaries' and builds a novel through 'interweaving stratifications'. Crucially, Plesske uses these phrases in the chapter of her book entitled 'The Palimpsestuous City', and it is here that she draws on Dillon's distinction between 'traditional palimpsest reading' and an attendance to the more dynamic concept of 'palimpsestuousness'. To Dillon's mind, where the former prioritizes the removal of subsequent layers of text to get back to 'the original script', palimpsestuousness reading is more about examining – and celebrating – the original *as well as* the subsequent layers, and the many ways in which these interact. Returning to Freud, Dillon outlines how he later put forward an alternative model of memory to replace his 'first stratified topography of the unconscious, preconscious and conscious systems'; Dillon describes this updated model as a much more 'complex structure of cryptic incorporation' (Dillon 2005: 249). Meanwhile, having drawn earlier parallels between 'traditional palimpsest reading' and Foucault's concept of History, Dillon now highlights Foucault's concept of Genealogy instead; this she views as 'a form of palimpsestuousness reading that does not focus solely on the underlying text for to do so would be to unravel and destroy the palimpsest, which exists only and precisely *as* the involution of texts' (Dillon 2005: 254; her emphasis).

    In the context of literary studies, this more dynamic approach has been adopted by many critics when examining contemporary fiction. Michele Janette, for example, unpacks the numerous layers at work in Monique Truong's *Bitter in the Mouth* and describes – in terms reminiscent of Dillon's palimpsestuousness – how 'as an interpretative tool, the palimpsest asks us to see distinction and interaction simultaneously: to see individual textual layers and their significance and *also* to see the blended patterns produced as the layers combine' (2014: 155–6; my emphasis). Focusing on Truong's novel about an Asian-American woman coming of age in rural North Carolina, Janette identifies the ways in which 'the novel's palimpsestic style and structure *train readers in palimpsestic thinking* more broadly and offer the practice of such thinking as a basis for social engagement' (2014: 156; my emphasis). The 'social engagement' in question here is to do with issues of race and disability, as Truong's form encourages us to hold multiple truths at once and to witness the points of overlap between these intersectional issues. As Janette frames it, the novel 'asks us to dwell in the uncomfortable and sometimes jarring intellectual space of unreconciled complexity' (2014: 174). While O'Farrell's novel may differ significantly from Truong's, for the final section of this chapter I wish to outline how *The Hand that First Held Mine* adopts a similar formal approach to explore an 'intellectual space of unreconciled complexity' – in this case, that of motherhood and female identity.

O'Farrell's Palimpsestuous Women

I have already outlined how the novel's male protagonist, Ted, spends much of his time as a 'traditional palimpsest reader', hunting for traces of his repressed history. I have also mentioned how his wife Elina spends the opening chapters searching for the truth about her son's birth, only to uncover the traumatic memories thereof. However, even after Elina has achieved clarity, the novel flirts with the possibility of her embodying another kind of palimpsest – that is, another example of an old text being completely erased and supplanted by a new one – this time in the form of the classic mother/artist dichotomy. In her canonical text *Of Woman Born* (1976), Adrienne Rich unpacks the patriarchal construct of 'motherhood' that society forces on a woman as soon as she has given birth. Rich foregrounds how this construct actively seeks to supplant or obliterate any previous autonomous identity a woman might otherwise have had. More recently, Daniel Stern's book, *The Birth of a Mother* (1998), describes how a mother is 'born' much like her baby is, her previous self transformed into something wholly new, while journalist Rachel Bertsche asks, simply: 'When Your Name Becomes "Mom", Do Your Other Identities Matter?'

These questions are often seen as even more charged when it comes to women involved in artistic careers, and much has been written by theorists and journalists alike about the irreconcilable union of the mother and the artist figure. Woolf herself has described how 'the Angel in the House' – that is, the symbol of perfect domesticity – is in direct opposition to a woman pursuing a creative life, while critic Cyril Connolly famously declared that 'there is no more sombre enemy of good art than the pram in the hallway' ([1938] 2008: 116). O'Farrell has described Connolly's as 'a loathsome assertion', explaining how she 'always detested the twisted misogyny of it' (2003); these words feature in an article she wrote for the *Guardian* while pregnant with her first child. During this time, she explains, she was in receipt of constant (unsolicited) warnings about how becoming a mother would jeopardize her identity as a writer – a warning she both resented and sought to unpack:

> These people are suggesting that it's asking too much to want children and novels, that it's impossible to look after a child and to have the time and mental capacity necessary to write. Is it unforgivable chutzpah to think you can do both? [. . .]
>
> Will I be fine and become, under my new stringencies, more focused and productive? Or will I turn into a cabbage-brain and never write another word? Ask me again in a few months' time. (O'Farrell 2003)

Of course, after the release of this article – and the birth of her son – O'Farrell went on to publish eight more books, have two more children and win countless international awards, thus undermining Connolly's assertion once and for all.

Within the context of *The Hand that First Held Mine*, after the birth of her son, Elina has to repeat her name over and over again to try and remember who she even is. A health visitor comes to the house and refers to her by the wrong name, but Elina does not have the confidence – let alone the energy – to correct her, so proceeds under this alien identity. Later she attends a GP appointment and is asked for her name, but mistakenly gives the baby's instead; even after they clarify that they are looking for hers, Elina momentarily forgets the answer. Elsewhere, thinking of her former self – that is, her artist self – Elina admits she 'cannot fathom, cannot grasp what happened to that person' (O'Farrell 2010b: 49). Searching for answers, she finds her old diary up in the attic – the space which also used to be 'her room, her studio, back when she was Ted's lodger' (O'Farrell 2010b: 63). Interestingly, the attic is also home to 'the only full-length mirror in the house', which Elina now uses to examine her scar – the 'ghostly trace' of her traumatic labour (O'Farrell 2010b: 63).

After Elina became Ted's girlfriend and moved down into the house proper, they built a studio in the back garden in which she could paint. Now – much like the symbolic parallels between the city and the self – this studio serves as a spatial embodiment of the previous incarnation of her identity. Staring at it, a new mother, Elina admits 'she cannot remember how you be an artist, what you do, how you spend your time. Her life in that small wooden building, all the hours she's spent in there, seem as distant as her time in kindergarten' (O'Farrell 2010b: 23). Only once does Ted come home to find Elina – and their son – in the studio; Ted regards her through the glass – another framed portrait of the past: 'She looks, Ted sees, like she used to. Like she did when he first met her' (O'Farrell 2010b: 142). This moment, however, is short-lived – Ted enters, the baby starts screaming and any possibility of artistic work is thwarted once more. After that, the studio isn't mentioned again until much later in the novel when Elina complains about how wild the garden has become, the growth threatening to swallow the studio completely: 'You can barely see it any more for all the weeds. Another few weeks and it will have completely disappeared. When I finally do have the chance to work I won't be able to get in there' (O'Farrell 2010b: 267). We can read this as a metaphor for Elina's previous artistic self being swallowed by the wildness of her new reality – a reality that threatens, to her mind, to completely erase what was there before.

Ted, though, is determined not to let this happen; we find him one afternoon down on his hands and knees clearing the grass and weeds away. And yet, for all his frantic gardening – all his determination to strip back the overlaid text – Ted's language here is key: 'He wants to have if not his old life then some kind of life, not this constant lurching from one day to the next' (O'Farrell 2010b: 267). For the first time, Ted acknowledges they cannot – and maybe do not even want to – go back to exactly how they were before, all he knows is that access to the studio should still be a part of their life – and, crucially, part of the woman Elina now is. Interestingly, at this moment in the garden, Ted has yet another 'bizzy', the literal and metaphorical palimpsest hunting once again taking place side by side: 'perhaps it is some confluence of elements causing a new connection because it is suddenly as if he has fallen through a trapdoor or down a rabbit hole' (O'Farrell 2010b: 268). Ted has another flashback from his youth; afterwards he finds himself 'back in his life [. . .] But at the same time he is also a little boy, crouching at a lawn edge' (O'Farrell 2010b: 268). This moment of simultaneity marks a crucial shift from Ted's earlier 'bizzies', as the past and present seem to coexist. Similarly, as Elina starts to find her feet with the baby (despite the chronic sleep deprivation), we watch her doze in and out of consciousness where she sees the veranda on her mother's house in Nauvo, she sees the curve of Jonah's head in the dark, she sees the flat water of the archipelago on a windless day, she sees her brother walking away from her down a gravelled track, she sees a painting she was working on before Jonah was born, she sees the grain of the canvas beneath a thick layer of paint, she sees Jonah again, still sucking, she sees the pattern of intersecting tramlines on a Helsinki street corner, she sees—

Suddenly she is wide awake, back in the bedroom. (O'Farrell 2010b: 225)

In mentioning 'the grain of the canvas beneath the thick layer of paint', O'Farrell once again puts us in mind of a literal palimpsest; however, this description is more than just seeing below the surface – it is, to use Dillon's words, to observe the 'complex structure of cryptic incorporation' that is Elina's identity. Past and present, England and Finland, mother and artist all intersect to form the palimpsestuous woman she now is.

Returning to Lexie, after Innes's death we are told that 'existence as Lexie had come to know it ended and another began: she dropped [. . .] out of her life and into another' (O'Farrell 2010b: 236). This also entails a physical relocation – she finds a new bedsit and a new job, filing and proofreading at the *Daily Courier* on Fleet Street, and vows she will 'never return to the grid of streets that made up Soho, not even once' (O'Farrell 2010b: 236). Eventually she finds a new boyfriend too – an actor named Felix by whom she ultimately gets pregnant. After the birth of their son, Lexie writes an article called '*the women we become after children*', O'Farrell once again alluding to the traditional narrative of a woman's identity being supplanted by motherhood (O'Farrell 2010b: 263). The article lists all the ways in which Lexie – like all new mothers – now differs from her previous self: '*We change shape. [. . .] We lose muscle tone, sleep, reason, perspective. Our hearts begin to live outside our bodies. [. . .] We get used to not getting where we were going. [. . .] We learn to look less in the mirror*' (2010b: 264). And yet, for all these changes, Lexie doesn't give up work, she doesn't change her name – despite Felix's constant offers, she doesn't marry and settle down. Instead, she and their son move to a flat in Dartmouth Park where Lexie 'peeled up the rotten carpets and old, damp lino, scrubbed the boards and varnished them. She whitewashed the back of the house. She rubbed the windows with newspaper and vinegar until sunshine glowed through' (O'Farrell 2010b: 263). Rather than covering up the past then, Lexie is exposing it – embracing it. She also hangs her paintings – Innes's paintings – on the wall, surrounding herself with his legacy. At work, too, she 'gives herself away' (O'Farrell 2010b: 243) – that is, she reveals her past experience with and intimate knowledge of the art world, and is thus invited to branch out and start writing reviews and artist interviews for the *Daily Courier*. We discover that she ultimately spent the rest of her career (until her untimely death) writing a column called 'From the Frontline of Motherhood', but also writing about art – it wasn't a case of one or the other, it was both; her past and present self intertwined.

At the very end of *The Hand that First Held Mine*, it is Elina who finds all these articles – she digs through a newspaper archive and uncovers the wealth of material left behind by Lexie, then brings them home to Ted who has been plunged into a deep depression. Elina sits by his bedside and reads Lexie's words aloud; when she pauses, Ted says: 'Keep going, El [. . .] keep going', and the novel closes with the simple clause: 'And so she does' (O'Farrell 2010b: 374). This sense of ongoingness, of becoming, chimes with the novel's overall celebration of palimpsestuousness – not a prioritization of one layer over another but an invitation to move fluidly between different versions, noticing all the ways they intersect and coexist. We think back to the early assertion that our protagonist is 'made up of myriad Lexies and Alexandras all sheathed inside one another, like Russian dolls'. By the end of her Russian doll of a novel, O'Farrell makes it clear that a woman need not select one name, one identity, one version and erase all others; instead, she can relish the myriad possibilities of the female self.

4

Vantage Points

How Maggie O'Farrell Dissects a Marriage by Shifting Points of View in *This Must Be the Place*

Edward Matthews

Introduction

O'Farrell indicated that from the outset, *This Must Be the Place* was a reaction to the restrictive structure of her preceding novel, *Instructions for a Heatwave*. She wished to write something 'without any constraints' and the result was a 382-page novel spanning four continents, seventy-two years, twenty-eight chapters, fourteen focal characters and five different narrative points of view (O'Farrell Q&A n.d.). The scope could easily have become unwieldy, the lack of constraints unravelling into a chaotic narrative with no throughline, but O'Farrell carefully structured the novel to alternate focal characters and narrative points of view that layered the storyline until a comprehensive picture of a marriage emerged – that of its two protagonists: Daniel and Claudette. O'Farrell uses several narrative points of view to characterize these people – first person, first-person plural, second person, third-person close, third-person omniscient – but predominantly relies upon Daniel's first person and a close-third that follows several focal characters. My operating definition of close third-person point of view comes from Austrian literary theorist Franz Karl Stanzel's 'figural narrative situation' described by the narratologist Jan Christoph Meister as a 'third-person narrator [that] remains unobtrusive while the narrative information is filtered through the internal perspective of the reflector character' (qtd. in Meister 2009: 335). This is the form O'Farrell's third-person point of view predominantly takes as she examines Daniel and Claudette's relationship.

Both Daniel and Claudette make problematic decisions that invite readerly judgement. Daniel is an absentee father, lacks impulse control and has difficulty processing grief which leads him to deceive loved ones. Claudette has an affair with a director who she eventually has a child with, then abandons him while taking their child into hiding. What makes O'Farrell's narrative decisions effective is that she examines Daniel and Claudette's decisions through a multitude of narrative lenses from different characters' vantage points – their children, their exes, a parent, a sibling, an in-law, a stranger and so on – which allows the reader to visit and revisit these seemingly negative attributes with a renewed understanding.

This chapter seeks to demonstrate how O'Farrell's craft is deserving of the same level of literary recognition enjoyed by two of her peers – Zadie Smith and Colum McCann. I will show how *This Must Be the Place* is more effective in conveying the complexity of an intimate relationship by contrasting its narrative approach with Zadie Smith's 2012 novel *NW*, then will draw a comparison to McCann's 2009 National Book Award-winning *Let the Great World Spin*, the latter of which also alternates narrative points of view, but in service of a complex individual (rather than a relationship). To establish a standard of narrative effectiveness by which I can compare novels from these three authors, I am using George Saunders's axiom of quality storytelling: 'Always be escalating. That's all a story is, really: a continual system of escalation' (Saunders 2021: 153). The degree to which each novel shifts the narrative point of view in service of escalating the plot's tension is where I build my case that *This Must Be the Place* is the superior novel to *NW* and *Let the Great World Spin*. Through an exegesis of the narrative techniques of *This Must Be the Place*, I intend to show how O'Farrell earns her place among the best contemporary novelists.

How O'Farrell Crafts a Three-Dimensional Protagonist

There are two primary narrative points of view O'Farrell uses to accentuate her characters' personalities. Daniel's chapters are mainly told in first person and reflect his neurotic interiority and loquaciousness, whereas Claudette's sections are told in a close-third that examines the situation and her feelings but gives no access to the depth of these feelings or motivations. Daniel is an American linguistics professor; Claudette is a former movie star. Daniel visited Ireland on an impulse to recover his grandfather's ashes and stumbled across Claudette and her seven-year-old son, Ari, changing a tyre in Donegal, a county at the topmost point of the Republic of Ireland. Daniel is divorced and estranged from his two children who live with their mother in San Francisco after he lost a prolonged custody battle. Claudette is divorced and estranged from her ex-husband, who she left on a yacht before sunrise on the Swedish coast with their only child in tow. Their encounter represents a new beginning, allowing Daniel insulation from his familial obligations and Claudette from the fame she garnered as an actress. They fall in love, Daniel moves in and they have two children together (Marithe and Calvin). After steadying himself in this new life, Daniel reconnects with his first two children (Niall and Phoebe) who grew up in his absence, eventually accepting him back into their lives after some hesitancy. Claudette fills the loneliness of her isolation with their new family. In short, they heal. The plot complicates when Daniel hears that an ex-girlfriend and first love, Nicola Janks, died the same year they broke up and he is overwhelmed with the thought of having contributed to her death in some way.

O'Farrell parallels the past lives of Claudette and Daniel by interspersing flashbacks to each character at the key inflection points of their lives as they were deciding whom to be with and how to raise their children. When narrating Claudette, O'Farrell's close-third takes readers through Claudette's meeting with her first husband (Timou), film sets, life in London, Los Angeles. Her thoughts, desires and anxieties are on display but still at a distance – the distance that separates third person from first. In contrast, Daniel's sections are primarily first-person singular, and his thoughts/desires/anxieties are not only on display but inform the writing, dialogue, structure and rhythm of the text. The following is a representative passage of Claudette's close-third, a passage taking place on her film set in India where she balances the double life of movie star and mother:

> She is listening for the rhythmic pad of his feet, the mellifluous rise in his voice, saying, Maman, Maman. She has to hold that small body in her arms, has to press her cheek to the silk of his hair, has to look into those grave hazel eyes, she has to. Just for a moment. But the nanny is coming toward her: she has Ari's sweatshirt in her hands; she is holding her finger to her lips and shaking her head. 'He's just this minute gone to sleep', she is saying. The disappointment is physical: a plummet in the stomach, a clenching surge in her headache, a tensing in her forearms . . . She has to gulp at the air in the trailer so as not to cry. (O'Farrell 2016a: 203)

Readers are taken into her thoughts and her reactions, but the third person keeps us from her feelings towards these thoughts, these actions. It refrains from the editorializations that occur moment to moment in our minds, the little judgements that betray how we view the world and our relation to it. We see how her body reacts to the disappointment, but don't see whether she blames the nanny or envies her or feels a mix of gratitude and dismay towards her; we are prohibited from knowing the interiority of Claudette, like most of the others who interact with her – Timou (her ex-husband), Daniel (her future husband), the nanny holding her child, the personal assistant chasing after her. Claudette lets each person in only to a certain point, under certain terms, and her personality is revealed through layering the interactions with her mother, brother, sister-in-law, ex-husband, husband and children as the novel progresses. The reader assembles these pieces as they are given to form a whole picture of Claudette.

Then there is Daniel.

There's a clarity to Daniel's behaviour when he is in the moment – whether it be his first encounter with Claudette, a conversation with his estranged children, a friend he hasn't seen since college, a stepmother he's never met – but the irrationality of what led him from one encounter to the next reveals his own complexity. As opposed to the arms-distance of Claudette's third person, Daniel's first person comes with a barrage of information. Readers are given all the pieces of his personality at once and left wondering what sort of puzzle it's supposed to make.

The following passage comes from the aptly named chapter 'The Tired Mind is a Stovetop'. In it, Daniel has tracked down a college friend, Todd, who he hasn't seen in twenty years. Todd and Daniel were roommates at a university in England where Nicola was a young instructor with whom Daniel began a relationship. During his last night in the UK, the three of them went to a wedding together and did narcotics even though Nicola was unwell due to an eating disorder. Daniel left her unconscious in order to catch his flight early the next morning, leaving her in Todd's care. Twenty years later, Daniel learns that she died the same year – 1986 – and meets with Todd to see whether she overdosed the night of the friend's wedding. Todd confirms that she died that year – but months after the night of the wedding – and Daniel feels a mix of relief and remorse:

> I find myself swallowing and swallowing, as if to keep something down, as if there is something in me fighting to get out. I have to consciously push images from my mind: Nicola as frail as a bird, a hospital bed, her house, which was beautiful, painted dove gray with woven rugs on the wooden floors, bookcases lining the stairs. Who would have come to dismantle it, to cart away all those books and rugs? Who would have been the first over that threshold? Did they come with boxes and garbage bags? Todd is standing, lifting his bag, pulling out his wallet, and tossing money onto the table. My mind is thrumming, bruised, overworked, but somewhere a veil of fog lifts. (O'Farrell 2016a: 196)

Similar to Claudette's passage, we feel the visceral nature of this encounter, Daniel's bodily reaction, the stress and the desire. The passages have a similar staccato rhythm, abundant description, one detail leads to three others in rapid succession, the way our minds leap from one thing to the next. The difference is with Daniel's passage, the first-person point of view gives the reader rhetorical questions, editorializations, in addition to the visceral description. The narration gives a window into the conscious fight between mind and body, our inability to keep the past from interfering with the present, which is a core theme in *This Must Be the Place*.

What makes O'Farrell's structure effective is that readers become trained in Daniel's idiosyncratic thought patterns, his way of processing what is happening. Readers pick up the rhythm of these alternations so that the distance between a chapter *from* Daniel and a chapter *about* Daniel never becomes too great that we lose track of his rationale, his thinking and interpretation. The intimate understanding of his mind state and the external observations of his actions merge into a believable, three-dimensional person. The novel works because the narrative never strays too far from this focal point (Claudette and Daniel's relationship). It never goes five chapters without returning to Daniel either in the first person or in the close-third, establishing a pace that keeps his characteristics (impulsiveness, verboseness) top of mind as he collides with other characters and tension escalates therein (to return to Saunders's dictum about what makes a good story).

Claudette's narrative parallels Daniel's, the close-third point of view giving readers insights into her past trauma and her current marriage. When she and Daniel separate three-quarters of the way through the book, we are left guessing if they will be reunited by the end, because Claudette's motivations are obscured by the close-third point of view. We are only given her reactions to others, so the tension of the plot remains until the very last page. The last encounter Daniel and Claudette have is a collision of their characteristics that O'Farrell has shown us for nearly 400 pages – Daniel is effusive and charming, while Claudette is emotionally withholding and guarded. The final chapter yields an emotional payoff not only because of the plot point (Claudette chooses forgiveness and lets Daniel back into her life) but because O'Farrell has trained us on how to read this novel and controlled the perspective enough to keep readers invested without giving us all of the pieces – the tension residing in the distance between what we know (Daniel's thoughts revealed through first-person point of view) and what is unknown (Claudette's motivations kept hidden through close-third point of view). The alternations of focal character and narrative point of view provide an effective balance, one that is difficult to achieve, especially when we see how talented novelists like Zadie Smith can fall short of this balance.

Contrasting Narrative Structure of *This Must Be the Place* with Zadie Smith's *NW*

To better demonstrate the effectiveness of O'Farrell's narrative structure in *This Must Be the Place*, I will contrast it with Zadie Smith's 2012 novel *NW*, a book that also alternates narrative points of view as it characterizes its two protagonists – Leah and Natalie. Similar in length (both around 400 pages), *NW* is divided into five sections – 'Visitation', 'Guest', 'Host', 'Crossing', 'Visitation' (a second time) – each with a different focal character followed by a close-third point of view that occasionally breaks the fourth wall. The first section ('Visitation') follows Leah, a social worker in her early thirties happily married to a Frenchman named Michel. They live on modest incomes in northwest London on a council estate like the one in which Leah and Natalie were raised. Despite being lifelong best friends, a rift in their friendship that cuts along class-lines becomes clear. Leah and Michel get invited to dinner parties by Natalie, who became a successful barrister and married a banker named Frank. They live an upper-class lifestyle with friends who are fellow barristers and bankers. These friends are the tablemates at dinner parties where Leah and Michel feel subjected to being the local colour as they 'look down at their plates and cut their food with great care, letting Natalie tell their stories for them, nodding to confirm points of fact, names, times, places' (Smith 2012: 96). When Michel tries to have a conversation about the stock market with Frank, the latter dissuades him from day trading in an arguably condescending way, advising 'signing on with an online site' and 'playing with fake money' (Smith 2012: 74). Leah feels a perennial adolescence that Natalie seems to have moved on from, with her two kids, her wealthy husband, her big house that 'makes her feel like a child' (Smith 2012: 74). The main tension in 'Visitation' is Michel's desire to have children and Leah's unwillingness, which takes the form of lying about taking birth control which she stole from Natalie. The landmarks of growing up punctuate *NW*, a novel that is entirely character-driven.

Smith's gift for characterization is her most distinguishing skill. The people created within a Zadie Smith novel are fully formed and lived-in. Each page reveals a new valence. Readers follow Leah for 106 pages with the big reveal about birth control coming near the end of 'Visitation'. The novel takes a detour from the main Leah/Natalie story arc to follow Felix, a Black resident of northwest London who extricates himself from one relationship while deepening another, then meeting a tragic death when he is robbed and stabbed. This crime is tangentially related to Leah and Natalie in that it occurs in the vicinity of their neighbourhood and is perpetrated by an old classmate of theirs, Nathan Bogle, whom Natalie encounters in the final section 'Crossing'. But other than displaying Smith's gift for characterization and fleshing out the setting more comprehensively – revealing other dimensions about life in northwest London – the sections dividing Leah's from Natalie's do not illuminate any new aspects of their friendship. They do not escalate the narrative trajectories of Leah or Natalie in a meaningful way.

When discussing *NW*'s narrator, I agree with Krasniqi and Tahiri's observation of 'a third-person narrator who does not intrude over the narrative but recounts the story from the four characters' angles, constrained in the knowledge imparted and transforming stylistically by taking on the attributes of each of the reflectors in turn' (2022: 143). Applying this framework of focal characters-as-reflectors to both *This Must Be the Place* and *NW*, it's clear that O'Farrell uses the shifting point of view technique to move the plot forward, underscore the main theme and heighten characterization – the reflectors service three areas simultaneously as they culminate towards the reunification of Daniel and Claudette. In *NW*, I argue, the multiple third-person point of view techniques serve only to layer characterization without moving the plot forward (Krasniqi et al. 2022: 138).

Smith's point of view decisions are surrounded with other postmodern stylistic choices – alternating between quotation marks to denote dialogue and em-dashes, snatches of contextless dialogue, prose poems, subsections that jump back and forth through time – making the alternating points of view feel like an avant-garde flourish, rather than a necessary device to make the plot work. The reason O'Farrell's shifting point of view works is because each time it reflects a new aspect of the story and escalates the tension of the plot. Readers do not have to wait 100 pages for relevant new information that intensifies the central plot. The past invades the present regularly enough for the reader never to forget the central question of the novel: Can regrets from Daniel's past be integrated into a presently healthy person that Claudette will accept? Or the simplified version: Can Daniel change?

The two pivotal years of Daniel's narrative are 1986 (his mother dies, Nicola's abortion, leaving Nicola unconscious in the woods to catch his flight) and 2010 (making amends with his estranged children, reconnecting with Todd to find out about Nicola, unpacking these events to a suspicious Claudette). The latter years covered in the novel (2011–16) recount primarily how Daniel grapples with the original regrets and the subsequent communication of these past mistakes to his current wife. The point of view alternates between first person, third-close and third-omniscient rotating among six different characters who all accentuate different character traits of Daniel's. Each of these character traits are inflection points that escalate the tension of the central question, which, put differently is: Can he communicate honestly and deliberately instead of acting impulsively and making amends retroactively?

By approaching this question through the vantage points of key characters he hurts through these impulsive acts, it takes nearly 400 pages to properly address said question, one that readers never lose sight of because the intervals by which it is approached are frequent. The novel necessitates this length. The process to answering the central question surrounding the plot in Zadie Smith's *NW* (will Leah and Natalie reconnect as adults across divides of class and race?) is circuitous and takes points of view from focal characters (Felix and Nathan) that do not approach this central question or illuminate anything new about its two protagonists. Readers follow Leah for 100 pages, then wait another 100 pages to follow Natalie and connect the dots to approximate this question. By the time we return to Leah's pivotal plot point (taking birth control pills without Michel's knowledge), there is a distant recollection of Leah's voice, her worldview, her motivation for this decision, whereas Natalie's voice/worldview/motivation feels so immediate given the 150+ pages spent following her in the 'Host' section. The intervals between the shifting points of view (the close-third following Leah and the close-third following Natalie) have a hundred pages between them, so the emotional impact of Leah's decision and Michel's reaction (seen through Natalie's eyes) does not land with the intended force. Put simply, in *NW* the time spent away from the protagonist dilutes the impact of Leah's decision once revisited.

O'Farrell structured *This Must Be the Place* to change focal characters and points of view often enough that no chapter carries on for longer than thirty-five pages (with most being 10–20 pages), thereby creating a rhythm for the changes in point of view, focal character and timeline. O'Farrell establishes this rhythm early on and continues it throughout the narrative, so the reader expects a change of chapter to bring a change in point of view or focal character, making for fluid reading when this change occurs. These changes layer as the book progresses and culminate in moments that land with impact, making the characterization double as plot progression. This structure allows the story to escalate with each passing chapter, a key point George Saunders makes in his exegesis of great Russian short stories (Saunders 2021: 153, 230).

The brilliance of this structure is that each chapter (whether it occurs in 1944, 1986, 1996, 2010, 2013, 2014, 2016) feels immediate in its narration, rather than a pre-processed memory the reader is made privy to. This immediacy stems from the multiplicity of narrative voices – with each voice having a different motivation, agenda, set of concerns and perspective on the situation. In Todd's chapter, we learn that Daniel, even in college, is a natural-born leader, someone people are drawn to follow (O'Farrell 2016a: 160). In Niall's chapter, we learn that Daniel is always pleased to see his son, that he doesn't force him to chat and that he brings something to occupy Niall's time while they sit together for a doctor's appointment (O'Farrell 2016a: 47). In Nicola's chapter, we learn that Daniel is (or at least she perceives him to be) 'set apart' from other men given he was raised with 'a strong mother and a clutch of sisters' making him 'much more evolved' and a 'better lover' (O'Farrell 2016a: 280).

As O'Farrell layers these descriptions, a full character emerges, one capable of being a good father and a terrible friend, an impulsive boyfriend but a resolute husband. Had O'Farrell decided to narrate the entire story from Daniel's first-person point of view, the reading experience would be entirely different because he'd become an unreliable narrator when discussing his attributes as a father and his evolution as a lover. It would be a less effective novel because the characterization would be one-dimensional, consumed with Daniel's frenetic, self-absorbed thought patterns. It'd be difficult to get any kind of objective, holistic understanding. Or if, like *NW*, the novel followed Daniel at a close-third for 100 pages, building character and exposition solely for his storyline, then switched to following Claudette for 150 pages, readers would lose sight of Daniel's idiosyncratic method of dealing with his past (acting impulsively in the present to combat past regrets) and Claudette would be reacting to a Daniel who felt immediate to her but not to the reader. By truncating the distance between different portraits of Daniel, given by each chapter's focal character, O'Farrell sketches a person who is at once damnable, sympathetic, narcissistic, compassionate – each focal character accentuating or drawing out one or more of Daniel's traits. It's a masterful technique that raises the narrative stakes and makes the answer to the plot's central question complicated.

Comparing Characterization Techniques in *This Must Be the Place* and Colum McCann's *Let the Great World Spin*

Another purveyor of shifting narrative point of view is the renowned Irish novelist Colum McCann, who is best known for his 2009 novel *Let the Great World Spin*. In it, he chronicles Philippe Petit's high-wire walk on 7 August 1974, between the towers of the World Trade Center that captivated the attention of New Yorkers. The novel begins with a kaleidoscopic five-page prologue that conveys the experience among viewers who felt time stop at 7.47 am that morning, as a third-person omniscient narrator roves the streets and offices and shops describing a communal moment of awe. The novel proceeds with a polyphonic narrative divided into four books and ten chapters, each chapter taking a different focal character. If the main point the plot orbits around in *This Must Be the Place* is the marriage of Claudette and Daniel, the main point *Let the Great World Spin* orbits around is Corrigan. Like Petit on the high wire, Corrigan's life connected disparate lives – artists, bartenders, sex workers, Jesuits – a model that called them to a higher point. In McCann's words, Corrigan is 'the force around which the voices spin' (qtd. in Cullingford 2014: 87).

McCann's ten characters represent a wide swathe of ethnicities, classes, demographics and experiences, making a connective thread a narrative problem to be addressed. The question that *Let the Great World Spin* poses is this: Is there something in modern life that can transcend culture and reveal interconnectedness?

Rather than answer this question, McCann decides to frame it accurately for the reader (to use an axiom from Chekhov) (Saunders 2021: 58). The novel takes as its focal characters: sex workers, a minister, a group of grieving mothers whose sons died in Vietnam, social workers, socialites, computer programmers and a judge. While maintaining a somewhat decentralized narrative structure – alternating points of view and focal characters with Petit's walk being the main constant – the novel returns to Corrigan more often than the others. An Irish Jesuit minister, Corrigan befriends a group of sex workers which include Tillie and her daughter, Jazzlyn, who work the Bronx area outside his apartment.

The first chapter is told in first person from the perspective of Corrigan's brother, Ciaran, who follows him from Dublin to New York to reconnect with him after the death of their estranged father. Corrigan is comfortable in the company of outcasts and content serving the overlooked – a modern St Francis. He gets beaten up by pimps and advocates for a group of sex workers (Tillie and Jazzlyn) outside his Bronx apartment, even when they get arrested for robbery. This chapter is told through the lens of a brother, one who filters the narration through the unforgiveness Corrigan held for their father and the love he had for their mother. The first chapter ends with Corrigan and Jazzlyn (the daughter of Tillie) dying in a car accident on their way back from the courthouse, an accident witnessed by the narrator of chapter three, Lara, who was in the car that rear-ended Corrigan and took off afterwards.

Each focal character examines Corrigan's life from a different lens. Adelita is a social worker who falls in love with Corrigan, she being the only woman he has loved: her lens is that of a lover who will never move on. Tillie, even after years of being a sex worker, has never felt judged by Corrigan and loves him for the unconditional love he has shown her; her lens is that of a fellow outcast who will never feel truly known by another soul.

The novel exists in the shadow of 9/11, an event that McCann was writing about arguably as much as Petit's tightrope walk, the former being the epitome of human disconnection at its most extreme, the adverse of Petit's performance. To approach a city as multitudinous as New York and a life as incomprehensibly selfless as Corrigan's, McCann needed Petit to contextualize each character in a time and place, then needed a wealth of vantage points from which to describe the transcendent, something inherently indescribable, something akin to the feeling that Gloria, one of the mothers who lost children in Vietnam, had when she saw the children of the deceased Jazzlyn being taken away by social workers: 'I knew almost right off. Them two babies needed looking after. It was a deep-down feeling that must've come from long ago' (McCann 2009: 285).

The characterization of Corrigan mirrors that of Daniel – both in the frequency they are returned to and the filters from which they are viewed, that is, the different lenses each focal character views them through. Every other chapter involves a direct observation of the protagonist. Where the novels diverge in structure is the pivotal reason why I believe *This Must Be the Place* is better executed than *Let the Great World Spin*, using as my standard the aforementioned quality of narrative escalation, as defined by Saunders (2021: 153). Every chapter of *This Must Be the Place* clarifies, contextualizes or reveals something new about the protagonist, even if he is never mentioned, which escalates the plot's tension, building up to the final encounter with Claudette. The same cannot be said for *Let the Great World Spin*, which features a lengthy exchange in a phone booth in chapter five when a character is briefly introduced only to describe Petit's walk and then is never featured again in the novel. Similarly in the preceding chapter, we follow a graffiti artist who wants to be a photographer, his narrative arc ending before it gets going. Each of these comes in Book Two, about one-third of the way through the novel, before it's clear who the protagonist is and how many voices are going to compose the narrative. After these chapters, the rest of the novel returns to Corrigan in some way, directly or obliquely.

O'Farrell shows more precision in drawing out the interconnectedness of each life through the focal point of a single life and does so in a way that never leaves the reader wondering: Why this vantage point? How does this escalate the narrative stakes? The chapters that appear to be deviations at first – 'Teresa, Brooklyn, 1944' and 'Rosalind, Bolivia, 2015' – find their connection to Daniel by serving as nodes for relevant influences in his life, chapters that provide important background we would not otherwise have. The former is a third-person close narration of how her mother fell in love with another man when she was engaged to Daniel's father yet carried on with the engagement anyway. This clarifies our understanding of Daniel's parents' marriage and the latent unhappiness her mother felt, which led to the resentment of his father and, ultimately, Daniel rejecting his father (a feature that also influences why Nicola is attracted to Daniel, i.e., his being raised by strong women). Rosalind's chapter is also told in third-person close, recounting how her vacation spawned as a result of discovering her husband's affair that was kept hidden for many years. She comes across Daniel at a time when he is separated from Claudette and grieving Phoebe's death. Rosalind tells him to keep his promises, take his medication, get healthy, then to go to Claudette and tell her '[w]hatever it is you wish you'd said to her years ago, when you were still together', then sharing her theory that 'marriages end not because of something you did say but because of something you didn't' (O'Farrell 2016a: 351).

Teresa's chapter demonstrates that Daniel was raised in a household resultant from someone who did not take the advice he'd eventually be given by Rosalind many years later, advice Daniel acts upon in the denouement because it's earned wisdom. Each of these chapters comes from voices we hear only once in the narrative, but each plays an essential role in the characterization of Daniel and the trajectory of the plot; the same cannot be said for the interludes of the graffiti artist and phone-booth answerer in *Let the Great World Spin*, both of which feel tangential. In these two chapters O'Farrell uses third-person close narration to 'expand our cognitive repertoire and the repertoire of what is altogether tellable and narratable' to demonstrate how the past impacts the present (Skov Nielsen 2011: 86). This is the function of polyphonic narratives that unify around a single focal point and do not deviate from it – they expand our narratable repertoire in a coherent way.

Conclusion

Every author operates within the realm of their skillset, leveraging these strengths to execute an effective narrative. Zadie Smith, Colum McCann and Maggie O'Farrell all excel in characterization across ethnicity, gender and class, bringing to life an ensemble of believable, lived-in characters that energize their novels. Smith operates best, arguably, in third-person close point of view, limited to the interiority of an individual and examining the world from one lens. Smith creates a character that resonates to this degree because of how carefully she scaffolds the development of Natalie – starting as a girl with the birth name 'Keisha' and growing up with an aptitude for completism, a 'compulsion' that 'manifested as "intelligence"' a quality that she is praised for despite it being a 'reflexive habit' (2012: 207–8). And yet, this quality is rewarded frequently enough that she 'began to exist for other people' resultant from the chasm between 'what she believed she knew of herself' and 'her essence as others seemed to understand it' (2012: 208). Smith sows the seeds of a personality in Natalie's childhood that come to full fruition about 150 pages later, through a seamless progression of this core character trait, as we follow her through college and law school where others mistake this 'mutation of the will' for determination (2012: 208).

Given that the starting point for Natalie's character is a bookish, devout Christian girl and the ending point is a married, mother of two who absconds to have a threesome with men almost half her age, it's remarkable that Smith maintains the suspension of disbelief. And yet, she does, and this individualistic characterization is what makes her exceptional. But where the reading experience lags is in the space between characters – she is not as adept in conveying the complexity of a relationship as she is an individual. O'Farrell is. This skill becomes crucial when examining the dynamics within a relationship played out over several years. Rather than Smith's approach of following the protagonist from childhood to adulthood, O'Farrell unravels Daniel's individuality by way of other characters' points of view, her narration appropriating their biases and lenses that colour their portrait of Daniel and inform the reader's understanding of his marriage, leading to a fuller explication of the space between characters.

McCann arguably excels most when characterizing a place as opposed to an individual or a relationship, making New York City the optimal setting for showcasing his talent. McCann renders a quality portrait of Corrigan, but deviates in favour of describing distinct parts of New York that do not meaningfully contribute to Corrigan's portrayal or to the plot. Description in *Let the Great World Spin* is an articulation of a time and place that can never exist again. When describing the feeling of being on a tightrope hundreds of feet in the air, or the interior of a wealthy judge's penthouse, McCann is a writer nonpareil. But there are times when the description of the city gets too far from the focal point of Corrigan's humanity and then the novel loses momentum for periods at a time, even as it still excels in the lens through which it views the city. O'Farrell never loses the plot.

The multitude of settings in *This Must Be the Place* do not become dizzying for the reader because each is imbued with an emotional resonance specific to the character, each building towards Claudette and Daniel's final encounter. Each place contains a memory and the details used to flesh out that setting are in service of the emotional tone of the memory and the character living it. If McCann's supreme talent is an encyclopaedic rendering of a particular city, O'Farrell's is knowing how to use place to amplify and accentuate character. *Let the Great World Spin* ends up being more New York City's novel than Corrigan's, at the expense of narrative continuity and plot escalation. To O'Farrell's credit, *This Must Be the Place* is concerned more with how people shape places, rather than how places shape people. What's encyclopaedic about her novel is not the fabric of a city but that of a relationship.

Given the ambition, scope and difficulty that *This Must Be the Place* approaches, I argue that it executes its goal more effectively than Smith in *NW* or McCann in *Let the Great World Spin*, even though these latter novels have enjoyed more acclaim than O'Farrell's. The precision of O'Farrell's central focal point of the novel – Daniel and Claudette's marriage – makes the proliferation of settings, characters and points of view fall into place in a seamless way, something that cannot be said of *NW* which deviates from the central focal point (Leah/Natalie). Similarly, McCann's tangents in *Let the Great World Spin* are intriguing descriptive forays into 1970s New York, but do not illuminate anything significant about Corrigan's character. This is the core reason why *This Must Be the Place* deserves more recognition for the contribution it has made to contemporary literary fiction, putting O'Farrell on par with the best of her peers.

5

Lost in Translation

The Dis-located Structures of Maggie O'Farrell's *My Lover's Lover*

Sarah Gamble

Introduction

Maggie O'Farrell is a writer who has enjoyed considerable commercial success, although her work has been little discussed in an academic context thus far. O'Farrell has published nine novels to date and has been awarded some significant accolades: most recently, being awarded multiple prizes – including the 2020 Women's Prize for Fiction – for *Hamnet* (2020). Her recognition has been consistent from the early years of her career, as evidenced by the fact that there was some surprise expressed when she was excluded from Granta's 2003 list of best young British novelists. The *Observer* had named her in their advance list of likely contenders and subsequently cited her as one of the 'five who missed out' following Granta's publication. In a similar spirit, the British Arts Council included O'Farrell in an alternative list entitled 'Best of the Rest'.

My Lover's Lover, published the previous year, in 2002, was said to have been the stumbling block to O'Farrell's placement on Granta's list. As reported by the *Observer*, the editor of Granta, Ian Jack, took exception to the novel's narrative games: in her article 'Women Writers Top Class of 2003', Vanessa Thorpe wrote that O'Farrell 'was apparently discarded because of a bit of dubious plotting in her second novel, *My Lover's Lover*, which was described by Jack as "a stunt"' (Thorpe 2003, npn.). Yet this essay will argue the contrary view that *My Lover's Lover* illustrates O'Farrell's skills as a writer, foregrounding her interest in depicting the subjectivity of experience and her intricate plotting of both physical and textual space. While the novel might, at a stretch, be described as a love story, it follows the domestic gothic tradition in portraying the dark underside of the romantic narrative, focusing on the point when relationships tip over into obsession and psychological manipulation.

Far from being a 'stunt', *My Lover's Lover* is an intricately constructed narrative that combines references to a tradition of female-authored domestic gothic with an astutely observed depiction of contemporary urban spaces and relationships. In typical gothic fashion, O'Farrell elides the past with the present in such a way as to destabilize both, exemplifying Christine Berthin's assertion that 'The Gothic is inherently analeptic, as it stages the return of the past generations [*sic*] in a present that is never present. This distortion of chronology and logic affects the very notion of subjectivity' (Berthin 2010: 67). There is no space within O'Farrell's text, be it internal or external, that is not haunted; moreover, the narrative is all too aware of the vulnerability of language itself to phantasmic possession. As Berthin says:

> communication and textuality, far from constituting a natural channel for the expression and constitution of the self, seem to generate interference. Interference precipitates the sense of the erasure of the subject. . . . The spirits of the dead are everywhere: the subject, a mere heir, a transmitter and transcriber, is condemned to be the voice of another. Displacement is at the core of textuality, as both reader and writer are the unsuspected vehicles of unknown messages. Haunting is the form of all textuality. (Berthin 2010: 108)

My Lover's Lover draws attention to the 'interference' inherent in language by making translation a central theme within the text. Not only is one of the main characters a trained translator but all the protagonists are burdened with the necessity of interpretation as they move through densely populated urban environments echoing with utterances that are multiple, fragmented and often bereft of context. The plot itself hinges on a moment of drastic mistranslation, indicating the extent to which language falls short as a vehicle for meaning, and as an anchor for a secure sense of self. O'Farrell's characters are adrift in an environment they cannot ever quite make sense of, even as they cannot make sense of themselves, and as a result, the reader too becomes disorientated in their efforts to comprehend motivations, space and place.

Translation and the Uncanny

If a tendency towards analepsis is inherent to the gothic then translation is an inherently gothic act, since the words that are being spoken are always ones that have been said before. There is no such thing as truly simultaneous translation since it can only follow, and never anticipate, the utterance in the source language. As a result, translation cannot escape its own belatedness: it is a literal enaction of the 'compulsion to repeat' (Freud [1919] 2003: 145) that Freud defines as intrinsic to the uncanny experience.

Yet it is also an act of repetition that is doomed to fail since it creates a 'double' of the original utterance which can only ever be an inexact duplication. As Walter Benjamin argues in his essay 'The Task of the Translator' (1923), 'translation, instead of making itself resemble the meaning of the original, must lovingly, and in detail, fashion in its own language a counterpart to the original's mode of intention' ([1923] 1996:161). A successfully translated text is thus not a simple *copy* of the original, but its *counterpart*, and there is an essential difference between these two concepts. A counterpart exists in a relationship of correspondence with its source, of which it is not necessarily an exact duplicate. Thus, to quote Carol Jacobs's commentary on Benjamin's essay, 'the relationship between translation and original . . . is always on the verge of eluding understanding' (Jacobs 1975: 758), because it draws attention to the contingency of meaning itself. Jacobs argues that 'For Benjamin, translation does not transform a foreign language into one we may call our own, but rather renders radically foreign that language we believe to be ours' (Jacobs 1975: 756), a statement that recalls Freud's definition of *Das Unheimlich*, as 'that species of the frightening that goes back to what was once well known and long been familiar' (Freud [1919] 2003: 124). The translated text, as a non-literal, belatedly uttered, counterpart of its original source, arouses the same anxieties that Freud ascribes to the double, in challenging distinctions between 'self' and 'other', 'same' and 'different', 'past' and 'present'.

Furthermore, Freud's essay itself can be regarded as an exercise in translation (and it is also worth remembering that for readers who do not know German, this is a text that is only ever comprehended in a translated form). In the first part of 'The Uncanny', Freud engages in an etymological search for the term in other languages, only to find that 'the dictionaries we consult tell us nothing new, if only perhaps because we ourselves speak a foreign language. Indeed, we gain the impression that many languages lack a word for this particular species of the frightening' ([1919] 2003: 125). Such a claim ensures that the extended examination of the usage of *Heimlich* and *unheimlich* that ensues is itself rendered uncanny, since German – the native language of the author and the essay's first readers – has now been defamiliarized by having already been rendered 'foreign'. So it could be argued that Freud's attempt to 'translate' the concept of the uncanny into other languages by trying, and failing, to find an exact equivalence, bears out Benjamin's belief that 'translation is merely a preliminary way of coming to terms with the foreignness of languages to each other' ([1923] 1996: 157).

To look into the etymology of the noun 'translation' and its associated meanings uncovers further correlations with the uncanny. Although in contemporary English it most commonly denotes the act of changing words from one language into another, historically 'translation' conveys a number of other meanings. The *OED* provides a long list of definitions, but two in particular are pertinent to my discussion. Both have relevance within an ecclesiastical context: the first defines 'translation' as 'transference; removal or conveyance from one person, place, or condition to another', and was primarily used to describe 'the removal of the body or relics of a saint to another place of interment'; while the second signifies 'removal from earth to heaven, *orig.* without death'. Whether concerned with the movement of bodies (whole or in part) or a direct passage to the afterlife, in both usages translation is associated with mortality: moreover, its Latin root, *translatus*, which means 'to carry over', identifies it as a term crucially concerned with mutability, transition and transformation.

As a Gothic text, *My Lover's Lover* is crucially preoccupied with all of translation's uncanny effects. In O'Farrell's novel, language, bodies and even the material composition of the contemporary cityscape itself, are all perpetually on the move from one form to another. While the elements of which its storyline is composed are familiar – and therefore in many ways predictable – what O'Farrell does is to play on that sense of familiarity (*Heimlich*) in order to render it foreign (or *unheimlich*). Analepsis plays an important part within this process, since in spite of the fact that the majority of the novel is narrated in the first-person present, its use of multiple narrators causes it to constantly double back upon itself in order to retell the same story from different perspectives. The characters' narratives do not link to form a pattern of chronological progression but instead overlap to create sedimentary layers of text.

In essence, the book depicts a triangular relationship between three people. It opens with Lily, a young and rather naïve girl, beginning a relationship with Marcus, an architect. Moving into his converted warehouse flat, she finds her new room still filled with the personal possessions of Marcus's former girlfriend, Sinead, whom, following Marcus's pronouncement that 'she's no longer with us' (O'Farrell 2002: 35), Lily assumes to be dead. Subsequently, she is haunted by Sinead's phantom presence, which manifests itself at various locations in the flat; but when she sees her predecessor in the street, Lily discovers that Sinead is actually alive and well. Disturbed by Lily's overt fascination with her, Sinead then tells the story of her relationship with Marcus and its breakdown due to his compulsive infidelity. Coming to realize that as far as Marcus is concerned, she is only an unsatisfactory substitute for Sinead, Lily leaves him. This triangular relationship is complicated by O'Farrell through the introduction of a second male character, Aiden, Marcus's best friend and fellow flatmate. Aiden is Marcus's competitor for much of the novel since he, too, desires Sinead, but he is also strongly aligned with the female figures in the text, primarily due to the fact that he shares their role as point-of-view narrator. Indeed, of the quartet that makes up the novel's main group of characters, only Marcus is not allocated a direct voice, making him an enigma around which the other figures in the narrative revolve. It is this opacity that places Marcus at the epicentre of the novel's preoccupation with translation, as the character who is most demanding of interpretation.

The Translator as Vacant Subject

Although *My Lover's Lover* moves with gradually increasing rapidity between Lily, Aiden and Sinead, if there is the central point of view within the text, it belongs to Lily, to whose perspective the novel persistently returns. The fact that she once worked as an interpreter, 'translating the strange desires, beliefs and objections of diplomats and politicians' (O'Farrell 2002: 24), thus brings the issue of translation – as well as its uncanny implications – to the immediate forefront of O'Farrell's novel. It is a career Lily has abandoned, due to the fact

> that after a few weeks she'd become unable to switch off the translating synapse in her brain. Like a tap left running somewhere, it became the constant background noise to her life. Having conversations with her friends, watching TV, part of her mind would persist in translating whatever she heard into French. And when the translating devil within her began to give a running commentary on each and every tiny act in her life . . . she decided she had to take some drastic action. These days, she has it largely under control; only occasionally does her inner interpreter start whispering to her about herself in French. (O'Farrell 2002: 24–5)

This resembles a description of the auditory hallucinations associated with schizophrenia and implies that for Lily, the act of translation is a catalyst for the uncanny splitting of the self. Like a spirit medium, she is a vessel for a voice from elsewhere; a voice that both is and is not her own. Her belief that she now has this compulsion 'largely under control' is proved to be erroneous, for she never appears in the novel as a fully unified subject: instead, she is simultaneously a prey to hauntings and a ghost who haunts others. Lily's first sighting of what she supposes to be Sinead's phantom is as she and Marcus have sex, when she opens her eyes to find 'near enough so that Lily could reach out and touch her. . . a girl with black Medusa curls and an angular white face' (O'Farrell 2002: 62). When Lily screams, Sinead vanishes, leaving the space where she has been 'blank, clear, hollow' (O'Farrell 2002: 62). Once Sinead is revealed to still be alive, Lily moves to occupy this vacancy and their roles reverse; now Sinead is flesh-and-blood, while Lily becomes increasingly phantasmic. When Lily accosts her in a bookshop, Sinead flees, leaving only 'the space where Sinead had been' (O'Farrell 2002: 133). The next day, Lily returns to the bookshop and takes over habitation of that space by 'translating' the scenario of the day before from Sinead's point of view:

> Back in the Covent Garden bookshop, Lily stands at the bookshelf, plants her feet where she estimates Sinead's shoes might have been less than twenty-four hours ago, reaches for the book Sinead had been looking at. Lily opens it, her eyes sliding over the words, and looks up. Repeats the action. Opens the book, looks up at the gap through to the other side of the shelves. Then looks to her right. That's what she saw. This view is what Sinead saw yesterday. . . . This is all exactly what she saw when I said her name – except with my face in the middle. (O'Farrell 2002: 138–9)

Lily's duplication of Sinead's original action of opening the book and scanning the shop not once but twice is suggestive of a Freudian compulsion to repetition, while the narration's elision of third and first person hints at a growing uncertainty on Lily's part as to where the ego boundaries between herself and Sinead are located. In this scenario, she is both the one who sees and the one who is seen: and when she utters Sinead's name, she also takes that name upon herself. Through her increasing obsession, Lily forces Sinead to occupy the role of uncanny double and to become a locus for Lily's anxieties concerning her own identity.

The notion that Sinead functions as a substitute or stand-in for the figure who is actually haunting Lily is reinforced when Lily first glimpses the 'real' Sinead on a London street, and is surprised by 'a memory [that] twitches then opens out in front of her – a day trip she took with her parents when they still had her baby brother Mark, before Lily found him in his cot, blue and cold as marble' (O'Farrell 2002: 131). Walking through a field of tall grass that 'came up to her neck' (O'Farrell 2002: 131), the child Lily is frightened by the possibility of disappearing forever, speculating, 'What if she was swallowed up and her parents couldn't find her again in this endless, rippling green sea?' (O'Farrell 2002: 131). Mark is only mentioned once more in the novel, when Lily, on the point of walking out on Marcus, recalls attempting to run away from home 'one day after baby Mark died' (O'Farrell 2002: 308), but is brought home by her mother. While both memories have the death of Lily's baby brother at their core, they are also both expressive of anxieties regarding the separation of parent from child. Although before Mark's death, this abandonment is involuntary, afterwards – although forestalled by the actions of Lily's mother – it is strongly willed.

The discovery of her brother's body appears to have affected Lily profoundly, and the fact that the first conscious memory of Mark represented in the novel erupts when Lily sees Sinead indicates that her mind suggests a connection between the two. Her obsession with Sinead can thus be regarded as the enactment of a far deeper and chronologically more distant traumatic event.

Lily can thus be regarded as a traumatized subject who is persistently haunted by dissociated memories. The resulting impact upon her psyche is summed up by her friend Sarah, who catches sight of Lily at a moment when she is unaware of being watched. As she subsequently tells Lily: 'You looked empty and . . . worn out and . . . you looked hollow, I'm telling you. Like a part of you was gone or missing or something' (O'Farrell 2002: 103 [ellipses in original]). It could be argued that Lily is a literal exemplification of Christine Berthin's observations that communication perpetually threatens the erasure of independent subjectivity since her 'hollowness' is precisely what makes her a talented translator. The psychic vacancy left by her suppressed traumatic memories makes her an empty channel for the words, thoughts and actions of others, which allow her to enact her predisposition towards repetition and re-enactment and accounts for her failure to achieve a fully coherent independent subjectivity.

Space, Translation and the Uncanny

The worlds of the spatial and the linguistic become persistently entangled in *My Lover's Lover*, a novel in which both buildings and language demand, yet also resist, the necessity of interpretation. A great many of the spaces in the novel, from walls to floors, are made of glass, which creates an illusion of transparency or clarity of meaning; yet, as the examples already discussed demonstrate, the opposite is actually true. These reflective surfaces disorientate and confuse, because of the way in which they blur demarcation lines between one space and another, one self and another. While, in all its slippery translucence, the (post)modern city may visually differ from the dark convoluted spaces of the traditional Gothic castle, there is little to distinguish the two. Because they are impossible to 'read' with any accuracy, they become spaces that enclose and conceal secrets; what cannot be said hidden in what cannot be easily navigated.

London's inhabitants, therefore, move through a densely populated cityscape which is both palimpsestic and analeptic: the layering of new architectural forms upon the old persistently pulling the viewer's attention away from the present and back to the past. Language's ability to function as a form of communication is in constant question in such a context, as the majority of the action is set in crowded urban environments permeated by anonymous voices and partial conversations, as well as meaningful non-vocal interactions. Because such overheard utterances and random contacts are frequently divested of the context that would give them meaning, they are rendered gnomic and mysterious, echoing through the text independently of origin and immediate significance. More than that, they often contain an intimation of menace. Leaving a restaurant in New York, Aidan passes 'a man carrying an albino child in a hooded blue anorak on his shoulders' and feels 'ashamed' under her 'knowing, searching, oddly prescient gaze' (O'Farrell 2002: 268). Lily, gate-crashing one of Sinead's lectures, overhears her neighbour in the lecture theatre describing food preparation in terms that sound like murder: "'And he got this squid and chopped it up. Just like that. Lengthways and, you know . . . sideways. It got *everywhere*'" (O'Farrell 2002: 142).

The use O'Farrell makes of verbal cacophony and physical proximity throughout *My Lover's Lover* is directly linked to her portrayal of contemporary urbanization, in that this layering of multiple voices and chance encounters arises from the conditions of the city itself. Doreen Massey uses the term 'throwntogetherness' to denote the 'chance of space [that] may set us down next to the unexpected neighbour' (Massey 2005: 151). A space of multiple occupation only increases those 'elements of chaos, openness and uncertainty' (Massey 2005: 153) that Massey argues are intrinsic to an experience of place. In her analysis, no site is ever stable, but 'formed through a myriad of practices of quotidian negotiation and contestation; . . . the *practising* of place, the negotiation of intersecting trajectories; place as an arena where negotiation is forced upon us' (Massey 2005: 154). Massey's particular focus of interest is in the political implications of throwntogetherness, but it can be appropriated as a way of conceptualizing O'Farrell's presentation of the urban, which in *My Lover's Lover* is formed through a multiplicity of contesting speech acts and physical collisions echoing off and across each other in order to form an ambiguous, inconclusive and always partial exegesis on the predicaments of the novel's central characters.

Although Lily has given up the practice of translation in order to avoid the unsettling commentary of her inner voice, it still emerges in the random words of the strangers that surround her. Lily's first meeting with Marcus takes place in a crowded art exhibition, during which he is accosted by his cousin, with whom he has a cryptic conversation:

> 'How are you doing?' Phoebe's voice is nearly a whisper. Something private, hidden, is being referred to. Lily looks from one to the other, suddenly wanting to be away from them both. Whatever this is, it has nothing to do with her.
>
> 'Well, I –' He stops. . . . Someone passes in the corridor beyond the kitchen door, saying 'And she never knew, never found out'. (O'Farrell 2002: 7)

The reader shares Lily's incomprehension at this point, as only much later in the novel is it disclosed that the exhibition takes place on the evening of the day Sinead leaves Marcus. Phoebe's concern for Marcus is counterbalanced by the comment of the anonymous speaker, which in retrospect can be read as a commentary on both Sinead's and Lily's ignorance of Marcus's deceptive nature; his enduring wish to indulge his desires without discovery or consequence.

Translation, Navigation, Revelation

It is this that becomes the knowledge encrypted at the heart of *My Lover's Lover*, hinted at in the chance utterances and meaningful glances of strangers, and lost in any attempt at direct communication. Sinead eventually reveals to Lily that since leaving Marcus – and hence for the entire duration of Lily's relationship with him – Marcus has been pursuing her with threatening relentlessness: 'He – he phones me twelve times a day. He follows me to work. He follows me from work' (O'Farrell 2002: 157). This gives a new significance to already-related incidents when Marcus has concealed half-written letters from Lily or prevented her from overhearing his telephone conversations: 'Marcus dials a number, hangs up, dials again, hangs up, redials, speaks inaudibly into the receiver before dragging the phone on its extension lead into his bedroom' (O'Farrell 2002: 47). From the beginning of the novel, therefore, Lily is surrounded by linguistic indicators that Marcus is not the caring boyfriend she desires him to be, but this information emerges in a fragmented form that is almost impossible to decode. *Almost*: but not quite, for if Sinead in her phantom form is approached as a manifestation of Lily's own traumas and obsessions, the fact that she is frequently seen attempting, soundlessly, to communicate indicates that at some level Lily may well be aware that she is deceiving herself. It is not insignificant that ghost-Sinead's first attempt at speech occurs after Marcus has excused himself from the breakfast table to take a phone call, whereupon Lily sees Sinead's 'lips . . . moving, as if she's speaking, as if she's trying to tell her something' (O'Farrell 2002: 75–6). Even after Lily has met the living Sinead, her phantom is still striving to pass on her message, 'a secret flood of words pouring out' of her mouth as 'she scans Lily's face, as if anxious for her to understand' (O'Farrell 2002: 140).

It is in the attempt to comprehend this secret that the gothic mode is activated, for Marcus is only the latest in a long line of literary gothic (anti)heroes who use the fascination they exert over women to exploit them and who preside over an interior space that serves to conceal their brutal exercise of patriarchal power. The fact that Marcus is an architect confirms him as a representative of the masculine impulse that has built, and continues to reshape, the city. His warehouse conversion, which divides the open expanse of the original factory floor into a series of smaller private spaces, reflects what Aiden describes as Marcus's 'spooky ability to completely compartmentalise his life . . . he can just put things into a box and shut the lid' (O'Farrell 2002: 294–5). In transforming a place of work into a place of habitation – a house – Marcus has created a gothic site par excellence since, as Anne Williams says, it is the home that 'makes secrets in merely being itself, for its function is to enclose spaces' (Williams 1995: 44).

It is true that Marcus is far from being a murderous '*homme fatal*' (Williams 38 [italics Williams's]) in the Bluebeard mode, as his crimes against women involve only infidelity, not murder. However, O'Farrell intimates that the boundary between the two acts may be thinner than we would like to think and that the concealment of one transgression may well lead to the necessity of concealing another, far more serious, crime. Marcus, a man who believes that 'Everybody should have . . . at some time or another . . . given in to their desires' (O'Farrell 2002: 263) is prone to using his physical strength to overpower his girlfriends. Lily wakes one night to find 'her wrists are pinned to the bed' (O'Farrell 2002: 151), just as Sinead is 'pinned down' on the ground with the joking warning: 'I misspent lots of my youth in judo classes. You might want to remember that' (O'Farrell 2002: 234). His living space hints at a capacity for violence: as Lily perceives, his preference for metal, glass and concrete in his warehouse conversion is disturbingly reminiscent of 'an operating theatre, or a morgue. Nothing would leave a mark in here that couldn't be washed or sponged away' (O'Farrell 2002: 59). The warehouse in *My Lover's Lover*, as the container for the guilty secrets and desires of its architect-owner, thus conforms to Anne Williams's definition of the gothic house 'with its secret room', which 'realizes, makes concrete, the structure of power that engenders the action within this social world' (1995: 41).

Anne Williams observes that the gothic narrative shows that the very attempt to conceal secrets can be the source of their undoing, arguing that the act of '[b]uilding walls and declaring boundaries . . . creates both the possibility – and the desire – to transgress any or all of them' (1995: 44). The rigidity and apparent permanence of the city's structures are frequently proved to be illusory in *My Lover's Lover*, where buildings – precisely because they are conversions from (or 'translations' of) earlier forms – present the characters with alternative navigational possibilities. Marcus's final unmasking is achieved at an architectural exhibition when Lily accidentally eavesdrops on a conversation in which his true attitude towards their relationship is revealed. Because the exhibition takes place inside a converted building, in a room that 'is really two rooms knocked into one', Lily realizes that the easiest way to reach Marcus through the crowd is to 'disappear through one door, walk along the corridor, and reappear next to him through the other' (O'Farrell 2002: 304). However, when she reaches 'the opposite side of the wall to them, their mirror image' (O'Farrell 2002: 305), she hears Marcus making a derogatory joke about her. In this moment, two different meanings of the word 'translation' are put into play: the movement of bodies in space leading to linguistic transformation and illumination.

Translation, Debt and Deferral

Translation in *My Lover's Lover* is a concept that is persistently linked to estrangement, belatedness and the distortion – rather than the clarification – of meaning. The result is a narrative of shifting identities and landscapes that can never quite be mapped or understood and which emerge as uncanny in their unsettling indeterminacy. The original Latin derivation of 'translation' is *translatus*, meaning 'carried over', which not only foregrounds the act of translation as one that is always on the move from one language to another but also evokes a meaningful association with the use of the term in a mathematical context. Here, 'carrying over' signifies the number that is left over when a number does not exactly divide into another. This remainder is what resists assimilation into a unified whole and which is persistently on the move from one column to the next in the quest for resolution. It is thus always in excess, and always *owing*, in the sense that an account with a remainder can never be balanced.

This concept of translation as supplement – as what always exceeds any calculation – is relevant to O'Farrell's novel, providing a pertinent perspective from which to understand the text's complicated – and often rather confusing – construction. The narrative is not anchored in a single point of view, nor does it progress chronologically; instead, different voices meet, overlap, interrupt and double back on each other in such a way as to render the space *of* the text as disorientating as the spaces *within* it. Meaning is in a perpetual state of deferral, migrating from one person, place and time-scheme to another in order to create the disconcerting sense of an instantaneous present which, in never quite arriving at a resolution, is suspended in a constant process of becoming.

The novel is divided into four sections, but because it does not proceed in chronological order, these sections interlink with each other in rather convoluted ways. The action begins in medias res with Lily's fall from the taxi outside the art gallery, creating a sense of freewheeling motion that is maintained by O'Farrell's use of the third-person present, thus placing the reader in the midst of the action as it unfolds. This is maintained throughout the first part of the text, which moves between the alternating viewpoints of Lily and Aiden. In this part of the novel, events do not exist prior to their representation; instead, the characters are situated in a dynamically unfolding 'now'.

This changes, however, in the second section of the text, which focuses exclusively on Sinead to tell two different parts of her story simultaneously – both of which predate the events already related by Lily and Aiden. The narrative shifts between two alternate periods: in the first – related in the third-person present – Sinead anticipates Marcus's return from a business trip to New York, while the second uses the first-person past to tell the story of how Sinead and Marcus met. O'Farrell creates a sequence of events that pull in two different directions: for while in one time-strand Sinead and Marcus are moving towards each other, in the other they are also simultaneously moving apart, an effect intensified by the rapidity with which the text alternates between these two perspectives. On leaving Marcus's flat for the last time, Sinead 'imagines that, in some parallel universe . . . her identity has bifurcated and somehow somewhere she – or someone who looks and sounds like her – is holding hands with Marcus as they walk through the streets to Phoebe's gallery' (O'Farrell 2002: 236); a fantasy that has already been fulfilled in the novel, where Lily has already met Marcus at that very gallery. Time in *My Lover's Lover*, then, is neither linear nor singular, but circular and multiple, constantly doubling back on itself in order to disrupt any sense of coherent chronology. Actions and objects appear in the text bereft of the background information that would give them significance; for example, Lily is fascinated by a dress that has been left in her bedroom wardrobe, and wonders 'Why, out of everything, has it been left? . . . Was it some kind of message, a private sign?' (O'Farrell 2002: 31). It is only later that the reader learns that this is the dress Sinead is wearing on the night Marcus confesses his infidelity to her, and that it is thus indeed an object with a history: albeit one to which Lily does not have access. While the present may well be 'only the past amended' (O'Farrell 2002: 41), that does not necessarily mean that the past is capable of being adequately understood. Instead, it more often appears in the text in the form of relics and reminiscences that remain unanchored in definitive meaning.

In the introduction to this essay, I quoted Christine Berthin's argument regarding the 'inherently analeptic' nature of the gothic, a mode in which the past 'returns . . . in a present that is never present' (Berthin 2010: 67). O'Farrell's depiction of space and chronology literalizes this assertion, situated as it is in a present that is also always a 'non-present', in the sense that it is not anchored in a linear chronology that would give it significance *as* the present. This brings us back to the concept of translation, which is always a delayed repetition of something that has already been said. In its stress on reiteration and reinterpretation, *My Lover's Lover* itself becomes an echo chamber within which words and actions are compulsively recycled and repeated, but never reach a point of resolution.

Conclusion

In *Gothic Hauntings*, Christine Berthin asserts that the adoption of a Gothic point of view entails a profound, and entirely disorientating, shift in perspective:

> [I]f Gothic were at the center, then everything else would have to be decentered, and we would have to see the world athwart from the distorting perspective of the ghost, and then things that were buried between the surface of texts would start appearing, forcing us to read differently. The past would be given pride of place as that which colors the present and the future, beyond our understanding and our control. (Berthin 2010: 57)

A tale told by ghosts, then, is one that demands an act of radical re-translation. Opening up the hidden spaces within a text exposes the analeptic and palimpsestic nature of narrative, which always contains traces of its own indebtedness to prior stories and past texts, thus evading final meaning. What Berthin terms the 'perspective of the ghost' is the dominant perspective of *My Lover's Lover*, which openly displays its desire to reverse the relationship between the centre and the margin in order to force the reader to read against the grain.

Berthin calls for an uncanny refocusing that will transform a familiar plot we think we all know into something *unheimlich*; for the act of displacing the hero from his privileged central position within the narrative draws attention to what hovers on the margins, waiting to tell their story. By the end of the novel Marcus – the character who most conforms to the stereotype of the gothic hero/villain – has not only been persistently denied a voice but has had all linguistic agency removed from him. When Lily returns to the flat for a final time in order to collect her belongings, she hears him on the phone, pleading with Sinead to return. Now in possession of the knowledge that enables her to translate his desires, she simply cuts him off: 'Without thinking about it, Lily moves towards the phone point, a white box low on the wall. Her fingers close over the small plastic plug and flick it out of its socket. She straightens up and waits. Marcus's voice blunders on, unchecked, oblivious, into the silence' (O'Farrell 2002: 309). Without an addressee, Marcus's words flow into a vacuum, becoming mere sounds deprived of meaning and significance.

The novel ends with the remaining three characters departing the claustrophobic environment of London for the open expanses of the Australian outback. Sinead accepts a lecturing job in Australia while – quite separately – Lily decides to go travelling. In a brief concluding coda, the two women, plus Aiden, are momentarily (and against all the laws of probability) brought together for a final time. Lily, in a truck parked on the side of the road in the middle of the outback, is passed by another vehicle going in the opposite direction, in which she sees 'a sight so familiar that it tipped over in to strangeness' (O'Farrell 2002: 321): Sinead and Aiden, their arms around each other.

This fleeting incident, however, does not constitute a reunion; rather, it suggests that however far they travel, these characters can never break free of an uncanny cycle of return and repetition. This is emphasized in the final image of the novel, which brings the narrative itself full circle, back to the twin themes of translation and dislocation that have dominated *My Lover's Lover*. Lily feels the 'scenery slid[e] into motion' (O'Farrell 2002: 322) around her as the truck begins to move away; simultaneously, she sees, '[f]ar away into the distance, a large-eared dog-like creature . . . standing on the edge of a crest of a rock, nose high, reading the air for her scent' (O'Farrell 2002: 322). Here, the translator, caught in the process of translation from one unidentified point to another, is herself translated: but this act of 'reading' – like all the others in the novel – does not facilitate communication so much as foreground the estrangement, mutability and mortality of the uncanny subject.

6

'A Small Victory for Love over Death'

The Haunted Narratives of *I Am, I Am, I Am, Instructions for a Heatwave* and *The Hand that First Held Mine*

Tasha Alden

Maggie O'Farrell's novels are full of characters struggling with a traumatic past that refuses to stay in the past, and her memoir, *I Am, I Am, I Am*, similarly dances around in time, in its compulsive, relentless repetition of O'Farrell's near-death experiences. The novels and memoir are full of secrets and ghosts; long-concealed manslaughter, the theft of children, (apparently) dead brothers and girlfriends, dead husbands, dead mothers and, ultimately, in the memoir, death itself. This chapter situates O'Farrell's use of realism, and her depiction of trauma, in the context of trauma theory which moves away from the Caruthian/poststructuralist 'first wave' model, and switches from focusing on a state of melancholia to focusing on mourning, as defined by Freud (Freud 1917).

Michelle Balaev suggests that 'trauma as the ultimate unrepresentable in the classic model maintains a tropological hegemony in literary criticism' (Balaev 2014: 5). In the model derived from Cathy Caruth's highly influential work, trauma is inherently dissociative and fragmenting. It cannot be fully assimilated into the psyche and memory; we can have 'approximate recall but never determinate knowledge' (Balaev 2018: 363). Trauma theorists such as Cathy Caruth (1996, 2013), Dori Laub and Shoshana Felman (1992) have suggested that this dissociation and fragmentation is best rendered in fragmentary, non-linear language, arguing that 'the breakage of the verse enacts the breakage of the world' (Felman and Laub 1992: 25). As Stef Craps explains,

[t]rauma theorists often justify their focus on anti-narrative, fragmented, modernist forms by pointing to similarities with the psychic experiences of

trauma. An experience that exceeds the possibility of narrative knowledge, so the logic goes, will best be represented by a failure of narrative. Hence, what is called for is the disruption of conventional modes of representation, such as can be found in modernist art. (Craps 2014: 50)

Craps counters this reading by arguing that the fragmentation model rests too much on one form of response to trauma, a Western one which focuses on single punctual traumatic events rather than, for example, the kind of insidious trauma suffered by people experiencing racism (see also Forter 2007: 260). This aligns with Balaev's argument that current trauma theory counters the 'monolithic concept of trauma's inexpressibility . . . thus expanding [its] interpretative potential' (Balaev 2014: 8). She argues that '[t]he recursive and repressed nature of trauma does not remove its expressive potential, but rather these elements allow trauma to be articulated' (Balaev 2014: 9), and realism – as Craps (2014) and Meretoja (2020) show in their readings of the realist texts *Memory of Love* and *A Little Life* – can offer powerful, ethically oriented depictions of trauma without recourse to the kinds of literary fragmentation first-wave trauma theory focuses on.

In this chapter, I will suggest that Maggie O'Farrell's work can be productively read through trauma theory which doesn't hold trauma as showing the referential limits of trauma and history (Balaev 2018: 364) but 'questions the aesthetics of the unsayable' and posits that a more pluralistic, less universalizing response (in relation to postcolonial or queer trauma, for example) is necessary. Work by critics such as Ann Cvetkovitch, Greg Forter, Amy Hungerford and Naomi Mandel conceptualizes trauma as 'an event that alters perception and identity yet in the wake of such disturbance new knowledge is formed about the self and external world' (Balaev 2018: 366). This opens up the possibility of trauma's mediation through forms other than the modernist, fragmented mode associated with first-wave trauma theory.

Greg Forter (2003, 2011) offers a Neo-Freudian alternative to the Caruthian model of trauma, looking at the 'relationship between word and wound' (Kurtz 2018). He outlines a model centring mourning, where grief is incorporated psychologically into the sufferer's life, allowing the process of grieving to reach a definite conclusion, rather than melancholia, in which the past attachment cannot be relinquished and the sufferer is unable to move on (Forter 2011: 17). As this chapter seeks to demonstrate, this maps onto O'Farrell's narratives of loss which end hopefully, looking to the future. Forter cites Gregg Horowitz's description of the way mourning 'enables remembering precisely through the process of letting go':

The mourner decathects the psychic traces of the lost object not to forget them, but to detach them from the lost object and thus render them memorable for the very first time. In this way, grieving preserves the intimacy with the lost object . . . despite its being lost to us. The loss always shadows, but it does not swallow, the mourner's love. The lost object is permitted to go its way, the decathected memory traces theirs, and thus the joy in having suffered love is sustained. (Horowitz 2001: 153, cited in Forter 2011: 21)

Moving from a state of fragmented, melancholic engagement with past trauma, to a state of mourning the past but beginning to re-engage with the world, as we see repeatedly in O'Farrell's writing, allows what Abraham and Torok referred to as a 'small victory for love over death' (Abraham and Torok 1994: 190). Susan Strehle describes O'Farrell's novels as being '[r]ealist rather than post-modernist in their assurance that secret histories can be uncovered, understood and survived' (Strehle 2017: 61); O'Farrell's texts are characterized by Abraham and Torok's small victories, questioning the aesthetics of fragmentation and showing, in different ways in each text, how narrative provides a way of engaging with trauma which neither asserts that it cannot be known nor that it can be 'mastered' (Meretoja 2020: 33). Hanna Meretoja's reading of realist fiction depicting trauma 'suggests that ultimately struggling to share one's experiences of pain with one's loved ones, no matter how difficult, may be the only way to bear a traumatic past' (Meretoja 2020: 33). Realist fiction, Craps and Meretoja suggest, 'can be a vehicle of stretching one's imagination towards what feels incomprehensible' and 'questions the aesthetics of the unsayable, emphasising how trauma can profoundly shape one's self-narrative (and not merely disrupt it as poststructuralism suggests) – in a profoundly damaging way' (Meretoja 2020: 33).

This chapter will explore the ways that Maggie O'Farrell's novels and memoir use psychological realism to show melancholia being worked through to mourning; each text does this differently, but always aligns narrative stories mysteries with family stories mysteries, and 'recovering what has been hidden out of shame . . . [which] enables the protagonist to face and understand the past in the present' (Strehle 2017: 67).

The Hand that First Held Mine, which won the Costa Novel Award, was O'Farrell's fifth novel. Like her previous work, it revolves around the emergence of a long-hidden family secret and has two plots which run alongside each other. The first plot, which begins the novel, is the story of Lexie Sinclair, a young woman who flees rural Devon for London in the 1950s, moving to bohemian Soho, beginning a relationship with married arts journalist and editor Innes Kent and developing her own career as an art critic and journalist. After Innes's death, she starts a relationship with a man called Felix, whose son, Theodore, she has. The present-day plotline starts in the second chapter with Elina, a new mother who is bewildered by the trauma of her emergency C-section and struggling to cope physically and mentally. But as this story develops and Elina recovers, her partner Ted starts to struggle, increasingly distressed and traumatized by what appear to be buried memories from his childhood now resurfacing as he looks after his new son. The memories Ted is beginning to recall will form the basis of the connection between the two plotlines, as it becomes slowly apparent that the woman he has grown up thinking was his mother is in fact not his birth mother; his birth mother is Lexie, whose death by drowning he witnessed as a three-year-old, all memories of which he has suppressed until now.

The Hand that First Held Mine is a psychologically realist text, which does use some innovative narrative techniques to enact the effects of trauma – the split plotlines, for example, offer a literal embodiment of the split Ted has created in his own mind between his life before and after the age of three, and they come together towards the end of the book as Ted recovers his memory of Lexie's drowning. It is clear from this, and from the description of Ted's emotional state, that he is in a state of melancholia. But while Ted has difficulties accessing his traumatic past throughout the book, the novel is always travelling towards his recovery of those memories, from melancholia to mourning. At the end of the book, Ted, with Elina's help, is beginning to integrate the difficult knowledge that not only did he lose his mother, but that his father Felix and Felix's wife Margot and mother-in-law Gloria lied to him and let him believe that he was Margot's son.

It is apparent from early on in the novel that Ted is repressing traumatic knowledge; he hasn't cried since childhood (O'Farrell 2010b: 25), he has a terrible memory (O'Farrell 2010b: 40), he has irrational fears that Elina will 'disappear' suddenly (O'Farrell 2010b: 87, 135, 143), as well as nightmares in which he cannot find her, but then finds when he does that she has someone else's face (O'Farrell 2010b: 226). He seems to go into a trance state increasingly frequently; during one of these, he remembers a song about crows from his childhood but can't remember past the line: 'The first crow was greeting [crying] for his ma, greeting for his ma', as though he half remembers crying for his mother but can't allow himself to (O'Farrell 2010b: 135). He never swims and seems to have a horror of it, as we're told just after we have seen Lexie drown.

The split in himself the child Ted created to survive the loss of his mother starts collapsing when he becomes a father, and the split in the text, between

Lexie's story and his, also starts gradually breaking down as he comes closer to recovering the truth. The first symptom of this is the return of Ted's 'bizzies', a visual disturbance where 'there is a space at the centre of his vision. The periphery is clear but he cannot see the very thing he looks at, as if a hole has been burnt in the centre of a lens' (O'Farrell 2010b: 88–9). This happens immediately after he has his first flashback: 'listening to the surprising sound of his mother arguing with someone who has come to the door', a man who waves to Ted '[a]s if [he] has an important message for him, as if he is beckoning him down to the street' (O'Farrell 2010b: 88). The 'bizzies' embody Ted's repression of his memories of his early life; like Pat Barker in her 1993 novel *The Eye in the Door*, O'Farrell plays with the metaphor of sight to represent the internal blinding of oneself by the traumatized person. What the child Ted saw, and knew, is unbearable, so he simply stops seeing it, and as Freud suggested, the repressed knowledge 'returns' in the form of physical symptoms, as well as dreams (Freud 1995: 28–9). The 'bizzies' reappearing after Ted's first fragment of memory resurfaces indicates the strength of his repression – he is, as Barker puts it in *The Eye in the Door*, trying to blind himself to something (Barker 1993: 75) – but it also indicates that the memories are starting to return again. 'It must be', Ted thinks, 'that having a baby leads you to relive your own infancy'; this must be why he keeps experiencing 'flashes of something else, somewhere else, like radio static or interference, voices cutting in from a distant foreign station' (O'Farrell 2010b: 191). He projects his own fears of losing a mother onto his son (O'Farrell 2010b: 96) long before he becomes aware of doing so when he suddenly remembers being on a woman's lap, and losing his grip on her, immediately after he has seen a photo of Lexie at the John Deakin exhibition.

O'Farrell's first draft of the novel was written 'from the point of view of Lexie from beyond the grave' (Couglan 2013), and while the final draft is not literally haunted in this sense, the past persists in the present in ways that often verge on the uncanny. O'Farrell signals the penetration of the present by the past in a series of episodes of prolepsis and narrative palimpsests. We are shown Ted sitting in the café that now occupies the office of *elsewhere*, the magazine Innes owned and Lexie wrote for, as the narrator picks out the overlaps across time: '. . . sitting at the table where Lexie's desk used to be is Ted. He comes here quite a bit. . . . He seems to be staring at the place where Lexie's pinboard used to hang. An untidy array of notes, proofs, lists, postcards, transparencies that only she understood. But, of course, he's just looking at the rain' (O'Farrell 2010b: 180). The past is very nearly within touching distance, but not quite yet. These moments disrupt the separation of the two narratives increasingly as Ted's memories return more insistently. The narrator teasingly overlays the present with the past and vice versa, with Ted and Lexie occupying the same physical spaces, decades apart. O'Farrell delineates the material traces of Innes and Lexie in their flat in the present day: '[t]here is a strong sense of them both in these rooms – that and the hope that time might blur and collapse and, if one were to turn round fast enough at the right moment, one might catch a glimpse of Innes' (O'Farrell 2010b: 125).

O'Farrell also plays with the theme of fragmentation, but whereas in a text conforming to first-wave trauma theory we might expect the fragmentation of the text to reflect the fragmentation of Ted's memories and emotions, and for the fragments to be indecipherable and irresolvable, because of the dual time frame the reader usually has the knowledge to interpret what Ted initially cannot. We can tell from his descriptions of her clothes that the woman he is starting to remember must be Lexie, not the very different Margot; it is obvious to the reader why he can't remember the words to the crow song beyond the detail about crying for a lost mother.

The John Deakin photo of Lexie and Innes which Elina and Ted happen upon at an exhibition their friend Simmy takes them to (neither of them knows Deakin's work) also functions as a fragment. While Elina and Ted can't recognize Lexie yet, and don't know what the truncated 'e l s e w h e r' (O'Farrell 2010b: 190) in the photo refers to, the reader does, and it tells them that for the first time since her death Ted is looking at a photo of his mother. Elina describes the photos as being 'melancholy' (O'Farrell 2010b: 191), which they are, in a literal sense, for Ted. Simmy replies that '[t]hat's because they're of the past. All photos of the past look melancholy and wistful precisely because they capture something that's gone' (O'Farrell 2010b: 191). The paradox of capturing something that is gone drives the book: how can Ted's loss of both his mother and of his trust in the parents who brought him up be assuaged, how can the two timelines be brought back together? They can't literally, of course, but as O'Farrell shows by bringing the timelines into parallel with each other in the final section of the book, melancholia is not the only possible response to Ted's loss, and a different ending can be written.

The two plotlines climax at the same time, with Lexie's death and Ted's being taken to Felix and Margot in the past plotline, and the adult Ted furiously demanding the truth from them in the present-day one, before collapsing into a state of profound grief. O'Farrell juxtaposes these two moments, with the child and the adult Ted catatonic with loss. The past section ends at this moment, with a deeply traumatized three-year-old Ted unmoving and almost silent. Ted's state is the thread that ties the end of the first timeline to the present-day one and links them together as the first storyline ends.

But this second ending is different; the first ends with Ted asking Margot if she is his mother, indicating clearly that he is in a melancholic state and has repressed the terrible knowledge of his mother's death (Felix, when asked why they let Ted believe Margot was his mother, replies – knowing how feeble this sounds – that '[t]he thing is, you sort of . . . forgot' (O'Farrell 2010b: 350)). In this second ending, Ted goes into a catatonic state again, not eating, sleeping in the day and not speaking, in a withdrawal from the world that mirrors his reaction to Lexie's death. But this time is different: he has confronted his parents, has been told the whole story, and has had a full, genuine apology from his father. This isn't enough to help Ted out of his profound state of melancholia, though; it is Elina's intervention in seeking out Lexie's writing in the newspaper archives that begins to partially restore Lexie to him. That it is writing that allows the adult Ted to get to know his dead mother in some sense is significant. We might compare the way that O'Farrell's narrative techniques, especially her use of a dual timeline, are engineered to bring Ted and Lexie together in Lyme Regis where their stories meet: Lexie drowns, and decades later, Ted remembers enough to collapse, then be sure that he has to confront his parents. Language, storytelling, O'Farrell is showing us here, can play a powerful role in the portrayal and working through of trauma at the level of both form and content. In the final palimpsest moment of the text, O'Farrell tells the story of the cracked tiles in Felix and Margot's hallway: this story covers almost a century and links Innes and Elina explicitly for the first time, closing a loop from someone who loved Lexie, at the start of the book, to someone who loves Ted, in the present. The novel ends with Elina recovering Lexie's writing from the archives for Ted. Ted doesn't respond until she tells him that she has found a column about him – which reveals that he once had a different name, and restores 'the facts' about him (O'Farrell 2010b: 50, 374). The novel ends with Ted speaking for the first time in a week, to say 'keep going' (O'Farrell 2010b: 374), a dually significant comment. We can hope that it means Ted himself might be able to keep going, that for the first time he wants to engage with the world, assimilating his new knowledge about the loss both of his mother and his previous sense of self.

Instructions for a Heatwave was O'Farrell's sixth novel, and once again uses the 'updated psychological realism' (Strehle 2017: 61) she is noted for. Strehle's observation that O'Farrell's novels often turn her characters 'into detectives ransacking the familial and cultural past' (Strehle 2017: 61) is true both metaphorically and literally in this novel, which begins with the disappearance of Robert Riordan, a retired husband and father of three adult children: Michael Francis, Monica and Aoife. At the start of the novel, Robert sets out to buy the newspaper at the same time he does every day. When he fails to return, his children are drawn back from their scattered homes to their bewildered mother, Gretta. Set in the heatwave of 1976, *Instructions for a Heatwave*'s title is ironic, as are the fragments of the *Drought Act 1976* O' Farrell quotes at the opening of each section: there are no instructions for a situation like this, and the family's panic and confusion drive the first section of the novel as the news spreads.

Unlike *The Hand that First Held Mine*, which uses its dual timeframe to build up to the disasters defining the story, *Instructions for a Heatwave* begins with a crisis. It becomes clear, though, that this isn't the only, or even the major, trauma of the novel. The secret that has suddenly, one baking hot morning, reached out to snatch Robert Riordan, a highly predictable, cautious, taciturn man, out of his everyday life without a sign is the first and the most obvious trauma we encounter, and Robert's disappearance itself is a trauma the family must face together. But as the book progresses, the individual secrets and traumas of each member of the family surface and are then worked through by the conclusion of the novel. It is arguably these traumas, which at first seem incidental to the main plot, which are the heart of the book and drive the shift from melancholic shame, alienation and fear to the stage of recognizing and incorporating losses and moving on.

Maggie O' Farrell structures the novel as a single narrative, but one told through the thoughts and memories of each family member, creating a jumbled collective family consciousness that has aired and worked through each character's key trauma by the time that Robert reappears on the last page of the book. While it may at first seem surprising that we never hear Robert's own story (there are some significant questions that are left unanswered), O'Farrell signals here that we don't need to hear his explanation for his disappearance. He is back; what will happen next is unclear, but what has become clear in the final section is that the hidden griefs, grudges and shame each character has been carrying have begun, at least, to be exorcized. The text thus ends looking to the future, in a mournful rather than melancholic relation to the trauma each generation of the family has endured, but has now begun to heal.

Setting up and working through these traumas takes up the majority of the novel. In 'Friday', subtitled 'Home', the characters variously reveal their shame (Michael Francis tells Aoife about his brief affair, and his fears that it has ended his marriage; Gretta is forced to tell her children she and their father never married), or are forced to confront badly buried feelings of hurt and rage (Monica is furious, and deeply hurt, that Aoife destroyed her marriage by telling her husband that she had an abortion rather than a miscarriage (or so she thinks)). Both Aoife and Monica chafe against old patterns of sibling behaviour and roles they feel forced into: the untrustworthy parental favourite; the feckless, hopeless baby of the family.

O'Farrell uses a classical tripartite structure to set up the plot, expand it and then resolve it. Having despatched Robert and introduced the fragmented family in 'Thursday', in 'Friday' O'Farrell slows the plot down before resolving it in 'Sunday'. The only significant plot development in 'Friday' comes at the end, when the children find a fragment of a letter with an Irish stamp, and cheque stubs that show Robert has been sending money to someone called 'Assumpta' regularly for years. Gretta is forced to tell them the story of Robert's brother Frankie eloping with Robert's wife on the day of their marriage, and the estrangement that followed. As she explains this, while her siblings assume that the shame and distress Gretta is showing is because Robert was divorced when they got married, Aoife realizes that the intensity of her mother's emotions can only be explained by the fact that their devout Catholic parents were never married. The chapter climaxes with this revelation, but other than that, the whole section moves at a pace and with a mood to match the stultifying heat. The plot gives way to a series of memories, some very brief, some extended, as experienced by Gretta and her children as they adjust to being together, and the children adjust to being in their family home again. 'Friday' is full of moments where the characters see the things of their childhood and are either taken back to early memories of them, and their associations (was Gretta's impulsive shopping an attempt at filling a void, as Monica wonders?), or are struck by the utter strangeness of the sameness of the unchanging house. Being thrown back into each other's company, and into their family home, is deeply unsettling for each of the children, though Gretta adjusts with ease, having never quite accepted that they had gone: while she slips happily back into the past, her children struggle, suddenly confronted with family tensions they had tried to suppress.

Over 'Thursday' and 'Friday' O'Farrell introduces then slowly expands the details of the traumas haunting each sibling. Who is Gina Mayhew, and why does she haunt Michael Francis? Monica's trauma is similarly revealed through fragments of memory suddenly resurfacing in unexpected places, before the reader can connect them: Why does the cat's death remind her of Aoife? What happened to the child who would have been almost three (O'Farrell 2013: 47), and what did Aoife have to do with that? Why is Monica's instant thought, when Michael Francis rings her, that Aoife has died? Aoife is similarly wounded – having fled to New York after her falling out with Monica, she obsessively watches families, as though searching for something she recognizes of her own, a dynamic, an echo of a face that would remind her of the echoes in her own family (O'Farrell 2013: 82). She will never get over what happened with Monica, she thinks – though the reader is still unclear about what did happen. Fear and shame are pervasive: Ben Gold suggests that this is 'a book about fear in all its forms: the fear of infidelity, of ridicule, of being unloved by one's family; the fear of riots, of bombs, of the distancing effects of racism' (Gold 2013). O'Farrell's mode of narration allows her to allow the reader some optimism, though: the tripartite structure hints at resolution and that it will not be tragic seems increasingly possible from the middle of the novel onwards, as the siblings start to communicate and reconnect. Susan Strehle notes that

> O'Farrell's wise, insightful omniscience represents characters of both genders and many different ages with more tender sympathy and greater understanding than they bring to each other; this narrative stance models the acceptance of failings and flaws that some of the characters achieve as the novels end. (Strehle 2017: 68)

O'Farrell's use of Free Indirect Discourse also encourages 'tender sympathy and greater understanding', placing the reader into the minds of each individual so that we understand the stories each of them tells themselves and how this helps or prevents them from seeing things as they really are. The use of Free Indirect Discourse is particularly powerful in relation to Gretta, whose rambling, free-associating trail of thoughts carefully prevents her from looking too hard at what she cannot bear to see, in an echo of Ted in *The Hand That First Held Mine*. A much darker version of her story about how she and Robert came to pretend to be married emerges very slowly, hinted at then fully developed. She frequently thinks to herself that her children will never understand what her life was like as an Irish immigrant, and as a pregnant unmarried woman, but O'Farrell allows the reader some insight, conveying Gretta's fear and pain through her stuttering and repetitive thought processes, and particularly through a striking extended metaphor that conveys Gretta's ability to repress difficult truths:

> It was like one of those holes in the road in London. They dig them up and it all looks so shocking, those gashes in the tarmac, the rubble and the scar, the bare earth and mud so near to the surface of the city. Then they fill them in, cover them up and it looks new and incongruous, the fill-in tarmac black and glistening and domed against the old gritty road. But then, after a while, it

becomes bedded down, dusty, indistinguishable, so that you can no longer tell the old tarmac from the new, you'd never know that anything had been amiss there at all. (O'Farrell 2013: 293)

This image shows very clearly that Gretta knows that what lies underneath the apparently smooth surfaces of roads and of her consciousness is still there. She has a sudden moment of clarity when she goes to find Robert at the convent and suddenly panics as she realizes, for the first time, that he might not want to see her – she has blinded herself to the more frightening possibilities, and then has to face a different frightening reality as she finds herself taken to sit with the dying Frankie, who she has never met and realizes may not even know who she is. At the end of the novel, Gretta is both much the same as before but also profoundly changed in one significant way. Now her secret is known, and she has survived its telling, not by denying it but by letting it be known and then finding that family life simply carries on. Every character has had a similar epiphany: Aoife has told her boyfriend she cannot read, and he has reacted perfectly; Monica and Aoife have resolved their falling out; and Michael Francis and his wife Claire are repairing their relationship. The book ends with Hughie, Michael Francis's son, spotting Robert walking off the causeway towards them, as simply and easily as he walked out of the book in the first chapter. By now, though, we don't need to hear his story; the way the other members of the family have repaired their relationships became the main story of the book a long time ago, and the novel's natural closing point.

In 2017, O'Farrell published her first extended piece of non-fiction, a memoir. Although the construction of *I Am I Am, I Am* is unusual, being made up of seventeen near-death experiences told out of chronological order, this collapsing of linear time also aligns it with O'Farrell's novels, as does its insistence on the power of realism and language to mediate and assuage trauma. We move through O'Farrell's life in a seemingly random manner, ending with a story revealing the severity of O'Farrell's childhood encephalitis and then another, bringing us back to the chronological present, about the life-threatening allergies her daughter lives with. Harriet Baker observed that 'Elaine Scarry wrote that pain obliterates language, but unlike Hilary Mantel in *Giving Up the Ghost*, O'Farrell uses language to write herself out of pain and to understand it' (Baker 2018). The last words of the book rewrite the title: 'I am, I am, I am' becomes 'She is, she is, she is' (O'Farrell 2017: 285), and the book offers what it knows is a partial victory – a 'small victory for love over death' in its shift from a state of melancholic fear to one of clear-sighted acceptance or mourning: writing cannot alter the reality, but it can offer the consolations of making meaning and connection.

The memoir, O'Farrell has explained,

> is a response to living with my daughter's life-threatening medical condition. How does a parent absorb and explain the near-death experiences suffered by a young child? How best to reassure them, make them feel safe? The only way I have found to do this is to tell my daughter stories, to transpose what has happened to her into narrative. Only then can she comprehend the illnesses, the threat, the pain. (O'Farrell 2018)

The book, listing the surprisingly high number of near-death experiences someone can have in forty-five years of mostly ordinary life, 'is a literary exercise in normalising the near-death experience' (Aitkenhead 2017) which was written, Decca Aitkenhead suggests, 'to help [O'Farrell's] children understand that her daughter's close proximity to mortality is not their unique curse, but in fact surprisingly common' (Aitkenhead 2017). O'Farrell explained to Kate Kellaway that '[d]uring the final copy edits I realised that trying to pin down in words what [my daughter] goes through was my way of trying to feel in control, but that that control was illusory' (Kellaway 2020). Threading their stories into a narrative, though, does give shape to the experience, and make it communicable: '[a] friend said recently, "you've basically revealed all the secrets you've spent your whole life hiding." But I did it for my daughter. I was tired of the silence, I think' (Aitkenhead 2017). Writing this memoir allows O'Farrell to speak out of the silence, to give her and her daughter's experiences a narrative shape to help them make sense of them.

Much of this is done through the way the text is structured. Like other trauma narratives, it does not follow linear chronology. This is not the logic of traumatic fragmentation, though, but a chronology arranged 'somatically', 'structuring her life according to pain, illness and immobility' (Baker 2018), creating a form of realism that is insistently grounded in the reality of the human body.

The memoir thus has a fluid, unexpected form and often uses narrative in a fluid and unexpected way within the stories, allowing O'Farrell to stress the extremity of the experiences she's delineating, but in a way that repeatedly brings us back to the body. She weaves some of the stories into each other, for example (such as the reference at the end of 'Neck (2002)' to the events of 'Neck (1990)' sixty pages before), so the narrative loops around in time in the stories themselves as well as in the arrangement of the stories.

This is also true of O'Farrell's interest in slippage, in the disjointing of the present from itself, and in relation to the narrator's sense of self. This slippage is a constant in her novels, and here too, in a variety of different forms. One of the most noticeable of these is the way the narrative shifts between the first, second and third person; most of the text uses the first person, so when it switches into second or third, we notice. The narrative voice goes from first person to third person in 'Bloodstream (1997)', in a story that begins with O'Farrell thinking about herself in her twenties, imagining her walking past as though she could see her 'in her weather-insufficient tights, short skirt and bright blue trainers. She has cut off her hair – it doesn't entirely suit her . . .' (O'Farrell 2017: 174). This jump into the present tense, as the past and present meet, begins the shift into the third person the story continues in; this is someone O'Farrell knows profoundly, but is also a stranger, someone she can only view from the outside. 'Cranium (1998)', which depicts a man and a woman in love with each other but unable to act on it easily for reasons that are only explained obliquely, explicitly refuses to tell us who the man is or what happened between them, and is similarly told at one remove, carefully putting a slight distance between the teller and the story. You don't need to know all about this, the narrator seems to be saying; this far and no further.

In the final two chapters, 'Cerebellum (1980)' (where she depicts the encephalitis that nearly killed her as a child, adding disturbing detail to the fragments of this story we have been picking up throughout the memoir) and 'Daughter (the present day)', the movements from first to second to third person again indicate the emotional charge of events.

'Daughter (the present day)' starts in first-person plural, in a state of emergency as O'Farrell realizes that her daughter is having a potentially fatal anaphylactic reaction in the back of the car. They are lost, though, on holiday in Italy, and without mobile or satnav signal: as she holds her, realizing that she is dying, she thinks 'she cannot die, not here, not now. I think: how could I have let this happen?' (O'Farrell 2017: 259). The next section answers this question with another story and is one of the longest passages in the third person in the book. O'Farrell jumps away from the crisis she's just unfolded and calmly begins the next sentence: 'There was once a girl who met a boy . . .' (O'Farrell 2017: 259). Over the next four pages, she tells their story: the boy and girl don't hit it off, then they do, then they have a baby. Then the girl has a miscarriage, then she can't get pregnant again. Then they try IVF. It doesn't work: the blood tests say so. O'Farrell switches back to the first person for the next stage of this story: the blood tests are – implausibly, miraculously – wrong. It is 'a brand of magic' (O'Farrell 2017: 263). The use of the third person here allows her to wrap up a huge amount of story, of emotion, and make it containable within the larger narrative of her daughter's condition. It distances in a different way later on when she poses the rhetorical question: 'The effects of living with a child who has a life-threatening condition, of loving someone who could, at any moment, be snatched from you? I think about this a lot' (O'Farrell 2017: 276). Here, the repeated 'you' draws the reader into a vividly detailed list of the exhausting, exhaustive demands keeping her daughter alive makes: the preparation, the precautions, the constant terror and the need to hide it. Aligning the reader with O'Farrell's almost unimaginable experience is a powerful way of giving us some sense of what that life might be like, a narrative manoeuvre she uses again in 'Cerebellum (1980)'. This story is mostly told in the first person, but jumps into the second person with the startling statement: 'When you are a child, no one tells you that you're going to die. You have to work it out for yourself' (O'Farrell 2017: 215). O'Farrell explains that this way of mapping emotions into language is how she manages the most challenging, most traumatic aspects of this experience (and others):

> I recall my encephalitis, in its most acute phase, in flashes, in staccato bursts, in isolated scenes. Some things are as raw and immediate as the moment they happened; these, I can inhabit as myself in the first person, in the present tense, if you like. Others I almost have to force myself to confront and I watch them as I might a film: there is a child in a hospital bed, in a wheelchair, on an operating table; there is a child who cannot move. How can that child ever have been me? (O'Farrell 2017: 226–7)

The memoir doesn't seek to answer that question directly, but does so implicitly, threading this memory into a whole alongside the others, creating a narrative of illness and recovery. The memoir is about illness, but the narrative techniques O'Farrell develops emphasize that it is really much more about survival. Like O'Farrell's novels, her memoir asserts the power of literary form, and specifically realism, to move out of melancholia, to achieve 'the small victory over death'.

7

The Taming Shrew

Agnes in Maggie O'Farrell's *Hamnet* as (Early) Modern Husbander

Nicholas Taylor-Collins

husbander, n. A person who husbands something (in various senses of the verb); esp. a person who makes careful use of resources, assets, etc., a thrifty or prudent administrator. Also (occasionally): a husbandman, a tiller of the soil. *(OED)*

husband, v. II. To manage to best advantage, to tend, to cultivate. *(OED)*

Maggie O'Farrell's award-winning *Hamnet*[1] (2020) loudly proclaims its affiliation with William Shakespeare's *Hamlet* (1599). It tells the story of Will Shakespeare's son, Hamnet, and the effect of his death on the Shakespeare family – particularly on his mother, Agnes (Will's wife). Hamnet's death overshadows the Bard so much that he goes nameless throughout *Hamnet*: clearly the emphasis of this book of grief is on the son, and not the father – not unlike Shakespeare's most famous tragedy, *Hamlet*. We might say that *Hamnet* husbands – tends, cultivates, lets grow – *Hamlet* in and into the twenty-first century. Stephen O'Neill (2021) has argued as much regarding the paratextual indexing of *Hamnet*'s motif of memory as a maternalizing response to, and correction of, *Hamlet*'s own injunction from the ghost to 'remember me' (1.5.91). *Hamnet* thus provides a reading of *Hamlet* that, in turn, is reconfigured to help us read O'Farrell's novel. While O'Farrell invites the turn to *Hamlet*, O'Neill offers a deep and nuanced reading that allows us to enjoy *Hamnet* on a richer level. Following O'Neill's lead, I explore the influence of early modern drama on O'Farrell, showing how *Hamnet*'s hero, Agnes, can tame her husband and become gentlemanly in his stead.

---

[1] *Hamnet* won the Woman's Prize for Fiction and the Waterstones Book of the Year awards in 2020.

Aside from *Hamlet*, throughout *Hamnet* there are nods to several Shakespeare plays including *Romeo and Juliet* (O'Farrell 2020a: 5), *All's Well that Ends Well* (27) and *Macbeth* (271). I turn to another, *The Taming of the Shrew* (?1590–2), to deepen our reading of the O'Farrell–Shakespeare connection. My argument builds on the idea that *Hamnet* adapts *The Shrew*, with a major theme of that play being the process of matrimonial husbanding through 'taming': Petruccio[2] becomes Katherina's husband by taming her into submission. During that taming, Katherina is associated with beasts and birds, and early modern husbandry manuals help us see how Petruccio's taming is in keeping with that growing practice. But it is with John Fletcher's later *The Shrew* sequel, *The Tamer Tamed; or, The Woman's Prize* (?1609–11), that I see *Hamnet* having a closer affinity. In this play, Maria – Petruchio's second wife – successfully tames Petruchio, often using the same tactics Shakespeare's Petruccio uses in the earlier play. Plainly, Maria cannot become Petruchio's husband, though she nonetheless tames him. Maria is, as I see it, a more useful forebear of O'Farrell's Agnes.

Another branch of gentlemanly self-fashioning and self-conduct is at the core of these three texts: falconry. The ability to tame a wild bird is not identical with husbandry – no land is cultivated, no food grown – but through hawking a gentleman may self-fashion. First, Shakespeare's Petruccio is the metaphorical falconer, controlling Katherina; then, Fletcher's Maria controls her husband as if he were a bird; and, in my trifecta, *Hamnet*'s Agnes develops the metaphorical husbandry of *The Shrew* into a literal practice and joins it with a literal falconry, through the joint skills of which she turns Will into William Shakespeare. This argument will allow us to re-think feminism in the early modern shrew discourse as well as illuminate the strengths of Agnes's character. Ultimately, I will demonstrate the importance of reading *The Shrew* and *The Tamer* alongside *Hamnet*, and therefore underline the significance that early modern drama continues to hold in contemporary writing.

'Haply to Wive and Thrive'

To start, I want to counter expectations: while it appears that *The Shrew* is about Petruccio becoming Katherina's husband, it is much more about Petruccio

---

[2] For the avoidance of confusion, I refer to Shakespeare's male lead as 'Petruccio', and Fletcher's equivalent character as 'Petruchio'. References to Shakespeare's *The Shrew* are parenthetically cited to the Arden Shakespeare Third Series, and references to Fletcher's play are cited to *The Tamer*, and the Munro (ed.) Bloomsbury volume.

making Katherina his wife. Two pronouncements early in the play amount to the same sentiment: that he is in Padua 'Haply to wive and thrive as best I may' (1.2.55 and see l. 75). It is under the banner of 'wiving' that Petruchio undertakes his bid for Katherina's hand and submission, whereas the idea of becoming someone's husband is voiced by the Lord in *The Shrew*'s Induction when he looks forward to Bartholomew calling the 'drunkard [Sly] husband' (1.132). 'To husband' is therefore to play around and mock others, whereas Petruccio's wiving is more about control – about 'taming'. While the way a husband exerted matrimonial control in the early modern period – and, if need be, 'tamed' his 'shrew' – was beginning to be questioned (with violent 'conduct [. . .] increasingly viewed as incompatible with ideals of companionate marriage' (Hodgdon in Shakespeare 2010: 43), the practice of violent domestic control nevertheless remained unsurprising.

For an early modern audience, the shrewish woman was not novel. Summarizing, Graham Holderness has written that 'From mediaeval devotional manuals to dramatic productions of the 1630s, the shrew is presented as a corrective exemplum of the need for patriarchal authority and wifely obedience' (2010b: 5). The seeking of financial compensation for marrying a shrew is part of this tradition going back to European folktales (Brunvand [1991] 2015) and demonstrates the precarity of Katherina's position. For instance, we are hardly into the play before the theme of shrewishness is connected to wealth when Petruccio's friend, Hortensio, 'promise[s]' him that 'she shall be rich, / And very rich' (1.2.58–62). Thus, along with the shrew comes the tamer – the man who can, through physical strength and wit, bring his woman to heel, by financial means or foul. In Shakespeare's play, Petruccio is that man. Before he takes on the task of taming Katherina, he negotiates with her father, Baptista, about her dowry:

> PETRUCCIO What dowry shall I have with her to wife?
> BAPTISTA After my death, the one half of my lands,
> And in possession twenty thousand crowns.
> PETRUCCIO And for that dowry I'll assure her of
> Her widowhood, be it that she survive me,
> In all my lands and leases whatsoever.
>
> (2.1.119–24)

This exchange is not merely filler for Shakespeare – nor just a sign that this play belongs to the shrewish tradition – but also reflects contemporary marriage practices (see Jeafferson 1872; Ranald 1979: 69–70). The play therefore hovers somewhere between comic social critique and social realism (see Hibbard 1964: 28). A similar discussion in *Hamnet* testifies to a comparable artistic process for O'Farrell: using realistic marriage practices as a narrative device to elucidate character. In *Hamnet*, we learn about John Shakespeare, Will's dad, and the power he wishes to wield over Agnes's family at Hewlands: 'This marriage [. . .] will be beneficial to [Will's] father, to whatever dealings he has with the sheep farmer's widow. His father is about to turn all this [. . .] to his own good' (O'Farrell 2020a: 99). Here John models an astuteness that benefits his own finances. Shortly afterwards, he organizes that Agnes will become Will's wife with a negotiation for her dowry that leads to her departure from Hewlands, and the cancellation of John's debt to her family. The decision is rushed 'and a bother to arrange, with her brother needing a special licence and [. . .] a protracted discussion (heated) about money' (109). This is but one way in which these texts share in early modern taming practices.

The taming of Katherina in *The Shrew* is a capricious affair, with Petruccio adopting various tactics. These include 'kill[ing]' a wife with kindness' (4.1.197), starving her like a keeper trains a falcon (4.1.179), treating her contrarily (4.5.1–21), calling her animalistic slurs (e.g. 2.1.208–25, l. 258, l. 261), and dressing inappropriately at their wedding (3.2.43–6). These tactics constitute the 'taming school' where 'Petruccio is the master / That teacheth tricks eleven-and-twenty long / To tame a shrew and charm her chattering tongue' (4.2.55–9). Through these methods, Petruccio can tame his wife and wive 'happily' (1.2.75). The taming's success is demonstrated in the final scene when, in a famous monologue – 'an essay on order, hierarchy and subjection reminiscent of the 1570 *Homilie Against Disobedience and Wylfull Rebellion*' (Holderness 2010a: 169) – Katherina confirms to her sister and the Widow that

> Thy husband is thy lord, thy life, thy keeper,
> Thy head, thy sovereign: one that cares for thee
> And for thy maintenance; commits his body
> To painful labour both by sea and land[.]
>
> (5.2.152–5)

In performance the actor playing Katherina could play this ironically, with a wink and nudge to the audience undercutting the manifest meaning of this speech. Nonetheless, the explicit meaning remains to the fore and in this conception of marriage, the husband, rather than the wife, goes through bodily labour; the husband is owed a duty by his wife; and the wife submits and shows obeisance to her husband. Katherina's final line confirms that she has been tamed 'happily'

– 'My hand is ready, may it do him ease' (5.2.185) – proving the success of Petruccio's venture to Padua.

We read a similar sense of happy domestication in *Hamnet* when Agnes moves from the farmland at Hewlands to the townhouse in Stratford upon her marriage. 'It seems strange to Agnes', we read, 'that she has, in the space of a month, exchanged country for town, a farm for an apartment' (O'Farrell 2020a: 137). As O'Neill (2021: 222) summarizes, until Part II of the novel, Agnes is exclusively associated with 'nature' and only then the 'domestic space of the house'. She is now domesticated into a hierarchy since 'there are the parents, then the sons, then the daughter, then the pigs in the pig-pen and the hens in the henhouse, then the apprentice and then, right at the bottom, the serving maids', rather than the utopian 'sprawl of generations, all working together' (O'Farrell 2020a: 137) at Hewlands. The different approach to work – and her general redundancy in Stratford – lead her to be domesticated on the fifth day:

> [Agnes] is up before the serving girls and out of the apartment's back door. [. . .] By the time they appear, she has fired the oven in the cookhouse and coaxed the dough into rounds, adding a handful of ground herbs from the kitchen garden. [. . .] It takes Mary a week or so to notice that the house is different. [. . .] It's only when she smells the distinct, pollen-heavy scent of beeswax in the parlour one day when she is entertaining a neighbour that she begins to wonder. (139–40)

This domestication is, I argue, a result of 'taming', if inadvertently achieved by Will. Agnes's housewife practice is in keeping with Gervase Markham's description of *The English Housewife* (1615), in which he advises on baking ([1615] 1986: 209–11), says that a housewife 'must know all herbs' (60), the importance of cleanliness (*passim*) and of making scented pomanders using wax (133). Agnes's shift from independent country woman to domestic wife and mother achieves the same end as Katherina's domestication by Petruccio: to be 'most obedient' (5.2.68). Agnes's assimilation into the Shakespeare household, and her assumption of domestic organization, makes her a housekeeper. Taken out of the wilds of Hewlands and removed to Stratford, Agnes has been tamed and wived.

It is no coincidence that Agnes is tamed on the fifth day, for on the fifth day of creation, God created the fish in the sea and (crucially) the birds in the sky. I will now turn to the significance of avian imagery in *The Shrew*, *The Tamer*, and *Hamnet*, and Agnes's association with the flightiness of birds – the reason she needs 'taming' at all.

Hawking: Gentlemanly Self-fashioning

When Will first sees Agnes, he is surprised by her appearance and demeanour:

> For a moment, the tutor believes it to be a young man. He is wearing a cap, a
> leather jerkin, gauntlets; he moves out of the trees with a brand of masculine
> insouciance or entitlement, covering the ground with booted strides. There
> is some kind of bird on his outstretched fist: chestnut-brown with a creamy
> white breast, its wings spotted with black. It sits hunched, subdued, its body
> swaying with the movement of its companion, its familiar. (O'Farrell 2020a:
> 33–4)

The 'young man' whom Will sees is Agnes, dressed in masculine clothes. Coupled
with her looking after this bird of prey – a kestrel – Agnes is cast as falconer:
a man who can improve himself and demonstrate that improvement through
taming wild birds.

Some characteristics of the kestrel are later symbolically applied to Agnes.
Will tells his sister, Eliza, that the kestrel "'is so different when it flies – it is
almost, you might think, two creatures. One on the ground and another in the
air'" (O'Farrell 2020a: 75–6), establishing the tamed wildness of the kestrel. It is
not difficult to see Agnes in this mould, since "'She is like no one you have ever
met. She cares not what people may think of her. She follows entirely her own
course'" (77). Later, when she has moved in with the Shakespeares, Will 'feels
the flex and pull of her shoulder-blade, as if she might fly, take to the air, like
her bird, if only she could' (95). The avian similarity develops when we read
that 'At this point he is aware of Agnes turning her head to look at him – he
can imagine her dark eyes on him, assessing, fathering information, like a spool
gathers thread' (96), imitating the 'alert, always alert' kestrel (79). Agnes's ability
to tame the kestrel's wildness is therefore mirrored in her self-disciplining and
control over her destiny: it is she who tells Will that she knows clandestine ways
of how to force her stepmother to let them marry and coordinates her loss of
virginity and the conception of their eldest child, Susanna. Rather than being
tamed, here, Agnes takes control and undertakes an extreme and rigorous self-
fashioning: she is the leader in this marriage.

Self-fashioning was described by Stephen Greenblatt as a breakthrough in
selfhood and individual identity in the Renaissance period. In *Renaissance Self-
Fashioning* (1980), he writes about how 'to fashion a gentleman', describing that
'manuals of court behaviour which became popular in the sixteenth century
[. . .] are essentially handbooks for actors, practical guides for a society whose

members were nearly always on stage' (Greenblatt [1980] 1984: 162). Examples of these handbooks include *The Court of Civil Courtesy* (1577), 'designed to help its reader to thread his way successfully through the labyrinth of social distinctions, to win at the game of rank' (163). George Turberville's *The Book of Falconry or Hawking* (1575, 1611) belongs to this discourse (see Hodgdon in Shakespeare 2010: 55) – and was a source for O'Farrell (2020a: 371). It is also behind many of the hawking references in *The Shrew*. Turberville's paean opening his book claims that falconry is a 'kind of sport [that] doth banish vice, and vile devises quight, / When other games do foster faults, and breed but base delight' (1611: n.p.). The skill involved 'reclaim[ing]' a female 'haggard Hawke', because 'she the fowle shall kill'. Furthermore, there is no 'greater glee' to 'make and man her in such sort, as tossing out a traine, / Or but the lewre, when she is at large, to whoup her in againe' (1611: n.p.). It is therefore the control and authority over a hawk involved in falconry that elevates the falconer to the appropriate level. Agnes's command over her kestrel in *Hamnet* belongs to this discourse of gentlemanly self-fashioning: another example of her surprising masculinity coming to the fore.

In his chapter on how 'To make your Hawke know your voyce', Turberville writes:

> IF your hawke be thus in foure or fiue dayes *manned* [. . .] then you shall first beginne to make her *know your whistle*[. . . .] But if your Falcon be not eager or *sharpe* set, then shall you do well to wash her meate some|times in fayre water[. . . .] It shall not be amisse also in the morning when she is *emptie* both in the *gorge* and pannell, to conuey into her a little Sugar candy [. . . which] wil make her eager[.] (Turberville, 1611: 144–5; my emphases)

When set in these terms, falconry hardly seems like modest husbandry of the natural world – a sense redoubled in Petruccio's soliloquy on his attempted, violent taming of Katherina:

> My falcon now is *sharp* and passing *empty*
> And till she stoop she must not be full-*gorged*,
> For then she never looks upon her *lure*.
> Another way I have to *man my haggard*,
> To make her come and *know her keeper's call*[.]
>
> (4.1.179–83; my emphases)

The emphases demonstrate the literal connection between Turberville's manual and Shakespeare's playtext, in which 'the imagery in much of the play indicates a perception of the matrimonial state as similar to the compact between falcon and keeper' (Ranald 1987: 119). Thereafter we can spot the alliance between gentlemanly self-fashioning and the violence inherent in the process; when applied to women – even to wives – Petruccio's husbandry of Katherina becomes assault. These methods of taming 'engage with a deeply gendered history' (Hodgdon in Shakespeare 2010: 55) of domestic violence that in the seventeenth century were practised on suspected witches. This is what I have described as wiving, earlier.

But for Agnes, the associations with her kestrel – and even her being the gentleman husband in her relationship with Will – are better contextualized alongside early modern husbandry. Benjamin Bertram has summarized that 'early modern husbandry manuals provided the country gentleman or yeoman with detailed information on farming techniques and household management' in order to lead 'pious, productive, and economical lives' (2013: 459). At root, 'A Husbandman is he which with discretion and good order tilleth the ground in his due seasons, making it fruitfull to bring forth Corne, and plants, meete for the sustenance of man' (Markham 1613: A3r). More broadly, the husbandman is committed to work to which we are all dedicated: to 'kéep[] the earth in order, which else would grow wilde' (A3v). The sense of bringing order to wild nature is evident in the primary motivation of hawking. Bertram demonstrates how a reading of the micro and macropolitical aspects of husbandry – Markham analogizes tilling the soil with a monarch looking after his nation – can help us read Shakespeare.

Bertram's focus is *Measure for Measure* (1604), but I find it useful for reading *The Tamer*. For instance, Bertram draws attention to the theme of 'waste' in the husbandry discourse to refer not only to uncultivated land but also to those who are not dedicated to improving it. Bertram cites Thomas Nashe's *Piers Penniless* (1592) as 'waste' meaning 'worthless people'.[3] Furthermore, Bertram points out the punning opening to Shakespeare's Sonnet 129 that references masturbation – 'The expense of spirit in a waste of shame' – to demonstrate the deep connection between early modern husbandry and procreation: being fruitful and multiplying is central to both. This latter argument invites me to consider the hitherto unaddressed moment in *The Tamer* when Petruchio, making a wager with the other men about his ability to tame his new wife, Maria, tells them that 'What may be done without impeach or waste / I can and will do' (1.3.33–4). Thinking of this as a dual reference to husbandry and

---

[3] This sense still maintains in the United States, especially when referring derogatorily to the working classes. See Nancy Isenberg (2016).

sexual waste – either his wife's barrenness or his own masturbation – allows us to identify the significance of husbandry in *The Tamer* and shrew narratives generally.

The primary reading of husbandry – as cultivation, control, tending the natural world – helps us to read *Hamnet*. The way Agnes husbands the natural world ranges from her deft command of the apiary at Hewlands, to caring for 'various animals and other creatures [that] she brings into the house' (O'Farrell 2020a: 204), to her transformation into the town apothecary. This behaviour represents perhaps the closest to the dictionary definitions of husbandry that head my chapter. Agnes is cultivating, tending and looking after the natural world, and here she feels more comfortable than when she plays housekeeper in the Shakespeare household. She is a husbandman in this pure sense, undermining the taming tradition that relies on these tropes and vocabulary.

Another way that *Hamnet* adapts the taming husbandry of *The Shrew* is through the transformation of the shrew's devilish and witchcraft behaviours into medical practice. Katherina is called a devil six times in *The Shrew* (out of twelve instances of the term), while in *The Tamer* Petruchio despairs when he asks the audience, following his wife, Maria's behaviour, '[A]m I / Keeping tame devils now again?' (3.2.215–16). Moreover, there are intimations in *The Tamer* that the rebellious women form a coven of witches. This is done subtly with a nod to Shakespeare's *Macbeth* when three Country Wenches come onstage for a six-line scene:

> FIRST WENCH How goes your business girls?
> SECOND WENCH   Afoot and fair.
> THIRD WENCH If fortune favour us. Away to your strengths;
>   We are discovered else.
> FIRST WENCH The country forces are arrived. Begone!
> SECOND WENCH Arm and be valiant. Think of our cause.
> THIRD WENCH Our justice! Aye, aye, aye, 'tis sufficient.

> (2.4.1–6)

Compare this to the style and vocabulary of *Macbeth*'s three Weird Sisters, whose 'Fair is foul, and foul is fair' (1.1.9) and later 'Where hast thou been, sister?' (1.3.1) are recalled in this short conversation. While not explicit – and nor are the Weird Sisters called 'witches' in *Macbeth* at any time – there are hints at shrews being or using witchcraft in their daily practice of rebellion.

In *Hamnet*, by contrast, the allegations are explicit:

> Agnes has a patch of land at Hewlands, leased from her brother, stretching from
> the house where she was born to the forest. She keeps bees here, in hemp-woven
> skeps, which hum with industrious and absorbed life; there are rows of herbs,
> flowers, plants, stems that wind up supporting twigs. Agnes's witch garden, her
> stepmother calls it[.] (O'Farrell 2020a: 16)

Elsewhere, Agnes gains a certain shrewish 'notoriety' because of her deft practice
with flora and fauna, and is described as 'perhaps mad', having 'learnt her crafts
from an old crone' (O'Farrell 2020a: 37). But in *Hamnet* Agnes's witchcraft is
viewed positively, like her falconry, as Agnes's husbandry and familiarity with
the herbs, plants and flowers lead to her vocation as the Stratford pharmacist.
This 'focus on her medicinal knowledge also plugs into the archives and to those
histories of how women in the period were actively involved in the business of
health and healing' (O'Neill 2021: 222) and demonstrates that Agnes adjusts the
discourse of husbandry in her favour, confounding the shrewish expectations of
a masculine woman. In the next section, however, I demonstrate how Maria in
The Tamer and Agnes in *Hamnet* not only confound expectations but become
totally new types of women.

Feminism and Husbanding Humans

I have already shown how Agnes is positively associated with her kestrel, and
how this positively spins the animalistic slurs thrown at Katherina. But I now
turn this on its head, first by returning to Holderness. Earlier, I cited the first half
of an important summary of shrewishness. The second half reads that 'in practice
[. . .] representations [of the shrew] frequently provoke resistance, argument, a
paradoxical destabilisation of patterns of authority and the dissolution of gender
norms' (Holderness 2010b: 5). Holly Crocker usefully notes that '"shrew" was
flexible in Shakespeare's day, though critical attention to "shrew" has usually
focused on the term as it was applied to women'. More critical still, Crocker's
research 'reveals a crucial connection between domestic order and self-control,
since medieval renderings characterize shrews as unable to rule the domestic
body' (Crocker 2010: 49). In other words, when we think about men as shrews
– and therefore logically in need of taming – we ought also to consider how
taming belongs to the discourse of husbandry: cultivating the land and bringing
it to order out of chaos (to quote Markham) is like bringing the shrew to heel.

Agnes, like Maria – 'I am she' who 'now shall [. . .] / [. . .] tame you' (*The Tamer*, 1.3.281–3) – might also be a tamer in her husbandry.

For instance, the way Agnes births her daughter Susanna demonstrates that her 'sense that animals' exist in the material and spirit worlds 'extends to people too' (O'Neill 2021: 222). Agnes undertakes this by returning to the forest where she and her brother Bartholomew used to play. The danger of giving birth is tangible; after all, Agnes remembers her mother's death while giving birth to Bartholomew, recalling a 'bed soaked red and a room of carnage, of violence, of appalling crimson' (O'Farrell 2020a: 55). Not coincidentally, this involuntary memory springs to Agnes's mind when she is watching her father slaughter a lamb: birth and death are quite often simultaneous.

Agnes takes on the birth like an animal, recalling births she has witnessed – not only 'neighbouring women' but also 'the pig, the cow, the ewes birth their young' (O'Farrell 2020a: 155). When she is ready for the final push, 'Agnes plants her hands in front of her, on all fours, like a wolf, and submits to another pain' (156). This act literally opposes Katherina's submission to Petruccio when she says that a woman's husband 'commits his body / To painful labour' (5.2.154–5). If husbanding animals involves midwifing their births, then Agnes is now husbanding herself – husbanding humans. After the birth, 'Agnes turns her [daughter] on to her side, as her father always did with lambs. [. . . Susanna] looks suddenly and completely, human. [. . . S]he begins to suck. Agnes lets out a laugh. Everything works' (O'Farrell 2020a: 160, 161). Agnes's ability to husband turns Susanna from a wolf-cub, as it were, into a human girl. Doing this alone, enacting a most literal Renaissance self-fashioning by herself, Agnes becomes what we now call a feminist.

The feminism (*avant la lettre*) in *The Tamer* is distinctly other from *Hamnet*'s, but nonetheless significant. Its irony is already evident in the play's other title, *The Woman's Prize*, as editors Celia Daileader and Gary Taylor make plain. In early modern England

> there were literally no prizes that a woman could win, because there were none for which she was allowed to compete. That is why *The Tamer Tamed* has an alternative, equally paradoxical title[. . . .] The prowess of the play's protagonist has to be troped in the male terms of warfare, jousting, and the competitive rhetorical exercises of a humanist education. [. . .] Fletcher, as a man, could boldly go where no woman in 1610 dared to tread: on to a feminist stage. (Daileader and Taylor 2006: 2–3)

This feminism is achieved first by representing rebellion. Maria recognizes that any 'childish woman / That lives a prisoner to her husband's pleasure / [. . .]

becomes a beast / Created for his use, not fellowship' (1.2.137–40). Bertram's reading of instrumentality in *Measure for Measure* focuses on 'use', arguing that in *Measure*, 'the self is put to "use" within various forms of exchange; it is transformed from something wasteful to something generative and thrifty' (2013: 466). We can read Maria's 'beast / Created for his use' as both a comment on patriarchy and husbandry. I extend this to account for Giorgio Agamben's examination of the Shoah, which begins with a reading of Aristotle's descriptions in *Politics*. Aristotle establishes that the work of the slave is the 'use of the body', with Agamben highlighting that for the ancients, 'in using the body of the slave, the master is in reality using his own body' ([2014] 2015: 14). Analogously for my argument, the women in *The Tamer* are fighting against the enslavement and oppression of their bodies in a patriarchal society. These early modern women overturn the idea that they are 'on the one hand, a human animal (or an animal-human) and, on the other hand [. . .], a living instrument (or an instrument-human)'. If they can overcome this animal instrumentality, they will gain 'access to the truly human condition' (Agamben [2014] 2015: 78).

The women's assuming the style and authority of *The Shrew*'s tamer, Petruccio, is the next step in this process. For instance, *The Tamer*'s Bianca adopts Petruccio's language when she talks about falconry and hawking (relevant terms emphasized):

> Now thou com'st near the nature of a woman.
> Hang those tame-hearted *eyases*, that no sooner
> See the *lure* out, and hear their husbands' hallow
> But cry like *kites* upon 'em; the free *haggard* –
> Which is that woman that has *wing*, and knows it,
> Spirit and *plume* – will make a hundred checks
> To show her freedom, sail in every air
> And look out every pleasure, to regarding
> *Lure* nor *quarry*[.]
>
> (1.2.147–55)

These women are not just fighting the innate sexism of the tamer and the taming tradition; they are also adopting the language and tactics of the tamer to tame him in return. This includes the several shocking references to the women wearing men's breeches (e.g. 1.2.146), and even their discovery and practice of sexual pleasure without men. They achieve this when they have decided to mimic the siege of Ostend[4] by walling themselves up together to punish their husbands:

---

[4] Between 1601 and 1604, the city Ostend in West Flanders was besieged by a Spanish general Spinola. The latter is directly referenced by Jaques (1.3.70), and the former by Sophocles (1.3.95).

JAQUES   They have got a stick of fiddles, and they firk it
         In wondrous ways; the two grand capitanos
         That brought the auxiliary regiments
         Dance with their coats tucked up to their bare breeches
         And bid the kingdom kiss 'em: that's the burden.
         They have got metheglin and audacious ale
         And talk like tyrants.

                                               (2.5.37–43)

The fiddlesticks here stand in for dildos, and while 'firk[ing]' means 'dancing', its innuendo intimates something much lewder. These women dare to imagine a gynocracy where they derive sexual pleasure independently and get drunk in the process. This parallels Agnes's rejection of help when giving birth to Susanna: she demonstrates self-husbandry that begins to render her husband redundant (Bartholomew mocks Will after the birth: '"You get the basket, [. . . i]f it's not too heavy for you"' (O'Farrell 2020a: 165)). Thus, not only are *The Tamer's* women in the process of taming the tamer Petruchio, but also 'taming' the stereotype of women, shrewish or not.

Ultimately, Maria tames Petruchio, 'adopt[ing] the identity of the headstrong female partner, or a "shrew," to turn Petruchio from his immoderate ways' (Crocker 2010: 60). She calls his bluff when he threatens to leave her, and in doing so achieves financial independence: 'What I ordained your jointure / [. . .] and half my house. / [. . .] /Your apparel, / And what belongs to build up such a folly, / Keep, I beseech ye' (4.4.123–8). This clearly echoes and counterbalances the financial independence that Petruccio sought from Katherina in *The Shrew*. As he is about to leave, Maria insists that Petruchio 'take heed you fly not back, sir' (l. 138) and urges him to starve himself – 'One meal a week will serve you' (l. 162) – before he can transform 'from a jade into a courser' (l. 171). Again we witness Maria's turning the rhetoric of taming on its head, and even Sophocles praises her 'an excellent woman to breed schoolmen' (l. 154), demonstrating how she, rather than her husband, is master of the taming school.

Fletcher's Petruchio tries one more trick to tame Maria – he plays dead – but Maria mocks the fact he lived a 'poor, unmanly, wretched, foolish life' because he was 'far below a man, [. . .] far from reason, / From common understanding, and all gentry[.] / [. . .] / He had a happy turn he died' (5.4.20, 24–7). The taming, in other words, is primarily about becoming a better gentleman than Petruchio was a husband and, in turn, improving Petruchio *as* a husband. Maria tends, cultivates and *husbands* Petruchio. It is only when Petruchio caves in his final trick – when he tacitly concedes victory to Maria – that Maria is happy to settle: 'I have tamed ye, / And now am vowed your servant' (5.4.45–6). Though the Epilogue (probably added later by William Davenant) claims this denouement as 'teach[ing]' both sexes due equality' (l. 7), it was 'Well laid and grounded' (l. 10) through Maria's headstrong, defiant and ultimately successful taming of Petruchio.

Agnes is in this mould of headstrong defiance, and we see her at her proudest and happiest as a wife and mother when she husbands Will. For instance, she organizes for Will to go to London to expand his father's business (O'Farrell 2020a: 189–94), before sensing an altogether different reason to tame her husband:

> Agnes looks at her husband and suddenly she sees it, feels it, scents it. All over his body, all over his skin, his hair, his face, his hands, as if an animal has run over him, again and again, leaving tiny pawmarks. He is, Agnes realises, covered in the touches of other women. (O'Farrell 2020a: 310)

The animalistic Agnes can 'scent[]' infidelity on Will. Her first response is to go back to Hewlands to 'tend[] her bees, pull[] up weeds, cut[] the blooms off chamomile flowers' (O'Farrell 2020a: 311): she returns to husbanding the land. However, this is insufficient compensation and so, in the throes of forgiving passion that night, 'She has a perverse desire to thwart whatever it is he is about to say. She will not let him off so easily, will not let him think [the fidelity] is all as meaningless to her as it is to him' (319). She tames and husbands him in the way she practised earlier that evening with the bees, weeds and flowers.

Will soon proposes buying her and the children their own home in Stratford where she can be master and husbandman. She assumes the mantle reluctantly at first, but then with gusto:

> She plants a row of apple trees along the high brick wall. Two pairs of pear trees on either side of the main path, plums, elder, birch, gooseberry bushes, blush-stemmed rhubarb. She takes a cutting from a dog-rose growing by the river and cultivates it against the warm wall of the malthouse. (O'Farrell 2020a: 328–9)

Here Agnes can be independent from the Shakespeares, but also from Will, albeit for different reasons. This is where, while the house has been paid for by Will's London earnings from theatreland, she can make the house into her home. However, problems remain at this new home: with her son, Hamnet, dead, she cannot find him anywhere she looks (2020a: 298) – even in the mystical spaces to which she turns to help her know her husband and the world. These animalistic spaces of scent and foreknowledge are closed to her after Hamnet dies: Agnes's command of the natural world fails, and with it her ability to husband, in any sense I have described.

The End of Husbandry

Agnes feels she has failed her husband and family because she could not prevent Hamnet's death from the plague. "'I did not see it," she whispers' to Will, claiming that "'I should have. And I should have known. I should have seen it. I should have understood that it was a terrible trick'" (O'Farrell 2020a: 277–8). The parallelistic conditional perfects ("'I should have . . .'") render the sentence nihilistic and underwrite her sudden inability to understand and control the natural world. For Agnes this is a failure as a mother, but it is also so intimately bound up with her practice of husbandry that it is difficult to separate the two. Her failure mystifies her:

> She cannot understand it. She, who can hear the dead, the unspoken, the unknown, who can touch a person and listen to the creep of disease along the veins, can sense the dark velvet press of a tumour on a lung or a liver, can read a person's eye and heart like some can read a book. She cannot find, cannot locate the spirit of her own child. (O'Farrell 2020a: 298)

Her witchcraft and her conversing with the non-material, non-present world pause while she grieves: 'This permeability of the boundaries between life and death becomes a particular challenge for Agnes' (Windberger 2021: n.p.). This is stressed through the switch between the simple sentence 'She cannot understand it', and the grammatically fragmented sentences that follow, with the 'She' marooned at the beginning of the sentences, her self-fashioning linguistically beginning to crumble. More than that, the natural world is now a source of shame and sadness when 'the hips' ripeness and their brazen colour are an insult, as are the blackberries turning purple, the elder tree's darkening berries' (O'Farrell 2020a: 293). Agnes's husbandry (of all stripes) now appears at an end.

Her upset is compounded by her husband's apparent diffidence. On the one hand, he too quickly "'abandon[s]'" (O'Farrell 2020a: 285) his family after Hamnet's death; on the other, 'He is the one who has caused this problem, this breach in their marriage' (313) through infidelity. Worst of all is his using his dead son's name in vain when he writes a new play:

> How can her son's name be on a London playbill? There has been some odd, strange mistake. He died. This name is her son's and he died, not four years

ago. He was a child and he would have been a man but he died. He is himself, not a play, not a piece of paper, not something to be spoken of or performed or displayed. He died. (O'Farrell 2020a: 344)

The depth of emotion can be plumbed not only by counting the times Agnes reminds herself that Hamnet died – four in this paragraph alone – but also by her bodily reaction. 'Agnes takes to her bed', we read, 'for the first time in her life' (O'Farrell 2020a: 345). Her daughter Susanna – earlier dismissive of her mother (62–3) – 'carries bowls of soup to her mother's bed, a posy of lavender, a rose in a vase, a basket of fresh walnuts, their shells sealed up' (345). Like the band of rebellious women in *The Tamer*, at Agnes's weakest point, the women close ranks to support one another.

Agnes recovers and travels to London. However, her true strength is restored when she finally realizes her husband's purpose in stealing her son's name: to 'writ[e] words for [a boy actor playing Hamlet] to speak and to hear' and that Will has 'instructed him, shown him, how to speak, how to stand, how to lift his chin' (O'Farrell 2020a: 365). Furthermore, 'As the ghost talks, she sees that her husband, in writing this, in taking the role of the ghost, has changed places with his son. He has taken his son's death and made it his own; he has put himself in death's clutches, resurrecting the boy in his place' (366). This restores strength to Agnes because 'An arm's length away, perhaps two, is Hamlet, her Hamlet, as he might have been, had he lived, and the ghost, who has her husband's hands, her husband's beard, who speaks in her husband's voice' (367). Not only is this restorative but also allows Agnes to see for the first time that Will's art is, like her own husbandry, alchemical and depends on faith in the invisible and the little understood. For Will it is in words onstage; for Agnes it is in husbandry of the natural world. Moreover, Agnes engineered this for Will, by slyly organizing that he be sent to London to expand his father's business, by catalyzing Will's becoming William Shakespeare.

But Agnes does not see the greatest achievement of her husbandry of Will, though it is 'well laid and grounded' (*The Tamer*, Epilogue, l. 10) on her labour. While he waits for the Globe to fill up with his audience, Will is watching the groundlings enter from 'the tiring house, just behind the musicians' gallery, at a small opening that gives out over the whole theatre' (O'Farrell 2020a: 353). Critically for him, this also is a restorative space because

He feels like a bird, above the ground, resting on nothing but air. He is not of this place but above it, apart from it, observing it. It brings to mind, for him, the wind-hovering kestrel his wife used to keep, and the way it would hold itself in high currents, far above the tree tops, wings outstretched, looking down on all around it. (O'Farrell 2020a: 353)

Will's symbolic transformation into his wife's kestrel is final confirmation that he has been utterly husbanded by her through her falconry skills. She introduced him to the kestrel; she was first associated with the kestrel's power and flight; but now he has assumed his wife's ability to appreciate the natural world not merely as a man 'Regard[ing] no more but onely to behold / The fleeing Hawkes', valuing 'The haughty Haggard [only] her weight in gold' (Turberville 1611: n.p.), but now as someone who can properly appreciate falconry. However, this appreciation is not, as it is with Petruccio, a means of taming his wife, shrewish or not. Rather it is to see the whole world and to immerse in its fullness. On this basis Will and Agnes end up with a marriage that 'teaches both sexes due equality' (Fletcher 2006: Epilogue l. 7), aligning it also with *The Tamer*. Indeed, 'Wifely obedience is clearly not at issue' in either text 'since Maria turns tame the instant Petruchio recognizes her authority' (Crocker 2010: 61) and Agnes forgives Will the moment she sees Hamlet resurrected onstage. In both texts we see the significance of women superseding men: it may be temporary, but it is decisive; it may start symbolically, yet it is effective; and though it seem countercultural, it provides the basis for establishing Maggie O'Farrell as a prize-winning, canon-shaping woman novelist.

8

Filling Historical and Emotional Voids

Hamnet

Laurie Maguire

Introduction

Dictating his will to his lawyer on his deathbed, Christopher Rush's fictional Shakespeare explains wryly that death is what he does best. 'I do deaths, you see. And I can do the deaths of children. "Their lips were four red roses on a stalk – that sort of thing"' (Rush 2008: 10). Death is also what Maggie O'Farrell does best, or, more precisely, the emotional response to death: grief. *After You'd Gone* depicts love and loss in marriage, dissecting the day-by-day and minute-by-minute pain of bereavement. Later novels focus on the loss of children. *The Vanishing Act of Esme Lennox* begins with young Esme alone with her dead baby brother, and the plot turns on the subsequent loss of her own child (2006c: 243). *The Hand that First Held Mine* portrays a new parent's fear of the loss of her infant (2010b: 48) and a linked plot chronicles the inverse: a child's loss of his mother. In *My Lover's Lover* (2002: 130) we are told that Lily, like the later Esme, had found her dead baby brother in his cot – an en passant detail that has no plot function but links emotionally to the response to Lily's attempted running away: 'Her mother snatched her off the pavement and pressed her to her, saying her name over and over. Don't go, her mother said in tears, don't ever go' (2002: 308). Like Shakespeare, O'Farrell can 'do the deaths of children': loss/bereavement is a recurrent theme.

O'Farrell's depictions of death and grief go hand-in-hand with depictions of parental love. Even when her parent-child pairs have a fractious relationship, the images for their linked identities are recurrently symbiotic. In *Instructions for a Heatwave*, the bond between Gretta and Monica is 'an invisible telegraph wire . . . all day long messages passed along it, without anyone else knowing' (2013:

194); Monica is Gretta's 'external heart valve' (300). When Lexie leaves the house in *The Hand that First Held Mine*, 'she senses a thread that runs between her and her son, and . . . she is aware of it unspooling, bit by bit. By the end of the day, she feels utterly unravelled' (2010b: 260).[1] O'Farrell conveys the permanent 'undertow of anxiety' (2010b: 307) that comes with parenting. When Daniel in *This Must Be the Place* faces the custodial loss of his children in divorce, the lawyer announces that they have 'come to the end of the road'. Daniel protests: 'It's parenthood. There's not supposed to be an end of the road' (2016b: 17, 18). In *Hamnet*, then, O'Farrell's career-long interests come together: loss, grief, parenthood.

William and Anne Shakespeare had three children: Susanna, born in 1583 (baptized 26 May), and dizygotic twins, Hamnet and Judith, baptized on 2 February 1585. Susanna lived until 1649, having married a celebrated local doctor who predeceased her in 1635. Hamnet died, presumably unexpectedly, aged eleven and was buried on 11 August 1596; his twin sister lived until 1662, buried on 9 February, aged seventy-seven (her husband, a vintner, whom she married in 1616, probably died after her as she is named as his wife rather than his widow in her burial entry). The death of Shakespeare's only son, Hamnet, was dynastically 'the end of the road' for the newly successful, upwardly mobile playwright.[2] The events of 1596 are simultaneously known (Hamnet died) and unknown (his cause of death, the responses of parents and siblings). O'Farrell's *Hamnet* takes the raw fact of Hamnet's death and imbues it with raw emotion: the novel's focalizing point is the grieving mother. This terminal event occurs mid-novel and the story then follows the mother's response to the death of her son.

How does one write a historical novel about Stratford's most famous family or about a wife and children whose lives lack historical and legal documentation? Several writers have tried to fill in the gaps: novels about Judith Shakespeare by William Black (in the nineteenth century) and Grace Tiffany (in the twentieth) and a film by Kenneth Branagh, *All is True* (in the twenty-first). O'Farrell's first pre-twentieth-century historical novel avoids the clichés of Tiffany (where Judith wants to be an actor) or of Branagh (where Judith competes with her dead

---

[1] The same image is used for romantic closeness in relationships. When Aidan parts from Sinead in *My Lover's Lover*, 'he feels as though he is holding on to the end of one of his essential fibres and that every step he takes away from her is, bit by bit, unravelling him' (2002: 315).

[2] Many Elizabethan parents, having lost an heir, conceived another. The Shakespeares did not do so; in fact, they had no further children after the birth of the twins eleven years earlier and it is probable that difficulties associated with multiple births impaired or made dangerous Anne's ability to conceive.

twin for her father's approval via poetic composition). Instead she offers a novel in which parental grief takes centre stage thematically, and her compositional tactics are defamiliarization and inversion.

Naming – for instance, calling the heroine Agnes rather than Anne – is part of the defamiliarization. Names were fluid in the Elizabethan period: an Ellen was also a Helen, Katherine not separate from Katharina. Hamnet Sadler (godfather to Hamnet and Judith) appears in the Stratford records as both Hamnet and Hamlet. In his will, Richard Hathaway refers to his daughter as Agnes; the name is pronounced francophonically Ann-yis or Ann-ya, hence its overlap with Anne. Elizabethans were particularly interested in onomancy: the (sometimes superstitious) relationship between name and identity. O'Farrell novels share this interest. In *My Lover's Lover* the choice of 'Gabriel' is discussed (2002: 208); in *Instructions for a Heatwave* Irish Ronan becomes English Robert to assimilate (2013: 180). In *The Hand that First Held Mine* Ted and Elina name their baby Jonah, a choice not approved by friends because of its associations (2010b: 181); the plot begins with the changing identity of Alexandra to Sandra to Lexie, and its twist turns on the revelation of Ted's 'longer name, never used' (49) and the belated identification of his mother as Margo (284). Like Shakespeare, O'Farrell explores 'what's in a name'.

Names in *Hamnet* are held at a distance: Shakespeare's dead sister Anne cannot be named (O'Farrell 2020a: 42). Agnes's mother 'went by the name of the tree' and her grieving father 'never let [the name] past his lips' (156).[3] Acrimony between the Shakespeares and the Hathaways means that Agnes's father 'will never even speak [the Shakespeares'] name' (75). The cabin boy registers Alexandria's strangeness by holding the place name at a distance: 'this place called Alexandria' (170). The name that is most obviously held at a distance is that of William Shakespeare, who is positioned only relatively (in both senses): he is the glover's son, the Hathaways' Latin tutor, Susanna/Judith/Hamnet's father, Eliza's brother, Agnes's husband.

If not naming Shakespeare is part of the defamiliarization, focusing on Agnes rather than the eponymous son is part of O'Farrell's inversion. Although named after the son, this is a novel about the mother; we think the twin daughter will die until we find out it is the son; the novel's geographic centre is Stratford, with London offstage until the end. Periphery thus becomes centre in terms of both character and location.

---

[3]   Historically, Agnes's mother's name is unknown but O'Farrell's choice of Rowan enables her to effect a symbolic moment when a sprig of rowan drops on Agnes on her wedding day, conveying the beneficent presence of her dead mother (2020a: 120).

In this essay, I explore the novel's theme of bereavement through its concentration on Agnes; in particular, I examine Agnes's agency as a playwright figure. I look at the novel's thematic use of twins and pairs: O'Farrell's plot is dependent on things being doubled and swapped, paralleled and compared, conflated and compounded. Agnes encounters these doubles therapeutically in the two-in-one of theatre so my essay examines doubleness in theatre; and since *Hamnet* is O'Farrell's first historical novel, I conclude by considering how she creates an Elizabethan world.

Mourning and Playwriting

In one sense *Hamnet* is a rewrite of *Hamlet* with the positions of the deceased and mourner reversed. Hamlet loses a father; the Shakespeares lose a son.[4] Like the play, the novel explores what it means to remember (another recurrent O'Farrell theme) and to be haunted by unbidden memory.[5] Agnes's deceased mother, whose souvenir lock of hair is discovered in her husband's pocket when he dies, 'live[s] in [her daughter's] memory' (*Ham* 2.2.385–6); Anne Shakespeare, the playwright's sister, who died just before her eighth birthday, is commemorated by Agnes: 'Anne, we know you are there, you are not forgotten' (O'Farrell 2020a: 129). When Agnes and her mother-in-law, Mary, prepare Hamnet's body for burial, Agnes realizes that Mary has shrouded children before (268), shared tragedies that silently bond them.[6]

In *Hamnet*, Agnes's loss of her mother is thematic background: the emotional focus is the loss of offspring. Just a few pages into the novel we meet the kitchen-cat's kittens, at risk of drowning by the matriarch of the Henley Street household, Mary Shakespeare. But the cat successfully prevents the intended felicide: 'the cat thwarted her, keeping her babies secret, safe' (9). By the end of the novel, these kittens have become cats who 'have kittens and, in time, those kittens have kittens'. (No end of the road here.) The kittens evade drowning by the cook who,

---

[4] In the first revenge tragedy to explore parental grief, Kyd's *Spanish Tragedy* (*c.* 1587), which influenced Shakespeare, Hieronimo and Isabella lose their only son.

[5] When Hamlet complains, 'must I remember?', he is describing involuntary memory, very different from the speaker of Sonnet 30 who 'summon[s] up remembrance' (line 2, my emphasis).

[6] William Shakespeare's two older sisters, Joan and Margaret (born in 1558 and 1563), died in infancy (a later Joan, born 1569, survived). Anne (the deceased sibling referred to in *Hamnet*) was born in 1571 and died at the age of seven. Shakespeare, the first surviving child, was born in a plague year (1564); biographers and historians assume that his parents sent him to the safety of his maternal grandparents in Wilmcote, where the uncontaminated air and lack of congestion ensured his survival.

enjoying the rodent-free house, eventually 'has to admit that there are advantages to living alongside a dynasty of cats' (331).

It is this animal instinct to protect her offspring, 'keeping her babies . . . safe' that Agnes, like other O'Farrell parents (both fathers and mothers) feels so strongly: 'she will fill . . . these children with life. She will place herself between them and the door leading out' (239). When plague threatens, she fights back: 'she will find that door and slam it shut' (239). Where the cat succeeds, however, Agnes fails: we are told, pointedly and poignantly, that the kittens, unlike the novel's eponymous son, 'escaped an early demise' (10). The cats inhabit a benevolent (in Elizabethan dramatic terms: a comic) universe in which a cook can change her attitude and the next generation survives to reproduce. Agnes is thwarted by a tragic universe where timing and coincidence conspire to bring plague to Stratford.

Agnes offers the instinctive response to tragedy: counterfactuals. 'Later, and for the rest of her life, she will think that if she had left there and then, . . . she might have changed what happened next' (18). In a chapter which provides what Stephen Greenblatt calls the ultimate in 'contact-tracing' (Greenblatt 2021, n.p.) O'Farrell offers what is essentially a theory of tragedy: 'For the pestilence to reach Warwickshire, England, in the summer of 1596, two events need to occur in the lives of two separate people, and then these people need to meet' (O'Farrell 2020a: 166). One can imagine this as a statement of dramatic principle in a Writers' Room, modern or early modern, plotting a play. For this is a novel about a playwright: not the Swan of Avon but his wife.

Agency and Identity

Agnes is presented as a playwright figure, engineering the life-changing moment in the family fortunes and her husband's mental and professional well-being when she facilitates his departure to London. Contemplating her husband's melancholy, she realizes that a glover's life is at odds with Shakespeare's ontology: 'A glover will only ever want the skin, the surface, the outer layer.' Her analysis tacitly invites contrast with the profession of playwright: the glover discards 'the heart, the bones, the soul, the spirit, the blood, the viscera' (144). Working on her brother to work on her father-in-law, she provides her husband with personal and professional opportunity: 'she has put these circumstances together . . . as if she were the puppeteer, hidden behind a screen, gently pulling on the strings of her wooden people, easing and guiding them on where to go. . . . She has created this moment' (208–9).

Anne Shakespeare's illiteracy is assumed by biographers (Germaine Greer is an exception) but O'Farrell's Agnes is a skilled reader: of people, of animals, of situations. Her interpretive abilities are specifically depicted in terms of literacy. She 'can read a person's eye and heart like some can read a book' (298). When she pinches the adductor pollicis (the muscle between thumb and index finger, which is her technique for gleaning the essence of a person; 57–8), 'she has the expression of a woman reading a particularly hard piece of text, a woman trying to decipher something' (44). She instinctively reads the A-frame architecture of her marital home alphabetically: 'They remind her, these rooms of the initial letter of her name . . . the apartment is formed like the letter, sloping together at the top, with the floor across its middle' (133, 134). Her whole body is literate: hair strands 'write themselves in damp scribbles on her neck' (195) and when she walks a route in reverse, her feet are 'a quill', 'inking over old words' (214). She assesses emotional situations grammatically: 'Agnes conjugates, he is going, he will be gone, he will go' (208).[7]

Unsurprisingly, her husband is also a reader: 'adept at . . . reading the thoughts of others, at guessing which way they will jump' (35). Despite the difference in ages and economic circumstances – Shakespeare is the underage son of a no longer financially successful tradesman, Agnes the 24-year-old daughter of a prosperous farmer – their emotional kinship is stressed as observers, readers, children of 'quick-tempered' parents (35). (This shared experience of maltreatment later bonds the cabin boy with the monkey on the quayside in Alexandria with tragic consequences (169).)

The husband-and-wife union – qua union – is signalled from the beginning. When Shakespeare is accused of having made a promise to Agnes Hathaway, Agnes corrects: 'we made a promise to each other' (99). In love-making, Agnes 'feels herself as a separate being, a body apart, dissolve, until she has no idea, no sense of whose skin is whose' (318). Identity – fused or fractured – is a recurrent theme in the O'Farrell canon. Reflecting on her marriage to John in *After You'd Gone*, Alice explains, 'I never felt incomplete before I met him but with him I felt finished, whole' (O'Farrell 2000: 281). In *Instructions for a Heatwave* Michael is 'for a moment, exactly the person he is meant to be. . . . No difference, no schism, between the way the world might see him and the person he privately knows himself to be' (O'Farrell 2013: 14). In *The Hand that First Held Mine*, Finnish Elina is baffled by the English idiomatic implication that identity is plural ('how are we today?'; (O'Farrell 2010b: 32)); elsewhere in the

---

[7] Cf. *After You'd Gone*, 87.

novel Lexie is made up of 'myriad' identities, 'all sheathed inside one another, like Russian dolls' (70). In *This Must Be the Place* Niall's severe dermatological condition results in bifurcation: 'There is him and there is his condition. They are two entities, forced to live in one body' (O'Farrell 2016b: 50).[8] Immigration also forces two identities to inhabit one body: *Instructions for a Heatwave* notes the Anglo-Irish experience of 'belonging yet not belonging' in London (2013: 262) and *The Distance Between Us* extends this with Italian-Scottish immigrants as 'the hyphenated people' (2004: 237) and Jake's Hong Kong identity versus his European skin.

O'Farrell's recurrent way of exploring ontological fusion and fracture is through twins, actual and metaphorical. In *Instructions for a Heatwave*, the ten-month age gap that places Michael and Monica in the same class means that 'people took them for twins' (2013: 58); in *My Lover's Lover*, Jodi is Aidan's twin sister (2002: 246) and like the severed Shakespeare twins, he feels her absence acutely (246). *The Distance Between Us* explores the closeness of siblings Nina and Stella, one year apart in age, whose closeness distances both their mother and their classmates. Images of heart chambers, of scissors, represent the 'twinness' of the sisters, and when Nina repeats a year in school, the sisters assume the educational position of twin siblings: in the same class. (Post-*Hamnet*, Alfonso in *The Marriage Portrait* is a Jekyll-and-Hyde character and the plot's climactic twist is enabled by the fact that Lucrezia and her maid Emilia look similar.) So O'Farrell's canon has a twenty-year warm up to the story of the twins, Hamnet and Judith.

Twins

Shakespeare shares O'Farrell's fascination with twins and twinned states: the Plautine lookalikes, the Dromios and Antipholuses (*Comedy of Errors*); the brother-sister Sebastian and Viola (*Twelfth Night*); childhood friends, Hermia and Helena, who 'grew together, / Like to a double cherry, seeming parted, / But yet an union in partition' (*Midsummer Night's Dream* 3.2.208-210). In *Hamnet* Shakespeare observes his infants' symmetry:

---

[8] For a sophisticated analysis of this disjunction, see Oakley (2007: 11–30), 'Although we live in our bodies, our social and personal identities are separate from them. But mostly we assume that bodies and identities are the same. When we introduce ourselves, we don't say, "I'm Ms Smith and this is my body"' (15).

He pushed two slivers of apple across the table to them. At exactly the same moment, Hamnet reached out with his right hand and gripped the apple and Judith reached out with her left.

In unison, they raised the apple slices to their lips, Hamnet with his right, Judith with her left.

They put them down, as if with some silent signal between them, at the same moment, then looked at each other, then picked them up again, Judith with her left hand, Hamnet with his right.

It's like a mirror, he had said. Or that they are one person split down the middle. (O'Farrell 2020a: 279)

Here we see the origins of *Twelfth Night*'s denouement when a bewildered Antonio asks Sebastian and Viola: 'How have you made division of yourself? / An apple cleft in two is not more twin / Than these two creatures' (5.1.218–20). (*Twelfth Night* was written in late 1601, just before *Hamlet*.[9])

But O'Farrell does more with this moment than just explore laterality. In making Judith left-handed, she subtly explains the historical conundrum of Judith signing a legal document in 1611 with a mark rather than a signature. This is in contrast to the fluency with which Susanna both writes and reads.[10] Why would Shakespeare's daughters not both be literate? Until the mid-twentieth century, left-handers were forced to write with their right. O'Farrell's Judith 'refuses to use her right hand, saying it feels wrong' (O'Farrell 2020a: 332) and Susanna, instructed by their father to teach her sister to write, eventually abandons the task. O'Farrell also hints at dyslexia – to Judith, the *d*s and *b*s 'look entirely the same' (333). Judith's dyslexic confusion is ironically a graphic version of twinned states, with *d* and *b* mirror images that can deceptively swap places, as the young Hamnet and Judith playfully do.

If Hamnet and Judith are biologically antimeric creatures – left-hand, right-hand – they are also presented as two halves of one entity. Hamnet feels 'they fit together . . . like two halves of a walnut' (199). Later the grieving Judith will say 'I am only half a person without you' (337). This is the language of Nina and Stella in *The Distance Between Us*: 'without Nina, Stella had no idea how to behave, how to live her life, what to say, what to do all day' (O'Farrell 2004: 198) and the novel takes its epigraph from De Beauvoir on her sister: 'She was my alter ego, my double, we could not do without each other.' In one of *Hamnet*'s

---

[9] Taylor and Egan (2017: 534–5).

[10] Literacy at this period viewed reading and writing as separate skills; many had the former without the latter. Susanna could sign her name in full and she gifted a book to Queen Henrietta Maria.

most poignant dialogues Judith explores the inadequacy of language to convey her ontological amputation as the remaining half of a duo. Seeking the twin equivalent of 'widow' or 'orphan', she asks her mother: 'What is the word . . . for someone who was a twin but is no longer a twin?' (O'Farrell 2020a: 292). (She concludes, sadly, that there isn't one.)

Hamnet is populated by doubles, twins, parallels, hybrid states. The two kittens have 'identical striped faces and white-socked feet' (295). Agnes is initially seen as a boy with a woman's figure (33–4, 38–9). The kestrel she flies is 'two creatures. One on the ground and another in the air' (76). Agnes is unafraid of the owl's screech – an Elizabethan ill omen – and notes approvingly that the bird seems 'to exist in some doubled state, half spirit, half bird' (131). Her young husband, frustrated and trapped by his career as a glover, is 'split in two. He is one man in their house and quite another in that of his parents' (145). The cabin boy is fascinated by Venice: 'a hybrid place, half of sea, half of land' (175).[11]

Many O'Farrell characters, not just those in *Hamnet*, are split in two, their cognitive rational sense observing their emotional, impulsive or social self. Elina in *The Hand that First Held Mine* 'feels curiously like two people. One is standing on the threshold. . . . The other is calmly watching her' (2010b: 67). In *This Must Be the Place* 'there is a man at the desk and the man is me' (2016b: 29). In *Instructions for a Heatwave*, Michael, with his arm round his wife, is 'jealous of himself. As if he is looking at a scene' (2013: 280). The most extended depiction of non-twin dual states in *Hamnet* comes when Agnes realizes the severity of Judith's illness (at this stage of the novel, it is Judith, who is infected by plague). 'Agnes seems to split in two. Part of her gasps at the sight of the buboes. The other part hears the gasp, observes it, notes it: a gasp, very well. Tears spring into the eyes of the first Agnes. . . . The other Agnes is ticking off the signs: buboes, fever, deep sleep' (2020a: 124–5). Agnes moves through this scene in split focus – 'She hears herself telling Hamnet . . .' – and her motor skills function independently: 'her hands are reaching out to find the stoppered pots' (125).

This is a novel about things that are paired then split apart. Twins, obviously. The husband and wife's shared parental grief manifests differently and interferes with their intuitive understanding of each other. After Hamnet's death, Agnes assumes Shakespeare will stay in Stratford; he feels the need to leave. She is

---

[11] In the apple store at Hewlands, where Agnes and Shakespeare first make love, the apples function as a comic example of how things that should be separate can come together: 'The fruit has been placed with care . . . The skin mustn't touch that of its neighbour . . . Except that something is moving the apples' (2020a: 81).

appalled to hear he is writing a comedy; he feels comedy to be a safe world where grief cannot 'ambush him' (303). His letters become shorter and fewer; certain words cannot be said – 'plague' for instance (329). What brings them together is theatre.

Theatre and Memory

Theatre provides the ultimate expression of doubles. Unlike the world of prose fiction, drama is never pure representation. The fictional character is embodied by an actor and we are always aware of the actor behind the role. Indeed, in many circumstances, it is the actor-in-the-role that we go to see: Richard Burbage's Hieronimo, David Tennant's Hamlet. As Keir Elam notes, when we see a scratch on a character's leg, we do not know if it belongs to the character or the actor (2002: 8). The two-in-one of twins and doubles that fascinates O'Farrell, and receives particular focus in *Hamnet*, reaches a pinnacle in the novel's denouement.

Agnes is initially outraged that her husband has written a play with her son's name. Her stepmother Joan maliciously shows her the playbill advertisement. Agnes fixates on the name, its associations: 'how could he take up his pen and write it on a page, breaking its connection with their son?' (2020a: 363). The Elizabethan link between name and identity that we saw earlier now receives extended scrutiny. Resolving to visit London and the Globe theatre, 'it is just as [Agnes] feared: he has taken that most sacred and tender of names and tossed it in among a jumble of other words' (363). Standing at the Globe, Agnes summarizes her impressions, giving a definition – a negative definition – of theatre: 'A wooden stage, declaiming players, memorised speeches, adoring crowds, costumed fools' (364). She is baffled by the tense opening scene and the absence of the named character. But when the actor-Hamlet appears, she is mesmerized both by his similarity to her son – 'how can this player, this young man, know how to be her Hamnet when he never saw or met the boy?' (365) – and by theatre's doubleness: 'Hamlet here, on this stage, is two people, the young man alive, and the father, dead. He is both alive and dead' (366).

The bereaved Alice experiences the same shock, acoustically rather than visually, at the end of *After You'd Gone*. Trailing the father-in-law who has refused to meet her, and has disowned his (now dead) son, she eavesdrops on him in his local library. 'His voice. His voice is so like John's. It is John's. It has a slight Polish edge to it but the tone, the inflection, the pitch are identical. It could have been him speaking.' However, the doubleness only accentuates her widowed loss: 'but it wasn't and she cannot bear it' (2000: 361). O'Farrell replays this scene in *Hamnet* but turns it into a redemptive moment. Theatre, the playwright, the bereaved father 'has brought [Hamnet] back to life, in the only way he can' (2020a: 366).

Sceptics about the correlation between Shakespeare's writing of *Hamlet* in 1602–3[12] and the death of his son six years earlier point not only to the time gap but to the reversal in situation: *Hamlet* is about the loss of a father not a son; a closer biographical parallel therefore lies in the death of John Shakespeare in September 1601. O'Farrell takes this reversal of situation and makes it part of the novel's definition of parental love.

'Agnes finds she can bear anything except her child's pain' (270). In novels and interviews O'Farrell talks about the parental instinct to protect one's child from pain by swapping places with them: taking on their suffering.[13] Because he is a twin, Hamnet in the novel is able physically to substitute for Judith. The novel's twins, like many sixteenth-century and twenty-first-century twins, are premature, and Judith's fragile health is contrasted with her brother's robustness.[14] Faced with the unthinkable prospect of losing Judith, Hamnet capitalizes on the twins' ability to confuse people and tries the same *trompe l'oeil* with death, 'to pull off the trick he and Judith have been playing since they were young' (200). In a version of 'to be or not to be', Hamnet whispers to his twin, 'I want you to take my life. It shall be yours. I give it to you' (201). Returning to the pallet, Agnes sees not Judith, or Judith and Hamnet, but two Judiths – the ultimate in doubles. The twin can effect the substitution desired by parents.

But the playwright can also do a version of this as Agnes realizes in the novel's final moments. Writing *Hamlet* is not a sacrilege, a severing of the name and identity of her son, nor is it an act of resurrection: it is a substitution of father for son. Whereas earlier we saw a parent as playwright (Agnes), we now see the playwright as parent. 'He has, Agnes sees, done what any father would wish to do, to exchange his child's suffering for his own, to take his place, to offer himself up in his child's stead, so that the boy might live' (366). The substitution is further reified in O'Farrell's use of the tradition that William Shakespeare acted the part of the ghost in *Hamlet*.

---

[12] Taylor and Egan (2017: 542–8).
[13] See, for instance, interview with Ann Patchett.
[14] Since statistically one twin is often weaker than the other, this is often invoked as explanation for Hamnet's death. In fact, if an Elizabethan child survived infancy, their chances of a long adult life were high.

This restitution – this piercing of the boundary between life and death via the boundary between play and audience, between real life and fiction – is all the more important in Agnes's journey in grief because Agnes is privately atheistic. As a child witnessing her mother's death, she saw what another O'Farrell character calls 'the appalling irreversibility' of death (*After You'd Gone*, 2000: 294). The child Agnes shouts to God in her grief: 'I am finished with you. After this time, I will go to your church because I must but I shan't say a word there because there is nothing after you die' (2020a: 56). In her later adult grief at the loss of her son, Agnes finds 'that it is possible to comfort your daughters with assurances about places in Heaven and eternal joy and how they may all be reunited after death and how he will be waiting for them, while not believing any of it' (288). When the vicar supplies conventional consolation – 'God had need of him' – Agnes's unspoken response is 'I had need of him' (290).

We are here in familiar *Hamlet* territory: the rejection of conventional memento mori wisdom. The grieving prince rejects Claudius's attempts at consolation in the first court scene. Death happens, says Claudius: nature's 'common theme / Is death of fathers' (1.2.103–4). But aphoristic generalities are no help when it is *your* father that dies. *Hamlet* is a play in which young people lose fathers – Hamlet, Ophelia, Laertes – and they move from seeing death as unnatural – something accompanied by portents, meteors, ghosts – to something natural: 'if it be not now, yet it will come' (5.2.199–200). In the play's first scene Horatio describes the night before Julius Caesar's assassination: the sky was full of portents and 'the graves stood tenantless' (1.1.114). Immediately, we meet a grieving Hamlet, who cannot accept that Gertrude and Denmark have moved on: Gertrude has remarried, and the burghers of Denmark have switched allegiance from Old Hamlet to the new king. It is this resumption of normal life that Hamlet cannot understand. But by the time he meets the gravedigger in Act Five, his attitude to death is calmly practical: interested in identifying skulls, and in the technicalities of decomposition ('how long will a man lie i'th'earth ere he rot?'; 5.1.154). He now dispenses the memento mori wisdom he had previously rejected: 'get you to my lady's table and tell her, let her paint [apply cosmetics] an inch thick, to this favour [face] she must come' (5.1.182–4). In other words, nature's 'common theme is death'; for Hamlet, the play is a journey in grief and recovery.

After Hamnet's death, the domestically efficient Agnes no longer sees the point in sweeping the floor (2020a: 289), and is astonished at the way life can continue for others. The residents of Stratford, understandably, go about their normal business (291). Mary, eventually, feels it is time to move on. Agnes's daughters start to recover: Susanna assumes competent direction of the household and takes over some of her mother's pharmaceutical activities. Recovery from grief – like time – travels in 'divers paces with divers persons' (*As You Like It* 3.2.299-300).

Agnes's recovery, like Hamlet's, is enabled by a theatre performance. In *Hamlet* the players come to Elsinore. In *Hamnet*, Agnes goes to the players (for the first time, the novel moves from Stratford to London). Like Hamlet, she comes to realize that moving on is not the same thing as forgetting. Memory of the dead is highlighted early in the novel: the child, Anne Shakespeare, the mother, Rowan Hathaway. The novel begins and ends with the ghost's injunction in *Hamlet*: 'remember me' (1.5.91). Grief and memory are interlinked and to explore one is to explore the other. O'Farrell's rewriting of *Hamlet* is itself an act of memorial 'inspired by the short life of a boy who died in Stratford, Warwickshire, in the summer of 1596' (2020a: 369). The homage continued in 2022 when O'Farrell planted two rowan trees in Holy Trinity Churchyard in memory of Hamnet and his sister Judith.[15]

History

Susanna, who died in 1635, is buried in the chancel of Holy Trinity Church, alongside her mother, her father, her husband and her son-in-law. (Her daughter, whose second marriage took her to Abington, Northamptonshire, is buried there in the Church of St Peter and St Paul.) Why Judith is buried in the graveyard (in an unmarked site) is not known. In 1596, when Hamnet died, there would have been no reason – of status or finance – to bury him in the church. And if he died of plague, then he would not have been buried in the town – Stratford dug plague pits in the Welcombe Hills.

That Hamnet died of plague makes for a dramatic plot but is extremely unlikely as the cause of his death. While August is a high month for plague deaths in urban centres, the burial register for Stratford in 1596 records only five deaths that month, including that of Hamnet. This is average for that year. There were five deaths in July (including one in childbirth), six in June (including two in childbirth), and seven in May (one was a drowning); September saw six deaths, and October just one. The scribe notes plague deaths – marked 'P' or 'pestis' or

---

[15] Judith is also commemorated in the titles of North American and German editions where the novel's title is *Hamnet and Judith/Hamnet und Judith*.

'hic incepit pestis' when there was an outbreak of plague – but there is no such notation in 1596.[16] An accident is possible – Stratford scribes frequently record the causes of death when they are unusual such as drowning – although since there is nothing systematic about the registers, nothing can be inferred from the lack of explanation. All we know is that Hamnet, like Alexander, 'died, . . . was buried, . . . returneth to dust' (*Hamlet* 5.1.198–9).

Hamnet was O'Farrell's first historical novel. *Esme Lennox* is part-historical (one plot is set in the 1930s) and *Instructions for a Heatwave*, set in the drought of 1976, is technically historical given that O'Farrell was only four that year. She researched this summer (*Instructions for a Heatwave*, 'The Imaginary People in the Kitchen', n.p.) just as she researched immigrant experience for *The Distance Between Us* and female hysteria and incarceration in the 1930s for *Esme Lennox*. Several of her novels list books to which she is 'indebted' (*The Distance Between Us*) or which she 'found inspirational' (*Instructions for a Heatwave*); *Hamnet* credits Shakespeare biographies, books about the Tudor world, Anne Hathaway, herbalism and falconry, and the guides of the Shakespeare Birthplace Trust and Holy Trinity Church. O'Farrell is a historical researcher.

Of note, then, is how little factual or historical detail is required to write an/ this Elizabethan historical novel. This is in marked contrast to *The Marriage Portrait* (2022) which makes use of sixteenth-century Florentine and Ferrarese politics, fashions and rivalries. In *Hamnet* O'Farrell creates history, location and Elizabethan life via atmosphere. Outhouses, mice, fires, valerian and campion conjure up a world; reference to a kirtle or a coif summons up the whole female ensemble; a few Elizabethan phrases locate us linguistically – a character is 'of means' [wealthy] (2020a: 63), no one 'is abroad' [out and about] (131), something is 'passing strange' (294). Images are drawn from the contemporary material world. Cursive handwriting looks like 'a skein of embroidery' (153); a voice is 'pinched and tight like an outgrown smock' (225); burned skin is 'puckered . . . like melted candlewax' (175); Shakespeare draws his father's anger 'like a horseshoe to a magnet' (31), anger which 'seems to unsheathe itself and stretch out from him, like a rapier. Hamnet can feel the tip of it wander about the room, seeking an opponent' (12). O'Farrell's career-long habit of drawing on the natural world becomes here her source of historical atmosphere: buboes are 'a pair of quails' eggs' (15); Bartholomew is 'someone who must be approached sideways,

---

[16] Deaths begin to rise (dramatically) in November 1596 and continue to do so until the following March. Many of these deaths are noted as being of paupers or almspeople; it was clearly an extremely harsh winter, making the poor and the homeless more vulnerable, and accounting for the increased burials.

with caution, as with a restive horse' (76); Agnes collects 'impressions as a wool-gatherer hoards wool' (142); the monkey 'has nails like apple pips' (168). She adds her trademark present tense (which here assumes a lyric quality) and a measured (slow) pace to conjure up this historical world. But, in a deliciously ludic moment, she also looks forward to Stratford's tourist industry: the local fame of Agnes as a healer, which brings a constant stream of visitors to Henley Street, leads Susanna to wonder wearily: 'will it ever end, this stream of people through their house?' (64).

O'Farrell describes this house at the start of the novel: it 'was built in a gap, a vacancy' (27). The description stands as a metonymy for the novel's intervention in the historical records. O'Farrell's concerns in this historical fiction are, like Shakespeare's, transhistorical: the human heart, human emotion, love and loss. Hamnet's death offers a narrative that was a ready fit for O'Farrell's twenty-year interest in what happens 'after you'd gone'.

9

Remaking the Duchess

Underpainting and Overpainting
in *The Marriage Portrait*

Elaine Canning

Introduction

In the 'Author's note' at the end of *The Marriage Portrait*, O'Farrell highlights her continued fascination with doubles and pairings: 'Alfonso II d'Este, Duke of Ferrara, is widely considered to have been the inspiration for Robert Browning's poem 'My Last Duchess'; Lucrezia di Cosimo de' Medici d'Este, Duchess of Ferrara, is the inspiration for this novel' (O'Farrell 2022a: 433). Indeed, the doublings in *The Marriage Portrait* are more complex than a mere transition from Duke to Duchess, from poem to novel. The Ferrarese marriage portrait which forms the basis of Browning's poem and which, O'Farrell states, 'is, to the best of my knowledge, entirely fictional' (O'Farrell 2022a: 435) is replaced by the marriage portrait of the book's title, a brand-new painting fashioned within the pages of the novel by multiple artists – themselves creations of the author herself, of course – which embodies multiple versions of Lucrezia. O'Farrell removes Lucrezia, Duchess of Ferrara, from obscurity and offers various iterations of her, as well as of her husband, in a novel about underpainting and overpainting not only canvases but people, perspectives and place.

According to Hughes-Hallett, 'This is a book about a picture, and it is also pictorial. There is a lot going on in it under and around the surface narrative, in the way that there are other stories being enacted in the backgrounds of Renaissance paintings of biblical scenes' (Hughes-Hallett 2022). The narrative starts where the story ends, in 'a wild and lonely place' – the *Fortezza* – the site of Lucrezia's fate which is foreshadowed in the opening paragraph: 'it comes to her with a peculiar clarity, as if some coloured glass has been put in front of her eyes, or perhaps removed from them, that he intends to kill her' (O'Farrell 2022a: 1). In a narrative that weaves together chapters like a row of non-chronological paintings in a gallery, the reader experiences Renaissance Italy as if having stepped inside an artwork. Moreover, the interplay between the illusory and the real is evidenced in a number of ways: the artifice of the staging of Lucrezia's marriage portrait is presented within the stark reality of a hierarchical marriage; there are the exotic beasts locked within the walls of a *Palazzo*, far from their natural habitat; and various dream sequences facilitate Lucrezia's stepping outside of herself.

In this essay, I consider how *The Marriage Portrait* is a novel about making art, and how the creative process both liberates and controls within the right/ wrong hands. I explore how the theme of underpainting and overpainting interconnects with both a narratological layering effect characteristic of O'Farrell's work, as well as the creation of multi-faceted identities in the cases of Lucrezia and Alfonso. Finally, I discuss the extent to which Lucrezia asserts her agency through creative pursuits and out-of-body experiences: her acts of defiance in the face of toxic masculinity.

Layering the Narrative: Art Within Art

In his review of *The Marriage Portrait*, Kelly writes that 'The Renaissance suffuses this novel. It is carefully patterned with images: fire, water, honey, horses. There is a degree of relish in the detail, particularly around food and tapestry, but never with any sense of flaunting one's research' (Kelly 2022). The key aspects of Renaissance art, which 'combined influences of an increased awareness of nature, a revival of classical learning, and a more individualistic view of man' ('Renaissance art' 2023) infiltrate the narrative structure in complex ways. First, there are the chapter headings, heavily influenced by nature and individualism, while also underlining status, title/entitlement and plot both directly and indirectly. 'Scorched Earth' for example, is a metaphor for Lucrezia's fever, a soul in torment burning from the poison she believes her husband has administered. 'Venison baked in wine' is a nod to the affluence of the court, as well as to the absurdity of the focus on food preparation and consumption when Lucrezia is conscious of Alfonso's real intentions:

> Her husband, who means to kill her, either by his own hand or by his order to another, takes up the end of his napkin and dabs at his cheek with its pointed

corner, as if a spot of soup on one's face is a matter of importance. Her husband, who intends her death, spends a moment brushing a stray hair from his brow, then finally tucks it behind his ear. Her husband, the murderer, says, over his shoulder to the servants, that the cook should be told to add more salt. As if seasoning is important to them now. (O'Farrell 2022a: 49)

In contrast, the chapter titled 'Honey water' alludes to the purity and sweetness of the natural medication prepared by Lucrezia with which she saves the life of the artist's apprentice, Jacopo. There are variations, too, in the naming of chapters after individuals, where relationships and status are more and less evident. 'Sisters of Alfonso II, seen from a distance' refers to Elisabetta and Nunciata, ladies of a particular standing within the dynastic infrastructure given their link to the Duke of Ferrara. However, the identity of the seer who witnesses them 'from a distance' is unclear: is it Lucrezia, Alfonso, the reader? The title playfully calls into question the nature of the relationship between both females, the married couple, reader and author.

Other titles are deliberately unambiguous. 'Man Asleep, Ruler at Rest' encapsulates Alfonso in all his dictatorial glory after intimate relations with Lucrezia for the first time. He has hurt her, despite promising that he won't, triggering an out-of-body experience for the Duchess in which she defines and brands him: 'Lucrezia stares at him, as if she were considering a sketch: *Man, Asleep. Ruler, at Rest*' (O'Farrell 2022a: 196). Lucrezia, too, is 'branded' as she becomes the centre of events, despite her protestations. She becomes 'The Duchess Lucrezia on her wedding day', the point at which her life changes forever (indeed, as a precursor which reinforces this, there is a chapter titled 'Everything changes' where her sister, betrothed to Alfonso, passes away, and Lucrezia is promised to him instead). Towards the end of the novel, the chapter 'The marriage portrait of Lucrezia, Duchess of Ferrara' underscores the motif of underpainting and overpainting which permeates the novel – Alfonso gets his painting, but there is much more to it than he will ever know. It resonates with the duality of all that has been forced upon Lucrezia in public and with what remains intensely personal to her – her resilience, her creativity: 'Lucrezia regards the portrait; she stares; she cannot look away. It is at once scaldingly public and deeply private. [. . .] She loves it, she loathes it; [. . .] She wants the world to see it; she wishes to run and cover it again with the cloth at the artist's feet' (O'Farrell 2022a: 376). Apart from Lucrezia, only one other individual recognizes this duality, but it is not Il Bastianino, who was meant to have painted the portrait. The portrait may be overpainted with Il Bastianino's name and reputation, but the real artist, the one who understands Lucrezia's predicament, is the one whom she saved, who offered her an escape by the back door: Jacopo. 'And [Lucrezia] can look at Jacopo and know that it was he who painted the portrait. It was him' (O'Farrell 2022a: 377).

The arrangement of the chapters by time and place in a non-sequential criss-crossing intensifies the shifting actions and reactions of both Lucrezia and Alfonso. In the first half of the novel, the narrative moves between the *Fortezza*, the star-shaped hunting lodge where Lucrezia will meet her fate and the *Palazzo* where she was conceived and grew up. We encounter a child who is different, 'so difficult, so intractable' in her mother's eyes (O'Farrell 2022a: 11) who grows up in the basement kitchen away from her siblings. She is a talented young artist and a fearless empathizer: after she reaches out and touches the back of the tigress which has recently been installed in her father's Sala dei Leoni, she is swiftly carried away by one of her father's soldiers against the backdrop of screams and shrieks. In a poignant foreshadowing of her own fate in the 'wild and lonely place' (1), she reflects on the tigress' plight: 'To be so alone in such a place! It wasn't fair or right. She would ask her papa to send the animal back' (O'Farrell 2022a: 45). This palimpsestic overlayering of place and action within a range of temporal shifts continues into the second half of the novel. Here, the action focuses on physical movement between the *Fortezza*, the *Castello* (the epitome of ducal and spousal responsibility) and the *Delizia* where, initially, 'so little is required of her' (O'Farrell 2022a: 216). And yet, it is at the *Delizia*, halfway through the novel, where the relationship between Lucrezia and Alfonso is problematized most acutely in a shifting pattern of alternating moods and expectations.

> During her days at the *delizia*, nothing is asked of her; at night, however, a great deal is expected. She has to give and surrender herself, to hand over her being to another, to grant him access and ingress, each night, every night. He is like a man possessed, a man on a quest: to conceive an heir, to ensure the continuation of his line. (O'Farrell 2022a: 221–2)

Indeed, while present at the *Delizia*, the Duke presents his wife with the rare gift of a long-maned, pure white mule; it is also the place where Lucrezia learns from her maid Emilia that Alfonso will punish his mother and sisters if they disobey him and go to France. Lucrezia experiences the roughness of the Duke's tone and grip on the night of a storm, when 'his hand closed about her upper arm like a manacle' (275). Moreover, in the same 'Honey water' chapter, Lucrezia's identity becomes increasingly blurred and fragmented: she saves Jacopo's life without him knowing she is the Duchess, and she overpaints her water-creature with a banal, acceptable still life of honey and peaches in time for her husband's return. The apprentice sketches of the portrait commissioned by her husband begin at the *Delizia*, while Lucrezia misinterprets her own reflection for that of her dead sister Maria, the Duke's first choice of wife. Ultimately, it is through recognition of the complex layers of her circumstances, or a palimpsestuous reading of the strata of her situation, to use Dillon's term (2005), that Lucrezia 'suddenly sees that some vital part of her will not bend, will never yield' (O'Farrell 2022a: 283). She realizes: 'If she is to survive this marriage, or perhaps even to thrive within it, she must preserve this part of herself and keep it away from him, separate, sacred' (283).

Hughes-Hallett maintains that *The Marriage Portrait* is 'set in a world as fabulous as a millefleurs tapestry' (Hughes-Hallett 2022). Among the colour and visual connectors to the Renaissance, together with the immediacy of the present continuous tense, the way in which Lucrezia sees her world accentuates the artificiality of it. When, for example, the Duchess is in the wedding carriage with her parents, the faces of the Florentines in the street 'are blurred by motion, daubs of paint dissolving in water' (O'Farrell 2022a: 127). Similarly, when she catches sight of Leonello and Alfonso in the courtyard some time later, she sees 'the bleached shapes of people. [. . .] The heat and the light seem to strip them of all colour and contour' (235). Her perspective, shaped by an artistically infused language, renders her undesired existence more illusory. In a further attempt at self-preservation, she turns the tables on Alfonso, making him the subject of her gaze. As Maurizio and Jacopo sketch, 'She allows her eyes to wander about the room; it is the only part of her permitted motion. Alfonso has folded his long frame into a chair; he sits, one arm draped over his knee, his head swivelling between her and the apprentices' (271). Thus, she reframes the narrative, if only fleetingly, within the confines of a fateful marriage.

Alfonso II, Duke of Ferrara: A Janus for the Renaissance

'[. . .] He is like Janus, with two faces, two personalities' (O'Farrell 2022a: 258). So says Maurizio to the Duchess, not knowing that he is describing her own husband to her. It is the duality of Alfonso's personality – the projection of a devoted, loving husband alongside an authoritative, frustrated abuser – that oscillates between the shifting time frames and settings of the novel. From this duality comes a proliferation of contradictory responses to which Lucrezia is exposed and which she alternately celebrates and condemns. He is, in turn, the attentive suitor, effusive in his joy at marrying his Duchess, regaling her with special gifts; he is the soft-spoken, caring husband during their first encounter alone after the wedding. The same man who takes her hand at the court banquet in a public display of affection very quickly transforms into 'a vengeful, irascible monster in human form, a devil in collar and cuffs' (279). Driven by a need to produce an heir, though it is rumoured that he never will, Alfonso is exposed for what he really is: a man consumed with anger who will exercise ultimate control over his wife and dispose of her when she serves no relevant purpose. It is unsurprising that in his statement of ownership, he refers to Lucrezia as 'My first duchess' (a nod to Browning's 'My Last Duchess'), then autocorrects to 'My beautiful duchess' (337). In her naivety, Lucrezia thinks: 'He meant "beautiful" all along. She is certain of it' (337), despite knowing that there are 'many Alfonsos, all fitted inside one body' (197). Indeed, the more sinister side to Alfonso's personality is mirrored outside of himself in the form of another male character, Leonello Baldassare. The Duke's main confidante, Leonello publicly manifests himself as a ruthless authoritarian in his maltreatment of a young boy. When Lucrezia questions his behaviour, she is warned by her husband never to undermine Leonello again (246). It can hardly be coincidental that the naming of this character recalls the lions which reportedly attacked and killed Lucrezia's tigress: a foreboding of Leonello's involvement in the Duchess' destiny as he doubles up as predator with Alfonso.

Re-creating the Duchess: Lucrezia's Paintings/Painting Lucrezia

It is through the act of painting and sketching – that is to say, overpainting – that Lucrezia asserts herself, alongside her dreamlike out-of-body experiences. The fifth child of Cosimo and Eleanora and a gifted artist, Lucrezia is reconstituted in a variety of ways as she exerts her agency and creativity.

Even before her betrothal to the Duke of Ferrara, Lucrezia is characterized as different, defiant and highly self-aware, traits which an arranged marriage threatens to bury. Her need for independence is highlighted very early on when she recasts the safe space of her father's *Palazzo* to at times feeling 'as oppressive as a prison' (O'Farrell 2022a: 22). Later, when she determines that Alfonso is going to kill her, she resolves that it will not be so, that she will not allow him 'to extinguish her' (50). Embracing the fire of her resolve and passion, she turns to counsel from her beloved, absent Sofia:

> 'You need a plan,' she hears – or seems to hear – her old nurse, Sofia, say, from a place near her elbow. 'To lose your temper is to lose the battle.' [. . .] So be it, she says to the invisible Sofia next to her. So be it. (O'Farrell 2022a: 50)

Lucrezia's sense of self becomes anchored in her art. It's the lifeline she desperately holds onto and which, she believes, saved her once before. After she became seriously ill upon hearing of the demise of the tigress, she didn't think she would have recovered or survived without her art tuition (59–60). But the same lifeline is threatened time and again. It happens even before her wedding day when Vitelli delivers the news that the Duke wishes to enter into marriage with her and traps her miniature painting of a starling inside his leather book, a premonition of Lucrezia's fate. It happens subsequently when the Duchess, racked with fever (an excess of choler in the doctor's opinion, much to Alfonso's rage) has her books, paints, vellum and chalks removed 'to prevent excitement' (394) as she continuously fails to conceive. In between, however, she engages in painting, including in underpainting, as described to her by the artist Vasari: 'A *tavola* or a canvas, Vasari explained, might have three or four different paintings on it, all existing in secret layers' (113). It's no coincidence that Lucrezia's parting gift to Sofia, 'the keeper of all her secrets' (152) is a tiny painting of a nurse with her fingers crossed. Later, her still life of fruit and honey will replace a scene featuring 'an aquatic creature, half man, half fish' (249), something too exotic which can only ever exist as an underpainting. Painting makes Lucrezia feel alive: 'she is absorbed in her work; she is her work' (261). And yet, as her understanding of her fate becomes clearer, she is conscious of Alfonso reshaping her, relegating her true self to an underpainting: 'She has changed her shape, shed her skin, been painted over, or remade in a new form' (285).

Lucrezia's out-of-body experiences enable her to exist in 'secret layers' as she attempts some degree of self-preservation. We witness the markings of this very early on, even before she steps outside herself after being physically hurt by Alfonso in bed, when husband and wife are first alone: 'He takes her fingers in his and raises them to his lips. She observes this, as if the hand belongs to someone else' (149). When she is forced to pose for the marriage portrait, 'She becomes other and elsewhere, as she does at night, with Alfonso, leaving just her skin and bone behind, in her stead; only her outer layers remain. The rest of her withdraws, escapes, slips away' (331). There are occasions when she physically steps outside herself in resolute acts of defiance – when she dresses up in her maid's drab clothing to wander at night; when she leaves her room against her husband's orders. She doesn't know if she can be saved, but she pushes the boundaries of what fate dictates until the end. Even when her paints and chalks are removed, she sketches the faces she sees on her visits to the confessor with ink and paper meant for letter writing. Those faces will turn to ashes when burned: identities metaphorically extinguished as Lucrezia herself soon might be.

As Smith contends, O'Farrell 'has given us an exhilarating, devastating look at women's captivity, creativity and ultimately, rebellion in a world run by some very cruel men' (Smith 2022).

Overpainting the Ending

In a final testament to the shifting parameters of the multi-layered narrative of *The Marriage Portrait*, O'Farrell engages in a final act of overpainting. The ending which both Lucrezia and reader await, sealed as it is within the dynastic and authoritarian control of Alfonso, becomes a form of underpainting itself. The true cause of death is concealed – it was a seizure, they say, never a murder – and O'Farrell overpaints Lucrezia, remaking her, rewriting her fate. 'Look', the author writes,

> Here is Lucrezia, a small figure in the corner of a landscape with a river, a forest, an imposing stone building. She is moving across open ground, through the dark winter night, running, running, with all her strength, towards the merciful canopy of trees. (O'Farrell 2022a: 432)

This rebirth of the Duchess, an adaptation of the novel's anticipated denouement, not only reasserts Lucrezia's agency but is symbolic of the duality that characterizes O'Farrell's novels generally. *The Marriage Portrait* not only calls into question the power of the dominant male over a young woman but highlights how the creative process can inform and liberate a woman's thinking and being, even if only temporarily. It is a novel about making art; but ultimately, it is also about the extent to which a narrative can transcend the cultural and stylistic boundaries of storymaking.

'Post-it Baby'

An Interview with Maggie O'Farrell

Elaine Canning

7 June 2022

EC: Here we are, Maggie, and what a joy it is to be in conversation with you this morning. I'd like to begin by asking you about your work in general. What I absolutely love about it is the way you navigate multiple time frames and narrative perspectives. You also give us complex worlds where identities are blurred, doubled, haunted and fragmented. Is this something you purposefully developed right from your debut novel, *After You'd Gone*?

MOF: I'm not sure if I would say I developed it; I think it's just the way I see the world, perhaps, and the way I see narrative. I've never been an adherent to chronology and I don't particularly like using it as a narrative structure. To me, stories are not linear; they don't go very neatly in a line from A to B. I don't think that's the way human brains work. I don't think our memories and sense of ourselves are neatly linear – it seems to me an arbitrary way to arrange a story. If you listen to somebody in a café or on a bus telling the story of what happened to them yesterday, it's actually quite unusual for them to begin: 'I got up in the morning and then I had breakfast and then and then and then . . .'. It seems to me that the way to create a narrative is not like that. I had a very good English teacher at high school and he gave us a story once about a boy who was trapped on top of a water tower (I think it was by an American but I can't remember who it was). It starts with him trapped and then goes right back to the beginning to explain how this teenager got to be at the top of a water tower. The teacher talked about the point at which the writer chooses to begin the story: he said if you imagine the narrative is a thin line, at what point on the line do you choose to jump in? That's always the tricky decision; that's one of the first decisions you have to make with a novel – where do I start it and at what point in the river of this narrative do I dive in? Sometimes you get it right the first time – there are books I've written where first time round, I think: I've got this, and I can see the structure of it. I can see at which point I'm going to enter and which point I shall move back to. But other times not, maybe halfway through or at the end of the first draft, you think: this has to be rearranged. I think that human nature is not neat, chronological or alphabetical. I think it's geological in a sense: layers and layers of experience as the bedrock and then there are extra layers of different eras, different strata of rock. Some come to the surface and some don't; some get easily eroded away and some are igneous.

EC: And everything that we remember is also subject to the way we process our own memory of it.

MOF: Exactly. Like geology, there are all sorts of external forces that alter that for you. Some will rise to the surface with some geothermal pressure.

EC: Within your work, love and loss feature as core themes and you situate them within a range of different places and spaces, infiltrating them with secrets, spectres and memories. When it comes to writing a novel, do you begin with character or setting or does it depend upon the story you're telling at that particular moment?

MOF: I think it depends on the novel, there's no hard and fast rule. That's the strange thing about novels. It's a bit like being a mother – you have one baby and there's a hugely steep, vertiginous learning curve that you have; and then you have a second one and you think: it's okay, I know about babies now. But then you realize that this is an entirely different human being with different needs, different joys and different challenges, so you have to relearn it all again. It's the same with novels. You think, I know about novels, I've worked out how to do it, but then with the second or third it's a different book, a different story, different characters and so on. In a way it's necessary to reinvent your method every time, otherwise you'd end up writing the same book. With every book I try to do something different, I try to learn something different. Or every book teaches you something. I remember when I wrote *Instructions for a Heatwave*, I studied polyphony. I wanted to study how other writers had handled multiple voices and multiple viewpoints, how you switch between one person's head and then another's all within the space of a paragraph. I remember that was something I consciously wanted to learn how to do and that's why I wanted to write that book the way I did. There are some books that creep up on you very stealthily: they don't even tap you on the shoulder and suddenly you turn round and they're there. And then there are other books which just fall into your lap, almost fully formed. It would be great if that happened every time! That's what happened with the last one I wrote, *The Marriage Portrait*. I wasn't even thinking about it, I was starting to write another book. I remember I was sitting in a car outside one of my friend's houses waiting for my daughter and I suddenly had this idea about the woman in the Robert Browning poem. I looked it all up on my phone, found out who she was, and by the time my daughter came out of the house, I had the whole thing! I had the sense of it: it was almost as if I could see it, as if I was holding it in my hands and could leaf through the pages. Obviously, I couldn't just go home and write it, but the sense of it, the shape of it was there. But as I say, that doesn't happen very often. I wish it did!

EC: I think that's what Elizabeth Gilbert calls 'Big Magic', that sense of living in a world surrounded by ideas and sometimes an idea comes along and is meant for you – you have to grab it with both hands. In terms of where you write, do the creation of your novels and characters determine where you base yourself? With *Hamnet*, you talked about moving yourself into a little potting shed to write.

MOF: If you're going to write and have children, there are two things, really: you've got to learn to be able to switch very quickly from your domestic life or your everyday life – your family life – to your writing life. You've got to be able to cross that bridge as quickly as you can and back again. It makes me very cross, that school of thought out there, that you can't do both. Obviously there are many examples of women who didn't have children or chose not to have children or couldn't have children, whatever the case may be, and wrote books. But there are also many cases of women who did have children and wrote books. There are many arguments for both sides. Whatever people choose is fine for them. But I hate that school of thought out there – there were people who said to me when I was pregnant with my first child that every baby costs you a book. It's a horrible equation and a horrible put-down. I'm not saying it's easy, but I think it's the women who have regular office jobs, who have to be in a certain place at a certain time, clock watching, those are the ones who have it hard. In many ways it's been a lot easier for me because I've been around at home with my children. You need to be able to make that switch very quickly. You can't be pencil sharpening or rearranging everything or waiting for the right place or the right moment or the right light. You just have to do it anywhere and everywhere. When my kids were small, I'd take them out for a walk in the buggy and then if they fell asleep, I'd sit on a bench and try to write – once or twice I've been writing in a notebook as I've been pushing the buggy along. You can't be precious about it. The only thing I really need is a bit of quiet. If I can hear music, I find it really distracting. I don't mind other people's conversations, that's fine. But you can't rely on waiting for the right wind, you just have to get on with it.

EC: It's so refreshing and reassuring to hear this. I often find that I'm sitting on the side of a court while my son is playing tennis and I'm scribbling something down or making a note in my phone! In terms of how you write, are you self-consciously writing in dialogue with your contemporaries or thinking about the relationship your work might have with that of your peers? Is that a consideration at all?

MOF: I try to eliminate any type of self-consciousness when I'm writing. I read all the time and try to read what my contemporaries are writing – I have a lovely stack of proofs on my bedside table. But certainly, when I'm writing, it's quite the opposite. I ring-fence that quite fiercely – any sense of self-consciousness is really bad for your writing; I think it's very antithetical to that process. It's one of the reasons why I never read my reviews. My husband reads them for me, which is very nice of him. But I really don't want to read them, even if he says it's a great review, they loved it: I think it's the worst thing you can do in a sense because when you're sitting down, wherever you happen to be, at your desk or in your studio or whatever, you don't want an awareness of how other people see you, whether you're trying to second guess what readers may want from you or whether you're trying to position yourself in terms of your contemporaries. You have to write the book you can't not write; you've got to write the one shouting the loudest or tugging most insistently at your sleeve. You have to write to answer a need in yourself, or to resolve something, or to create the thing you want to create. You can't tailor it to somebody else's wishes or to a market or readership. If there's something standing between you and your book, it's never going to be the right one. I think it's all part of the reason why I don't read my reviews and why I'm never on social media. It has to be guarded so carefully, the relationship between you and your novel has to be so hermetic. I never talk about a book I haven't finished, not even with my husband. Even though he is my first reader, I would never talk about it, not with him nor with my editor, Mary-Anne Harrington, who I've been with for twenty-odd years: not at the first draft stage. It's such a fragile thing, such a private thing, and it should be. So self-consciousness is a big enemy for me. I try to completely seal myself off. I think social media is a wonderful way to put yourself out there and publicize your book, but it's not really for me at all. It's a question of time too – and I'm sure you have to develop the right voice for it.

EC: I wanted to move on to ask you about the works themselves, beginning with some of your earliest novels. The way in which you are able to navigate gaps, distances and absences within your work to explore issues like grief, sacrifice and responsibility is really striking and fascinating. There's a wonderful quote from Michael Donaghy at the beginning of *After You'd Gone*: 'The past falls open anywhere.' In terms of how you manage time shifts and changes in perspective when you're drafting the texts, how do you land your characters where they need to be, or indeed remove them or change a particular perspective depending on how the narrative arc needs to work for you?

MOF: I'm not much of a planner in life or fiction! I have heard other writers talk about this and say they don't put pen to paper or hand to keyboard until they plan the whole thing – every single chapter, every part of the narrative. I'm the opposite. I tend to feel I can't visualize the book unless I'm actually writing it. I think of it like driving on a dark road at night – you don't know which way to turn the wheel until your headlights illuminate the cats' eyes. It's only when you're actually there that you see every curve of the road, and I feel like that about novels. I could never think about it in an abstract form and then write a whole plot – I need to start writing to see where I'm going, where my characters are going. That's not to say that I don't have any idea where the book will end: often, the point at which I always feel a book is working is when I think, perhaps, my characters are going from this place to that place, and actually, it changes. At some point in the book the characters will almost turn and say: we're not actually doing that we're doing that instead, and do a big left-hand or right-hand turn. That's the point at which I feel the book has momentum, or its own pulse. If I'm writing a book with a complicated time frame, like *This Must Be the Place*, I usually go out and buy a lot of coloured Post-it notes. It's different for every book, obviously, but I might have a different colour for a certain time frame and I'll have a whole wall covered in my studio or in my study. I'll move them around and spend a long time looking at them. And I might think, for example, there's too much of a time lag in a particular area. That's how I keep track of it. When I was writing *This Must Be the Place*, my youngest daughter was around a year old, maybe one and a half, and she'd seen me doing this. I'd been staring at the notes and she obviously realized they were significant. I was in the bathroom one morning cleaning my teeth and she came in saying, 'All gone, all gone'. I said: 'What's all gone?' and then I saw in her hand she had a multi-coloured ball of paper. She'd climbed on the desk and pulled them all down so efficiently, every single one! It was a terrible moment! And there are people at my publishers who still call her 'Post-it baby'.

EC: Oh my goodness, what did you do with the crumpled ball?

MOF: Well, all the ink had run, and she was horrified, she'd never seen me cry before. So we both cried for a little bit and I said: 'It's okay; it's going to be okay'. In a way, I like to think it made the novel stronger because I had to re-justify every decision. I did put the Post-it notes a lot higher up on the wall! She's now ten and she gets very embarrassed because I often say to her: 'Whatever you do, don't touch my Post-its'.

EC: That's a great story! I did wonder if, for a book like *This Must Be the Place* or *The Vanishing Act of Esme Lennox* which has such a degree of fragmentation within it, whether you were physically moving pieces of paper around during the writing process. I've heard of some poets doing similar things, such as pegging individual poems on an internal type of washing line to determine what order they should appear in their collection.

MOF: Absolutely. I've been writing children's picture books quite recently and I always find it fascinating that children's book editors don't talk about 'writing a book', they talk about 'making a book'. I find that distinction so interesting because obviously there is a huge symbiosis in picture books between the pictures and the text; there are places where they mesh and places where you hand the baton over to the illustrator and then the illustrator hands it back. When I'm looking at the final proofs, I'll lay them out and consider whether there are places where I can hand over to the illustrator and she can pick up. I can imagine if you're a poet working on a collection, you'd do a similar thing. The white spaces are so useful in stories, poems, pictures and novels as well: what isn't said can be so powerful and so redolent.

EC: That's one of the many things that intrigues me about your work, the absentees from space and the shift from the first to third person, as well as the white space on the page. I'd like to ask you about the reception of your work. I know you mentioned about not reading reviews and maintaining a little distance. Is that also true, for example, in relation to reception of your work outside the UK, translations of your novels etc? I'm thinking of translation in the context of *My Lover's Lover* which deals with translation, mistranslation and miscommunication. Is engaging with this kind of reception and translation something that you also prefer to keep at arm's length?

MOF: It sometimes depends on translation publishers: there are some with whom I have a close relationship and others I've never met. Sometimes translation publishers will very conscientiously send me all the reviews in a particular language, Norwegian for example, and it's quite nice because I can't read them at all! The idea of any kind of reception is something I consciously don't think about. I'm totally unnumerical, I think it goes back to my idea of chronology and sequencing. If you gave me a telephone number to read out, I wouldn't read it out in the right order. In a sense it's quite useful because I totally forget numbers, things like book advance amounts or book sales. I can retain them for possibly ten seconds and then like a goldfish, it's all gone. I think the only sense of success or lack of success that I should be engaging with is whether the book is working, whether the plot is interacting with the characters, whether the setting is the right one, whether the time frame or the tenses or the grammar are correct: that's my role in the process of putting a book out into the world. The other things like numbers and book sales and reception aren't my job. Once it's published, it will always be part of me and something that I'm proud of or frustrated with in varying degrees. My job is to do the writing.

EC: Yes, the handing over and allowing someone to take up the reins, whose job it is . . .

MOF: It's hard. I used to quite like this metaphor but it doesn't work anymore . . . in Scotland there's the Forth Rail bridge and apparently they used to constantly repaint it . . . it's so enormous, they would paint it from one end and by the time they'd finished, they'd be starting again, it would need to be repainted. But they've invented some great new paint and don't need to do that anymore! I always used to feel a little bit like that about books – I don't know if you find this with your books, but there is a point where you could keep on rewriting them and editing them and finessing them forever. I have reading copies – I had a terrible stammer when I was younger – and when I have a copy of a book I read aloud from, I have to tell myself where to breathe; I have to cross out words I won't be able to speak aloud and I cling onto those copies very carefully. But actually all the way through I'm thinking – why did I use that adverb? Why did I not cut this sentence? So you could, like the painters of the Forth Rail bridge, keep on going: you could rewrite and finesse into eternity. You need someone you trust – an agent, an editor, a spouse – who's going to wrestle it out of your hands.

EC: Of course, that important handover time. And in terms of your 2017 memoir, *I Am, I Am, I Am: Seventeen Brushes with Death*, the weight of responsibility when moving from fiction to non-fiction, particularly when you're writing about things so personal to you and your family, must be significant. Is it a coincidence that this came seventeen years after your debut novel?

MOF: Yes, it is a coincidence! I'd never thought of that – how funny. There were other things on the cutting room floor that didn't make it. And as proof of my terrible numeracy, quite late on in the process – it might have been when we were sending it to the copyeditor, or even to be typeset – Mary-Anne (my editor) phoned me up in a panic and said: 'There are only sixteen'. And we counted them and she was right! So I had to very rapidly pick one up from the cutting room floor and rework it. That's one of those books that crept up on me: I never thought I'd write a memoir – it was against the grain of anything I thought I'd ever do. I still feel very wedded to fiction. I was a journalist a long time ago, but I never thought I'd write about myself – it seemed like the last thing I would want to do. I'm quite a private person in lots of ways; but also, I always think of writing as the alternative life to the one I have to lead. It's much more interesting making stuff up. I was actually planning to write *Hamnet* at that point, but I was feeling a bit of vertigo about the whole going back to the sixteenth century, so I ended up starting to write these essays about times I nearly died. Looking back on it now, a lot of it was thinking about the near-death experience; it was of course to do with my daughter and her medical condition and trying to come to terms with that – what doctors were telling us and also, how you bring up somebody with that condition. I wanted to comprehend what she was going through as her mother, or as a carer. I wanted to write almost a manifesto on how we live our lives and how these experiences can change us, how we need to carry on: how we learn to live around them and adapt to them. It was a bit of a surprise, I never really expected to write a memoir.

EC: Did you keep a diary when you were younger?

MOF: Yes, I did. I've got some diaries from the age of five or six – obviously they're very sketchy – and then when I was ill as a child, I couldn't write. But I've kept them pretty regularly since I was about ten. I thought they would be quite useful, but the strange thing is they weren't. I do like looking back at them but I find them more useful in terms of creating, say, a teenage character. They were less useful for writing about my teenage self. Certainly, when I was writing a teenage character in *This Must Be the Place*, I did look back because diaries contain quite mundane details. You can read about something that happened when you were sixteen: you can remember that day, what you were wearing, the boredom of sitting in a classroom, taking an exam or having your packed lunch with your mates. Diaries are incredibly useful for pinning down the everyday; the larger things, certainly when I was a teenager, I didn't really write about. It was the small stuff. And that's the stuff you forget – the big stuff you remember anyway. It was a really interesting process writing the memoir and in some ways, it was easier than fiction because of course it's all there: you don't have to make it up or struggle with details or plot. It was a process of excavation, rather than creation. I approached it as I would a novel and I would never have wanted to write the kind of memoir that began: 'I was born in Northern Ireland and then I went to infant school' – I would have found that really dull. Structurally, it was quite liberating because if you write in a non-sequential, non-chronological way, there's quite a lot you can leave out. And you are in control of what you say about yourself, how much you reveal. There's a huge amount that isn't in there which is to do with my own privacy, but also to do with others. One of the interesting things that came up with that book was the idea of ownership of narrative which I'd never thought about before, because you don't as a fiction writer. When you're writing a memoir, your life obviously overlaps with thousands of other people's and at every point, I was asking myself: who does this story belong to? Is it mine? Or how much of it is mine? What's the ratio? I really didn't want to write the kind of memoir that was exposing for other people. You read some memoirs and it's horrifying what people reveal about themselves or others in their lives. I never wanted to write that kind of book which was an imposition on others. The idea of how much you own, and do you own your own stories, is really interesting.

EC: What was evident to me as I read it was that this was non-fiction in the hands of a very accomplished novelist. It's very much about you, the body, internal organs and the interiorization of the story: it's almost like you let everyone else just be. And then there are your children's books – what was that transition like for you to your first one in 2020, *Where Snow Angels Go*? And is it true that it was inspired by a conversation with your daughter in the back of an ambulance?

MOF: Yes, it was. One of the lesser-known symptoms of anaphylactic shock is that you suddenly get cold, and that's actually the most dangerous symptom there is because your blood pressure is dropping and your heart rate is slowing down: you're in danger of cardiac arrest. It's something you always have to watch out for and not many people are aware of that. I remember being in the ambulance and she was quite tiny – four, possibly, or five – and very frightened. She was suddenly shivering and turning very white. We were rushing along in the ambulance and I knew we weren't far away from A&E and I just said to her: 'It's a snow angel'. You know how you do when you're a mum, a parent or carer of someone with additional needs, you've just got to be inventive all the time. One of the very many interesting things about being a parent is that there is such a need for narrative: children need a narrative. It's a human necessity, a bit like care or love or sunlight. I think that your job as a parent is to metabolize something too difficult for a child to understand and hand it back to them in a form they can comprehend. Story is so useful like that – particularly if there's something really frightening happening to them, almost inexplicable to a young child – the way to do it is to use metaphor. So she was then distracted and wanted to know more about it. I was saying, he's wrapping his wings around you, he's here to look after you: he's like a guardian angel. If you ever feel unwell or cold, that's all it is: you mustn't worry. But also when my son, who's quite a bit older than my daughter, had been ill – he was three, I think – there was one night when I woke up and I suddenly felt that I needed to go and check on him. I went into his room and he was very sick – he'd actually got meningitis. He went to hospital and was fine in the end, but I always thought to myself – why did I wake up to check on him then? All these little stories came together and I remember telling my daughter that it was my snow angel who woke me that night, telling me to go and check on my son. I've always been fascinated by the idea of water and the water cycle and the axis between science and magic. The whole story came from lots of different places.

EC: It's such a beautiful story. I was really struck by the vulnerability of the snow angel character: the fact that he is confused, hesitant and frightened. And he negates the reference to himself as being magical. How important do you think those stories are for children in terms of looking at darker matters and more challenging issues? And is it fair to describe this story as magical even with a snow angel who refutes magic? It certainly feels magical to me.

MOF: There's an element of magic to science, isn't there? I actually really liked science and I loved chemistry – all the experiments and apparatus and coloured smoke – there is an alchemical fascination to it all. I wanted to write that book because I think there's a gap in books for children in a sense. There are picture books for the under-fives, some of which grapple with incredibly dark themes – you think about *Beatrix Potter,* associated with this pastoral English prettiness – but actually some of her books are terrifying: they're like Gothic novels for children. Even *The Tiger Who Came to Tea* or *Where the Wild Things Are* – there's a lot of dark and shade in them and they're grappling with quite difficult themes and difficult things that happen which, of course, children need. We all need a place, that's what books are for: they're a road map to tell us how to get from one place to the next, to tell us which turning we should take. And then, of course, before you get to the Harry Potters and Lemony Snickets, there's an odd gap which seems to have a lot of unicorns and rainbows. I do understand that, that when your child starts to read you don't necessarily want them going off to bed on their own reading about terrible stuff. But at the same time there's a lot that five- to nine-year-olds are dealing with – grappling with their first friendships, for example – there's a lot going on. I wanted to write a story for that age group which was dealing with harsh things, grappling with big things in life. I think children need it – we all need it. I also wanted

to write a book that could be, sort of, for any age. There are some books
which are timeless, which can be read by adults or older children, and
where younger children can see the illustrations. I was incredibly lucky to
be paired with Daniela Jaglenka Terrazzini. It was actually my daughter's
idea – we were trying to find the right illustrator and one day we came
across these incredible workbooks by Daniela where you cut things out and
make miniature bookcases and tiny books – my daughter was cutting and I
was sitting alongside her. And she said: 'This is who should draw the snow
angel'. And I thought: oh my God, she's right. Daniela's illustrations are just
so beautiful. We had a long discussion about the snow angel and what he
should look like. I'd been in Rome and seen Bernini angels, and I sent her
lots of photographs of those. It's such a joy to be collaborating because, as
you know, writing is a very solitary job. I love it, but there are times when
it's so fantastic to be creating a book with lots of other people – that's one of
the things I love about writing picture books for children.

EC: Can we expect more children's books from you?

MOF: Yes, we've got another one coming out – Daniela and I have done
another one which is coming out in October.

EC: Fantastic. And is it for the same age group? Five- to nine-year-olds?

MOF: Yes, that's right.

EC: I'll look forward to it very much. Before we end, let's talk about your two
fabulous, most recent novels, *Hamnet* and *The Marriage Portrait*. Is it true
that *Hamnet* is a book you always wanted to write?

MOF: I was looking back through an old notebook quite recently for another
reason – it's a book where I write down scraps of ideas or titles – and I
found this scrawled thing from about 2014 saying: *novel about Shakespeare's
son, Hamnet*. Later, I'd drawn square brackets around it as if to say: *good
idea: I need to go back to this one*. It's something I've wanted to do for a
long time, but I also had a strange superstition about writing it before my
own son was past the age of eleven. Every time I would think about it – I'd
got hold of lots of different books about Shakespeare and I'd read some of
them – I'd think I just couldn't do it until he was past that age. You never
know, you can't be too careful. I needed to wait until he was a bit older. I
made a couple of starts at it at various points and then I'd write another
book. I think I wrote three books instead of writing it! Definitely *This Must
Be the Place*, and definitely my memoir. Sometimes it's not the right time
and for whatever reason, it just felt like the right time when I started to do
it. You're never quite sure when you start a book whether it's going to take
flight. With *Hamnet*, I'd written about 15,000 words and I opened up the

document and I thought I'd started it at the wrong point. I thought: this is wrong and I need to start with him. He's got to be centre stage; he's got to be the first person the reader sees. So I wrote about him coming down the stairs, his fingers tightening around the door handle; I knew then it was just the right point in the story and the right point in my life to be writing it.

EC: How did you find the research process for a book like *Hamnet*, that transition to historical fiction within a sixteenth-century context?

MOF: The most vertigo I had was writing about Shakespeare – at times I thought: what on earth am I doing? It was more that than the time frame of it. I loved the research: there's always a point when you write when you hit a brick wall. If you're writing a contemporary novel, all you can do is put your head on the desk and think: I'm never going to finish this. But if you're writing a historical novel or a novel that requires research, you can just go off to the library and do more research on Tudor farming methods or whatever else you want to read! I found it endlessly fascinating. I tried never to think that I was writing a historical novel with a capital H because I just tried to approach it as I would any other novel. The kinds of historical novels I really enjoy are the ones that wear the history lightly or the research lightly. I don't like books that go into every single tiny detail where the novelist is wanting to show you they've done their homework. You need to know a huge amount to create a scene in, for example, an Elizabethan parlour. You have to know what the walls are like, what the windows are like, what characters are wearing, what cloth their clothes are made of, or what the floor is made of – but actually when you write the scene, you leave out 99 per cent of that, otherwise it reads like a PhD (that's not to say anything against PhDs, but it's not what should be in a novel). I think I realized that and it was an interesting way of approaching the story – you need to know so much, but actually you need to get rid of most of that material, edit it out.

EC: I know you've spoken at length about Agnes and the centrality of Agnes to the story, but I wondered about the use of tense in the novel, why you decided to write it predominantly in the present tense?

MOF: I think it was a question of immediacy. It was to do with trying to realign the story about Shakespeare and his works and his family. Obviously there's a very valid reason why works of scholarship, other novels, films etc, will focus on London, where the main story happens. But I wanted to tell a different story: I've always felt that the biggest drama of his own life happened off-stage in Stratford. It was realigning the story and giving the reader a heightened sense of immediacy. I used the present continuous tense for most of it. I leave the grammar of the story to the instinctive part of my brain – I never think: now I'm going to write a novel in the third-person past tense. Sometimes I'll start writing a novel and I'll use one tense – this happened in *The Marriage Portrait* several times and then I kept noticing that I was slipping into a different tense. But actually I ended up going with the one I kept slipping into. Often you have to listen to the material – the material will tell you what it needs to be: third person, past tense, first person etc. You have to trust the instinct, trust the story.

EC: In terms of the film adaptation of *Hamnet*, do you have a date for when that's coming out and are you involved in any way?

MOF: I've thought about writing the adaptations, but in a sense I've told the story the way I want it to be told and I'm happy to hand it over to somebody else. The idea of dismantling a novel I've written and putting it back together in a different form is not something that really appeals to me. I'm quite happy to let an expert do that job.

EC: That sounds very wise. And congratulations on the recent memorial to Hamnet and Judith!

MOF: It was fantastic – it made me so happy. It's something I've wanted to do ever since I went to Stratford to research *Hamnet* and walked up to the graveyard and realized there was no headstone for him or for Judith. It was so great that the Church were so open to it and the town were behind it. It was a really happy occasion.

EC: It was so lovely to be able to see it and follow it on social media. Finally, I'd like to ask you about your latest novel, *The Marriage Portrait*. It's set in the1560s, so you're back in the sixteenth century, and I love the story of how the idea about writing a novel about Lucrezia came to you. Within the book, some of the motifs from your earlier works reappear, such as doubles, reincarnations of identities, the pairing of places, families and so on. I was fascinated by the idea of 'underpainting' and 'overpainting' within the novel and the centrality of that to Lucrezia's affirmation of her agency. It's something that continues right to the end of the work. I wondered if you could say a few words about the way in which you shaped Lucrezia's character and how you've given her independence and resilience within the very claustrophobic conditions of her marriage.

MOF: One of the things that really struck me when I began researching Lucrezia and her siblings – she had many siblings – was that her father, the Grand Duke of Tuscany, Cosimo de' Medici, insisted on educating his daughters alongside his sons. That was quite unusual for their class and times, and the girls received the best tuition in what we now call the Classics, what they called Antiquity. These were girls who were fluent in Latin, they could hand draw a map of Mesopotamia if pressed and they were highly educated and highly intelligent. But their role in that dynastic society was to be wives and mothers, a kind of political pawn. The boys were trained as soldiers and Lucrezia's brother became a cardinal; it was all about consolidating the power of the dynasty and creating stability for their region. The girls were brought up to be married into other dynasties or to some ally or to form some kind of political alliance. It was an astonishing idea: what happens to all of that education? Where does it go? To be used as a uterus for the continuance of other dynasties or to align two houses. I just wondered what happens to it all. It doesn't just disappear. Actually, so little is known about Lucrezia – her sister Isabella de' Medici Orsini is a lot better known (she lived until thirty-five and was quite an influential figure around Florence. She had a horrific end to her life also). But in terms of Lucrezia, there is so little about her: she's not mentioned very much at all in her parents' letters – her parents wrote to each other quite a lot – and obviously she dies at the age of sixteen, so it's a very short life. It was the idea of this very highly educated person and these very confined circumstances, basically locked away in a gilded cage – it was interesting to me what might have happened to all that intellect and education.

EC: How difficult was it to write about art and to make art within a novel? Lucrezia's own creative process is, of course, integral to the book.

MOF: A lot of it was research – I wanted to find out about the different processes, how they did those paintings, different processes of oil and tempera, different surfaces they used. I spent my lockdowns doing research – I was either homeschooling or reading about ground-up pigments etc. I should say I'm absolutely hopeless at drawing, though I did have a shot at grinding up the pigments and adding to linseed oil. I think you can't write about something unless you've physically done it, and you feel the motion of it, you smell what it smells like: the difficulties of getting it all right. I absolutely loved it and it was fascinating. But it was very strange in that I did the book in a counter-intuitive sort of way: in a normal world, I probably would have gone off to Florence and Ferrara and I would have looked at all the locations and seen the art galleries. But because of lockdown, I couldn't go until I had almost finished it. I was on a third or fourth draft and only then could I go to Italy. It was quite nerve-racking because I thought: what if I've got it all wrong? What if the locations feel wrong? But actually by doing it that way round, I felt a very strong emotional connection with Lucrezia – she felt almost like one of my children in a way. I went to see her tomb and it was so sad: I went in September last year (2021) when Covid lockdowns had just eased. I went to the monastery and it was completely locked. I knocked on the door and in my very patchy Italian I said I really wanted to see the tomb of Lucrezia de' Medici d'Este. And they said to me that no one had ever come and asked to see her tomb. It was so sad: this sixteen-year-old girl who died far away from her family. God knows what they thought of me because I brought flowers and cried as I stood there.

EC: That's such a moving story. When I read the novel, I felt like I'd stepped into a Renaissance painting. And the chapter headings – they made me feel like I was entering another tableau or painting of sorts. Was that deliberate?

MOF: Yes, absolutely. They were meant to be like types of paintings, that was the idea behind the chapter titles. I did completely immerse myself in Italian Renaissance art, which was hardly a hardship, you know. I was incredibly lucky in that I met an academic at Edinburgh University – I got in touch with her and asked if I could buy her a coffee and go for a walk outside and ask some questions – and I was amazed at how generous she was. She told me all kinds of things and one of her theories was that she thinks the Renaissance is the first instance of feminism. There were quite a lot of fathers who trained their daughters as painters and also some like Cosimo who educated their daughters. Obviously not all women were educated and women were still being married off at the age of thirteen to twenty-five-year-old men, but I thought that was a very interesting idea: the idea that these women were just locked in their rooms isn't quite true, there's a shading to this.

EC: The novel is a fascinating read, the way in which Lucrezia becomes an 'overpainting' of herself in disguise and the art motif completely perpetuates the text. I can't wait for everyone else to read it; I feel very privileged to have had an advance copy to make it part of our conversation today.

MOF: That's very nice to hear. Thank you.

EC: The dedication of the novel to Mary-Anne Harrington (your editor) and Victoria Hobbs (your literary agent) is a beautiful sentiment and so apt in a novel dedicated to the resilience and visibility of a young woman.

MOF: I've worked with them for twenty-plus years and I thought it was high time they had a book dedicated to them. It's my name on the cover of the book, but it's a bit like the maxim about it taking a village to raise a child. The idea that it's just me is ridiculous. They've had so much input and so much influence on my work – I couldn't have done it without them.

EC: You make a wonderful team.

MOF: I'm very lucky to have them.

EC: It's been an absolute pleasure talking to you, Maggie. All the very best with *The Marriage Portrait* and your forthcoming new children's book, *The Boy Who Lost His Spark*.

MOF: Thanks very much.

Bibliography

Works Cited by Contributors

Abraham, N. and M. Torok, (1994), *The Shell and the Kernel: Renewals of Psychoanalysis, Volume 1*, ed. and trans. N. T. Rand, Chicago, IL: Chicago University Press.

'After You'd Gone' (2001), *Kirkus Reviews*, 1 January. Available online: https://www.kirkusreviews.com/book-reviews/maggie-ofarrell/after-youd-gone/ (accessed 4 August 2022).

Agamben, G. ([2014] 2015), *The Use of Bodies*, trans. A. Kotsko, *Homo Sacer*, vol. IV, 2, Stanford, CA: Stanford University Press.

Aitkenhead, D. (2017), 'I've Revealed the Secrets I've Spent My Life Hiding', *Guardian*, 12 August. Available online: https://www.theguardian.com/books/2017/aug/12/maggie-o-farrell-secrets-spent-life-hiding-brushes-with-death (accessed 20 May 2022).

All is True (2018), [Film] Dir. Kenneth Branagh, UK: Sony Pictures.

Andreasen, Nancy C. (2007), 'Book: A Tale of Madness and Sanity', *The Lancet*, 369 (9562): 633–4.

Augé, M. ([1995] 2008), *Non-Places: An Introduction to Supermodernity*, trans. J. Howe, London: Verso.

Baker, H. (2018), 'Pain Like a Sea Anemone: Diving a Life into the Parts That Hurt', *Times Literary Supplement*, 5 January. Available online: https://www.the-tls.co.uk/articles/maggie-ofarrell-death/ (accessed 20 May 2022).

Balaev, M. (2014), 'Literary Trauma Theory Reconsidered', in M. Balaev (ed.), *Contemporary Approaches in Literary Trauma Theory*, 1–14, Basingstoke: Palgrave Macmillan.

Balaev, M. (2018), 'Trauma Studies', in D. H. Richter (ed.), *A Companion to Literary Theory*, 360–71, Chichester, West Sussex: Wiley Blackwell.

Barham, P. (2020), *Closing the Asylum: The Mental Patient in Modern Society*, London: Process Press.

Barker, P. (1993), *The Eye in the Door*, London: Penguin.

Barry, S. (2008), *The Secret Scripture*, New York: Penguin.

Battisti, C. and S. Fiorato (2012), 'Women's Legal Identity in the Context of Gothic Effacement: Mary Wollstonecraft's *Maria or the Wrongs of Woman* and Charlotte Perkins Gilman's *The Yellow Wallpaper*', *Pólemos*, 6 (2): 183–205.

Benjamin, W. (1996), 'The Task of the Translator', in Marcus Bullock and Michael W. Jennings (eds), *Walter Benjamin: Selected Writings Volume 1 1913–1926*, 253–63, Cambridge, MA and London: Harvard University Press.

Berthin, C. (2010), *Gothic Hauntings: Melancholy Crypts and Textual Ghosts*, Basingstoke: Palgrave Macmillan.

Bertsche, R. (2020), 'When Your Name Becomes 'Mom', Do Your Other Identities Matter?', *New York Times*, 10 January. Available online: https://www.nytimes.com /2020/04/16/parenting/motherhood-identity-crisis.html (accessed 1 June 2022).

Bertram, B. (2013), '*Measure for Measure* and the Discourse of Husbandry', *Modern Philology*, 110 (4): 459–88.

Black, W. (1884), *Judith Shakespeare: Her Love Affairs and Other Adventures*, London: Macmillan & Co.

Bronfen, E. (1996), *Over Her Dead Body: Femininity and the Aesthetic*, Manchester: Manchester University Press.

Brunvand, J. H. ([1991] 2015), '*The Taming of the Shrew': A Comparative Study of Oral and Literary Traditions*, Oxford: Routledge.

Burnett, F. H. ([1910] 1994, 2021), *The Secret Garden*, Project Gutenberg. Available online: https://www.gutenberg.org/files/113/113-h/113-h.htm#chap01 (accessed 24 June 2022).

Busfield, J. (1999), 'Mental Health Policy: Making Gender and Ethnicity Visible', *Policy & Politics*, 27 (1): 57–73.

Campbell, P. (2020), 'Preface', in P. Barham (ed.), *Closing the Asylum: The Mental Patient in Modern Society*, 1–4, London: Process Press.

Caruth, C. (1996), *Unclaimed Experience: Trauma, Narrative and History*, Baltimore: Johns Hopkins University Press.

Caruth, C. (2013), *Literature in the Ashes of History*, Baltimore: Johns Hopkins University Press.

Casey, M. (2001), 'Bedside Manners', *New York Times*, 22 April. Available online: https:// archive.nytimes.com/www.nytimes.com/books/01/04/22/reviews/010422.22caseyt .html (accessed 31 July 2022).

Charles, R. (2020), 'Maggie O'Farrell's *Hamnet* Reimagines the Life and Death of Shakespeare's Only Son', *The Washington Post*, 21 July. Available online: https://www .washingtonpost.com/entertainment/books/maggie-ofarrells-hamnet-reimagines -the-life-and-death-of-shakespeares-only-son/2020/07/20/c949592e-ca95-11ea-91f1 -28aca4d833a0_story.html (accessed 4 August 2022).

Clark, A. (2020), 'Sebastian Barry: Family Stories Mean a Whole Different Thing in Your 60s', *Guardian*, 7 March. Available online: https://www.theguardian.com/books /2020/mar/07/sebastian-barry-family-stories-mean-a-while-dofferent-thing-when -you-are-60 (accessed 19 June 2022).

Connolly, C. ([1938] 2008), *Enemies of Promise*, Chicago, IL: University of Chicago Press.

Coughlan, C. (2013), 'Novelicious Chats to . . . Maggie O'Farrell'. Available online: https:// writingtipsoasis.com/novelicious-chats-tomaggie-ofarrell/ (accessed 17 May 2022).

Craps, S. (2012), *Postcolonial Witnessing: Trauma Out of Bounds*, Basingstoke: Palgrave Macmillan.

Craps, S. (2014), 'Beyond Eurocentrism: Trauma Theory in the Global Age', in G. Buelens, S. Durrant and R. Eaglestone (eds), *The Future of Trauma Theory: Contemporary Literary and Cultural Criticism*, 45–60, New York: Routledge.

Crocker, H. (2010), 'Engendering Shrews: Medieval to Modern', in D. Wootton and G. Holderness (eds), *Gender and Power in Shrew-Taming Narratives, 1500–1700*, 48–9, Basingstoke: Palgrave Macmillan.

Cullingford, E. (2014), 'American Dreams: Emigration or Exile in Contemporary Irish Fiction?', *Éire-Ireland*, 49 (3–4): 60–94. Available online: doi:10.1353/eir.2014.0013 (accessed 24 May 2022).

Day, E. (2010), '*The Hand That First Held Mine* by Maggie O'Farrell', *Guardian*, 25 April. Available online: https://www.theguardian.com/books/2010/apr/25/hand-that-first -held-mine (accessed 4 August 2022).

D'Erasmo, S. (2013), 'Bubbling to the Surface', *New York Times*, 28 October. Available online: https://www.nytimes.com/2013/07/28/books/review/maggie-ofarrells -instructions-for-a-heatwave.html (accessed 4 August 2022).

De Waal, K. ([2018] 2019), *The Trick to Time*, London: Penguin Books.

Dillon, S. (2005), 'Re-inscribing De Quincey's Palimpsest: The Significance of the Palimpsest in Contemporary Literary and Cultural Studies', *Textual Practice*, 19 (3): 243–63.

Dillon, S. (2007), *The Palimpsest*, London: Palgrave Macmillan.

Doyle, A. C. (2001), *The Penguin Complete Sherlock Holmes*, London: Penguin.

Elam, K. (2002), *The Semiotics of Theatre and Drama*, 2nd edn, London: Routledge.

Felman, S. and D. Laub (1992), *Testimony: Crises of Witnessing in Literature, Psychoanalysis and History*, London and New York: Routledge.

Fischer, S. A. (2001), 'A Room of Our Own: Rodinsky, Street Haunting and the Creative Mind', *Changing English: Studies in Culture and Education*, 8 (2): 119–28.

'Five That Missed Out: Highly-rated Young Novelists Who Didn't Make the Granta List', *Observer*, Sunday 5 January 2003. Available online: http://www.guardian.co.uk/uk /2003/jan/05/featuresreview.books (accessed 19 July 2011).

Fletcher, J. ([1609–11] 2006), *The Tamer Tamed; or, The Woman's Prize*, ed. C. R. Daileader and G. Taylor, Manchester: Manchester University Press.

Fletcher, J. ([1609–11] 2010), *The Tamer Tamed*, ed. L. Munro, London: Bloomsbury.

Flint, K. (2017), 'Victorian Roots: The Sense of the Past in *Mrs. Dalloway* and *To the Lighthouse*', in J. Acheson (ed), *Virginia Woolf*, 46–59, London: Bloomsbury.

Forter, D. (2003), 'Against Melancholia: Contemporary Mourning Theory, Fitzgerald's *The Great Gatsby*, and the Politics of Unfinished Grief', *Differences: A Journal of Feminist Cultural Studies*, 14 (2): 134–70.

Forter, D. (2007), 'Freud, Faulkner, Caruth: Trauma and the Politics of Literary Form', *Narrative*, 15 (3): 259–85.

Forter, G. (2011), *Gender, Race, and Mourning in American Modernism*, Cambridge: Cambridge University Press.

Foucault, M. (1980), *Power/Knowledge: Selected Interviews and Other Writings 1972–77*, ed. C. Gordon, Harlow: Longman.

Freud, Sigmund (1917), 'Trauer und Melancholie', *Internationale Zeitschrift für Ärztliche Psychoanalyse [International Journal for Medical Psychoanalysis]*, 4 (6): 288–301.

Freud, Sigmund (1995), *Five Lectures on Psycho-Analysis*, London: Penguin.

Freud, Sigmund (2003), *The Uncanny*, London: Penguin.

Freud, Sigmund and J. Breuer (2004), *Studies in Hysteria*, ed. R. Bowlby, trans. N. Luckhurst, New York: Penguin.

Gardam, J. (2006), 'The Vanishing Act of Esme Lennox by Maggie O'Farrell – Review', *Guardian*, 2 September. Available online: https://www.theguardian.com/books/2006/sep/02/featuresreviews.guardianreview19 (accessed 20 June 2022).

Gilman, C. P. [Stetson, C. P.], ([1892] n.d.]), 'The Yellow Wall-Paper', *[The New England Magazine] The National Library of Medicine*. Available online: https://www.nlm.nih.gov/exhibition/theliteratureofprescription/exhibitionAssets/digitalDocs/The-Yellow-Wall-Paper.pdf (accessed 14 June 2022).

Gilman, C. P. ([1913] 2011), 'Why I Wrote the Yellow Wallpaper', selected by Femi Oyebode, *Advances in Psychiatric Treatment*, 17: 256–65. Available online: https://www.cambridge.org/core/services/aop-cambridge core/content/view/9F08034 93F9D522712BB4B31BA5CCDC2/S1355514600014176a.pdf/why-i-wrote-the-yellow-wallpaper.pdf (accessed 14 June 2022).

Gold, B. (2013), 'Talking to Ireland'. Available online: https://guernicamag.com/talking-to-ireland/ (accessed 17 May 2022).

Greenblatt, S. ([1980] 1984), *Renaissance Self-Fashioning: From More to Shakespeare*, Chicago, IL: Chicago University Press.

Greenblatt, S. (2021), 'A Wisewoman in Stratford', *New York Review of Books*, 14 January.

Greer, G. (2007), *Shakespeare's Wife*, London: Bloomsbury.

Groskop, V. (2013), 'Instructions for a Heatwave by Maggie O'Farrell – Review', *Guardian*, 3 March. Available online: https://www.theguardian.com/books/2013/mar/03/instructions-heatwave-maggie-ofarrell-review (accessed 4 August 2022).

Harney-Mahajan, T. (2012), 'Provoking Forgiveness in Sebastian Barry's *The Secret Scripture*', *New Hibernia Review / Iris Éireannach Nua*, 16 (2): 54–71.

Hibbard, G. R. (1964), 'The Taming of the Shrew: A Social Comedy', in N. J. Sanders and A. Thaler (eds), *Shakespearean Essays*, 15–28, Knoxville, TN: University of Tennessee Press.

Hicks, C. (1988), *Who Cares: Looking After People at Home*, London: Virago.

Holderness, G. (2010a), '"Darkenes Was Before Light": Hierarchy and Duality in *The Taming of A Shrew*', in D. Wootton and G. Holderness (eds), *Gender and Power in Shrew-Taming Narratives, 1500–1700*, 169–84, Basingstoke: Palgrave Macmillan.

Holderness, G. (2010b), 'Introduction', in D. Wootton and G. Holderness (eds), *Gender and Power in Shrew-Taming Narratives, 1500–1700*, 1–10, Basingstoke: Palgrave Macmillan.

Horowitz, G. (2001), *Sustaining Loss: Art and Mournful Life*, Redwood City, CA: Stanford University Press.

Hughes-Hallett, L. (2022), 'The Marriage Portrait by Maggie O'Farrell Review – a Dark Renaissance Fable', *Guardian*, 26 August. Available online: https://www.theguardian.com/books/2022/aug/26/the-marriage-portrait-by-maggie-ofarrell-review-a-dark-renaissance-fable (accessed 28 August 2022).

Isenberg, N. (2016), *White Trash: The 400-Year Untold History of Class in America*, New York: Viking.

Jacobs, C. (1975), 'The Monstrosity of Translation', *MLN*, 90 (6): 755–66.

Janette, M. (2014), '"Distorting Overlaps": Identity as Palimpsest in *Bitter in the Mouth*', *MELUS*, 39 (3): 155–77.

Jeafferson, J. C. (1872), *Brides and Bridals*, 2 vols, London: Hurst and Blackett.

Kellaway, K. (2020), 'Maggie O'Farrell: "Having to Bury a Child Must Be Unlike Anything Else"', *Guardian*, 22 March. Available online: https://www.theguardian.com/books/2020/mar/22/maggie-ofarrell-novel-hamnet-interview-the-agony-of-burying-your-child (accessed 20 May 2022).

Kelly, S. (2022), 'Book Review: The Marriage Portrait, by Maggie O'Farrell', *The Scotsman*, 28 August. Available online: https://www.scotsman.com/arts-and-culture/books/book-review-the-marriage-portrait-by-maggie-ofarrell-3818484 (accessed 29 August 2022).

Krasniqi, L. and L. Tahiri. (2022), 'A Narrative of Different Voices: Stylistic Analysis of Multiple Points of View in Zadie Smith's *NW*', *Respectus Philologicus*, 46 (41): 132–44. Available online: http://dx.doi.org/10.15388/RESPECTUS.2022.41.46.114 (accessed 24 May 2022).

Kurtz, J. R. (2018), 'Introduction', in J. R. Kurtz (ed.), *Trauma and Literature*, 1–17, Cambridge: Cambridge University Press.

Kyd, T. ([c.1587] 1959), *The Spanish Tragedy*, ed. Philip Edwards, The Revels Plays, London: Methuen.

Lee-Potter, C. (2004), 'The Distance Between Us by Maggie O'Farrell', *The Independent*, 29 February. Available online: https://www.independent.co.uk/arts-entertainment/books/reviews/the-distance-between-us-by-maggie-o-farrell-71771.html (accessed 20 July 2022).

'Maggie O'Farrell – *The Vanishing Act of Esme Lennox*' (2016), [Radio], Interview with James Naughtie, BBC Radio 4 Book Club, 3 July. Available online: https://www.bbc.co.uk/sounds/play/b07hwwjx (accessed 19 February 2022).

Markham, G. (1613), *English Husbandman*, London: John Browne.

Markham, G. ([1615] 1986), *The English Housewife: Containing the Inward and Outward Virtues Which Ought to Be in a Complete Woman*, ed. M. R. Best, Montreal: McGill-Queen's University Press.

Massey, D. (2005), *For Space*, London: Sage.

McCann, C. (2009), *Let the Great World Spin*, New York: Random House.

McCarthy, K. (2017), 'Secrets and Grace in Sebastian Barry's *The Secret Scripture*', *Nordic Irish Studies*, 16: 37–54.

Meister, J. C. (2009), 'Narratology', in P. Hühn, J. Pier, W. Schmid, and J. Schönert (eds), *Handbook of Narratology*, 329–50, Berlin: De Gruyter.

Meretoja, H. (2020), 'Philosophies of Trauma', in C. Davis and H. Meretoja (eds), *The Routledge Companion to Literature and Trauma*, 23–35, London and New York: Routledge.

Muller, N. (2009), 'Hystoriographic Metafiction: The Victorian Madwoman and Women's Mental Health in 21st-Centruy British Fiction', *Gender Forum (Köln)*, 23: n/a.

Oakley, A. (2007), *Fracture: Adventures of a Broken Body*, Bristol: Policy Press.

O'Connor, J. (2008), 'Not All Knives and Axes, Rev. of *The Secret Scripture*', *Guardian*, 23 May. Available online: https://www.theguardian.com/books/2008/may/24/fiction1 (accessed 20 June 2020).

O'Farrell, M. (n.d.), 'Maggie O'Farrell Q&A on Her Novel This Must Be the Place', *Headline Books*. Available online: https://youtu.be/vLGE92CykGQ (accessed 31 May 2022).

O'Farrell, M. (2000), *After You'd Gone*, London: Headline.

O'Farrell, M. (2002), *My Lover's Lover*, London: Headline.

O'Farrell, M. (2003), 'Is the Pram in the Hallway the Enemy of Good Art?', *Guardian*, 17 March. Available online: https://www.theguardian.com/world/2003/mar/17/gender.uk (accessed 1 June 2022).

O'Farrell, M. (2004), *The Distance Between Us*, London: Headline.

O'Farrell, M. (2006a), 'The Vanished', *Guardian*, 2 October. Available online: https://www.theguardian.com/society/2006/oct/02/socialcare.genderissues (accessed 19 February 2022).

O'Farrell, M. (2006b), *The Vanishing Act of Esme Lennox*, New York: Harcourt.

O'Farrell, M. (2006c), *The Vanishing Act of Esme Lennox*, London: Headline.

O'Farrell, M. (2009), 'Climbing the Walls', *Guardian*, 9 January. Available online: http://www.guardian.co.uk/books/2009/jan/09/women (accessed 12 May 2021).

O'Farrell, M. (2010a), 'An Interview with Maggie O'Farrell', *BookBrowse.com*. Available online: https://www.bookbrowse.com/author_interviews/full/index.cfm/author_number/1491/maggie-ofarrell (accessed 1 June 2022).

O'Farrell, M. (2010b), *The Hand that First Held Mine*, London: Headline.

O'Farrell, M. (2010c), 'Maggie O'Farrell Interview', interview by A. Sooke, *Telegraph*, 17 April. Available online: https://www.telegraph.co.uk/culture/books/7597512/Maggie-OFarrell-interview.html (accessed 1 June 2022).

O'Farrell, M. (2013), *Instructions for a Heatwave*, London: Tinder Press, Headline.

O'Farrell, M. (2016a), *This Must Be the Place*, New York: Vintage Contemporaries.

O'Farrell, M. (2016b), *This Must Be the Place*, London: Tinder Press, Headline.

O'Farrell, M. (2017), *I Am, I Am, I Am: Seventeen Brushes with Death*, London: Tinder Press, Headline.

O'Farrell, M. (2018), 'Powells Q&A: Maggie O'Farrell, Author of *I Am, I Am, I Am*'. Available online: https://www.powells.com/post/qa/powells-qa-maggie-ofarrell-author-of-i-am-i-am-i-am (accessed 17 May 2022).

O'Farrell, M. (2020a), *Hamnet*, London: Tinder Press, Headline.

O'Farrell, M. (2020b), *Where Snow Angels Go*, illustrated by D. Jaglenka Terrazzini, London: Walker Books.

O'Farrell, M. (2021), In conversation with Ann Patchett, Parnassus Books, 10 May. Available online: https://www.youtube.com/watch?v=XJlS6aySW0Q.

O'Farrell, M. (2022a), *The Marriage Portrait*, London: Tinder Press, Headline.

O'Farrell, M. (2022b), *The Boy Who Lost His Spark*, illustrated by D. Jaglenka Terrazzini, London: Walker Books.

O'Neill, S. (2021), "'And Who Will Write Me?'": Maternalizing Networks of Remembrance in Maggie O'Farrell's "Hamnet", *Shakespeare*, 17 (2): 210–29.

Park, D. (2018), *Travelling in a Strange Land*, London: Bloomsbury.

Plesske, N. (2014), *The Intelligible Metropolis: Urban Mentality in Contemporary London Novels*, London: Transcript Verlag.

Ranald, M. L. (1979), "'As Marriage Binds, and Blood Breaks'": English Marriage and Shakespeare', *Shakespeare Quarterly*, 30 (1): 68–81.

Ranald, M. L. (1987), 'The Manning of the Haggard: Or *The Taming of the Shrew*', in M. L. Ranald (ed.), *Shakespeare and His Social Context: Essays in Osmotic Knowledge and Literary Inteprertation*, 117–33, New York: AMS Press.

'Renaissance Art' (2023), *Britannica*, 5 January. Available online: https://www.britannica.com/art/Renaissance-art (accessed 7 January 2023).

Rich, A. ([1976] 1996), *Of Woman Born: Motherhood as Experience & Institution*, New York: W. W. Norton & Co.

Rush, C. (2008), *Will*, London: Beautiful Books.

Saunders, G. (2021), *A Swim in the Pond in the Rain: In Which Four Russians Give a Master Class on Writing, Reading, and Life*, New York: Random House.

Shakespeare, W. (1979), *Midsummer Night's Dream*, ed. H. Brooks, The Arden Shakespeare Second Series, London: Methuen.

Shakespeare, W. (2006), *As You Like It*, ed. J. Dusinberre, The Arden Shakespeare Third Series, London: Bloomsbury.

Shakespeare, W. (2010), *The Taming of the Shrew*, ed. B. Hodgdon, The Arden Shakespeare Third Series, London: Bloomsbury.

Shakespeare, W. (2012), *Romeo and Juliet*, ed. R. Weis, The Arden Shakespeare Third Series, London: Bloomsbury.

Shakespeare, W. ([1959] 2013), *All's Well that Ends Well*, ed. G. K. Hunter, The Arden Shakespeare Second Series, London: Bloomsbury.

Shakespeare, W. (2014a), *Sonnets*, ed. K. Duncan-Jones, The Arden Shakespeare Third Series, London: Methuen.

Shakespeare, W. (2014b), *Twelfth Night*, ed. K. Elam, The Arden Shakespeare Third Series, London: Bloomsbury.

Shakespeare, W. (2015), *Macbeth*, ed. S. Clark and P. Mason, The Arden Shakespeare Third Series, London: Bloomsbury.

Shakespeare, W. (2016), *Hamlet*, ed. A. Thompson and N. Taylor, revised edn, The Arden Shakespeare Third Series, London: Bloomsbury.

Sherratt-Bado, D. M. (2020), 'Review: *Hamnet* by Maggie O'Farrell', *The Literary Review*. Available online: https://www.theliteraryreview.org/book-review/a-review-of -hamnet-by-maggie-ofarrell/ (accessed 4 August 2022).

Showalter, E. ([1985] 1987), *The Female Malady: Women, Madness, and English Culture, 1830–1980*, New York: Penguin Books.

Showalter, E. (2004), 'Mind the Gap', *Guardian*, 6 March. Available online: https://www .theguardian.com/books/2004/mar/06/featuresreviews.guardianreview21 (accessed 4 August 2022).

Skov Nielsen, H. (2011), 'Unnatural Narratology, Impersonal Voices, Real Authors, and Non-Communicative Narration', in J. Alber and H. Rüdiger (eds), *Unnatural Narratives–Unnatural Narratology*, 71–88, Berlin: De Gruyter.

Smith, G. (2022), 'The Marriage Portrait by Maggie O'Farrell, Review: Magnificent – and Just as Spellbinding as *Hamnet*', *INews*, 24 August. Available online: https:// inews.co.uk/culture/books/the-marriage-portrait-by-maggie-ofarrell-review -1812650 (accessed 31 August 2022).

Smith, Z. (2012), *NW*, New York: Penguin Books.

Stern, D. (1998), *The Birth of a Mother: How the Motherhood Experience Changes You Forever*, New York: Basic Books.

Strehle, S. (2017), 'Maggie O'Farrell: Discoveries at the Edge', in J. Acheson (ed.), *The Contemporary British Novel Since 2000*, 61–9, Edinburgh: Edinburgh University Press.

Sturges, F. (2017), 'I Am, I Am, I Am by Maggie O'Farrell – 17 Brushes with Death', *Guardian*, 18 August. Available online: https://www.theguardian.com/books/2017 /aug/18/i-am-i-am-i-am-by-maggie-ofarrell-17-brushes-with-death (accessed 4 August 2022).

Taylor, B. (2011), 'The Demise of the Asylum in Late Twentieth-Century Britain: A Personal History', *Transactions of the Royal Historical Society*, 21: 193–215.

Taylor, G. and G. Egan, eds (2017), *The New Oxford Shakespeare Authorship Companion*, Oxford: Oxford University Press.

Thorpe, V. (2003), 'Women Writers Top Class of 2003', *Observer*, 5 January. Available online: http://www.guardian.co.uk/uk/2003/jan/05/books.featuresreview (accessed 19 July 2021).

Tiffany, G. (2003), *My Father Had a Daughter: Judith Shakespeare's Tale*, New York: Berkley Books.

'Translation, n', *OED Online*. June 2011. Oxford University Press, 28 June 2021. Available online: http://www.oed.com/view/Entry/204844?redirectedFrom =translation.

Tuan, Y. F. (1975), 'Place: An Experiential Perspective', *Geographical Review*, 65 (2): 151–65.

Turberville, G. (1611), *The Booke of Falconrie; for Havvking or the Onely Delight and Pleasure of All Noblemen and Gentlemen: Collected out of the Best Authors, Aswell Italians as Frenchmen, and Some English Practises Withall Concerning Falconrie*, London: Thomas Purfoot.

Williams, A. (1995), *The Art of Darkness: A Poetics of the Gothic*, Chicago, IL: University of Chicago Press.

Windberger, E. M. (2021), '"Remember Me": Significant Absences and the Fragility of Family in Maggie O'Farrell's *Hamnet*', *Alluvium*. Available online: https://www.alluvium-journal.org/2021/05/07/significant-absences-and-the-fragility-of-family-maggie-ofarrellshamnet (accessed 5 May 2022).

Woolf, V. ([1927] 1981), *To the Lighthouse*, Boston: Mariner Books.

Woolf, V. (1985), 'A Sketch of the Past', in J. Schulkind (ed.), *Moments of Being*, 2nd edn, 61–160, New York: Harvest.

Woolf, V. (1996), *Mrs Dalloway*, Hertfordshire: Wordsworth Editions.

Further Reading

I. Works by Maggie O'Farrell

Novels

(2000), *After You'd Gone*, London: Headline.
(2002), *My Lover's Lover*, London: Headline.
(2004), *The Distance Between Us*, London: Headline.
(2006), *The Vanishing Act of Esme Lennox*, London: Headline.
(2010), *The Hand that First Held Mine*, London: Headline.
(2013), *Instructions for a Heatwave*, London: Tinder Press, Headline.
(2016), *This Must be the Place*, London: Tinder Press, Headline.
(2020), *Hamnet*, London: Tinder Press, Headline.
(2022), *The Marriage Portrait*, London: Tinder Press, Headline.

Memoir

(2017), *I Am, I Am, I Am: Seventeen Brushes with Death*, London: Tinder Press, Headline.

Children's Books

(2020), *Where Snow Angels Go*, illustrated by D. Jaglenka Terrazzini, London: Walker Books.
(2022), *The Boy Who Lost His Spark*, illustrated by D. Jaglenka Terrazzini, London: Walker Books.

II. Critical Material

Journal Articles

O'Neill, S. (2021), "'And Who Will Write Me?'": Maternalizing Networks of Remembrance in Maggie O'Farrell's "Hamnet", *Shakespeare*, 17 (2): 210–29.
Windberger, E.M. (2021), "'Remember Me'": Significant Absences and the Fragility of Family in Maggie O'Farrell's *Hamnet*, *Alluvium*. Available online: https://www

.alluvium-journal.org/2021/05/07/significant-absences-and-the-fragility-of-family
-maggie-ofarrellshamnet

Book Chapters

Lovelock, J. (2022), 'Maggie O'Farrell, *Hamnet* (2020)', in *The Business of Reading: A Hundred Years of the English Novel*, 162–70, London: The Lutterworth Press.

Strehle, S. (2017), 'Maggie O'Farrell: Discoveries at the Edge', in J. Acheson (ed.), *The Contemporary British Novel Since 2000*, 61–9, Edinburgh: Edinburgh University Press.

Newspaper Reviews

'After You'd Gone' (2001), *Kirkus Reviews*, 1 January. Available online: https://www .kirkusreviews.com/book-reviews/maggie-ofarrell/after-youd-gone/

Beckerman, H. (2016), '*This Must Be the Place* by Maggie O'Farrell Review – Technically Dazzling', *Guardian*, 17 May. Available online: https://www.theguardian.com/books /2016/may/17/this-must-be-the-place-maggie-ofarrell-review

Charles, R. (2020), 'Maggie O'Farrell's *Hamnet* Reimagines the Life and Death of Shakespeare's Only Son', *The Washington Post*, 21 July. Available online: https://www .washingtonpost.com/entertainment/books/maggie-ofarrells-hamnet-reimagines -the-life-and-death-of-shakespeares-only-son/2020/07/20/c949592e-ca95-11ea-91f1 -28aca4d833a0_story.html

Coughlan, C. (2013), 'Novelicious Chats to . . . Maggie O'Farrell'. Available online: https://writingtipsoasis.com/novelicious-chats-tomaggie-ofarrell/

Day, E. (2010), '*The Hand that First Held Mine* by Maggie O'Farrell', *Guardian*, 25 April. Available online: https://www.theguardian.com/books/2010/apr/25/hand-that-first -held-mine

D'Erasmo, S. (2013), 'Bubbling to the Surface', *New York Times*, 28 October. Available online: https://www.nytimes.com/2013/07/28/books/review/maggie-ofarrells -instructions-for-a-heatwave.html

Gardam, J. (2006), 'The Vanishing Act of Esme Lennox by Maggie O'Farrell – Review', *Guardian*, 2 September. Available online: https://www.theguardian.com/books/2006/ sep/02/featuresreviews.guardianreview19

Groskop, V. (2013), 'Instructions for a Heatwave by Maggie O'Farrell – Review', *Guardian*, 3 March. Available online: https://www.theguardian.com/books/2013/mar /03/instructions-heatwave-maggie-ofarrell-review

Hagestadt, E. (2010), 'The Hand that First Held Mine, by Maggie O'Farrell', *The Independent*, 9 June. Available online: https://www.independent.co.uk/arts

-entertainment/books/reviews/the-hand-that-first-held-mine-by-maggie-o-farrell
-1994895.html

Hickling, A. (2016), '*This Must Be the Place* by Maggie O'Farrell Review – An Audacious Account of Marital Breakdown', *Guardian*, 27 May. Available online: https://www .theguardian.com/books/2016/may/27/this-must-be-the-place-by-maggie-ofarrell -review

Hughes-Hallett, L. (2022), 'The Marriage Portrait by Maggie O'Farrell Review – A Dark Renaissance Fable', *Guardian*, 26 August. Available online: https://www.theguardian .com/books/2022/aug/26/the-marriage-portrait-by-maggie-ofarrell-review-a-dark -renaissance-fable

Kelly, S. (2022), 'Book Review: The Marriage Portrait, by Maggie O'Farrell', *The Scotsman*, 28 August. Available online: https://www.scotsman.com/arts-and-culture/ books/book-review-the-marriage-portrait-by-maggie-ofarrell-3818484

Lee-Potter, C. (2004), 'The Distance Between Us by Maggie O'Farrell', *The Independent*, 29 February. Available online: https://www.independent.co.uk/arts-entertainment/ books/reviews/the-distance-between-us-by-maggie-o-farrell-71771.html

Mullan, J. (2020), 'Maggie O'Farrell's *Hamnet*: A Brilliantly Observed Historical Novel', *The New Statesman*, 18 November. Available online: https://www.newstatesman.com /international-politics/2020/11/Maggie-ofarrell-hamnet-review

Scheeres, J. (2007), 'Seeking Asylum', *New York Times*, 18 November. Available online: https://www.nytimes.com/2007/11/18/books/review/Scheeres-t.html

Seymenliyska, E. (2013), 'Instructions for a Heatwave, by Maggie O'Farrell, Review', *The Telegraph*, 21 March. Available online: https://www.telegraph.co.uk/culture /books/9944065/Instructions-for-a-Heatwave-by-Maggie-OFarrell-review.html ?WT.mc_id=tmgoff_psc_ppc_dsa_culture&gclid=CjwKCAiAr4GgBhBFEiw AgwORrZgHnDq0Wwr2b4Y--hdpKvPgLgmTBw3E4j7mnS4XkBqN_CwXd -5eaxoClokQAvD_BwE

Sherratt-Bado, D. M. (2020), 'Review: *Hamnet* by Maggie O'Farrell', *The Literary Review*. Available online: https://www.theliteraryreview.org/book-review/a-review-of -hamnet-by-maggie-ofarrell/

Showalter, E. (2004), 'Mind the Gap', *Guardian*, 6 March. Available online: https://www .theguardian.com/books/2004/mar/06/featuresreviews.guardianreview21

Smith, G. (2022), 'The Marriage Portrait by Maggie O'Farrell, Review: Magnificent – And Just as Spellbinding as *Hamnet*', *INews*, 24 August. Available online: https:// inews.co.uk/culture/books/the-marriage-portrait-by-maggie-ofarrell-review -1812650

Speller, E. (2000), 'Her Family Can Be Brutal – As Can her Haircut', *Guardian*, 9 April. Available online: https://www.theguardian.com/books/2000/apr/09/fiction .reviews5

Sturges, F. (2017), 'I Am, I Am, I Am by Maggie O'Farrell – 17 Brushes with Death', *Guardian*, 18 August. Available online: https://www.theguardian.com/books/2017/ aug/18/i-am-i-am-i-am-by-maggie-ofarrell-17-brushes-with-death

General: Historical fiction; British novel

Acheson, J., ed. (2017), *The Contemporary British Novel Since 2000*, Edinburgh: Edinburgh University Press.

Baker, J. S. (2015), *The Readers' Advisory Guide to Historical Fiction*, Chicago, IL: ALA Editions.

Boccardi, M. (2009), *The Contemporary British Historical Novel*, Basingstoke: Palgrave Macmillan.

Cooper, K. and E. Short, eds (2012), *The Female Figure in Contemporary Historical Fiction*, Basingstoke: Palgrave Macmillan.

de Groot, J. (2009), *The Historical Novel*, London and New York: Routledge.

English, J. F., ed. (2006), *A Concise Companion to Contemporary British Fiction*, Oxford: Blackwell.

Lovelock, J. (2022), *The Business of Reading: A Hundred Years of the English Novel*, London: The Lutterworth Press.

Robinson, A. (2011), *Narrating the Past: Historiography, Memory and the Contemporary Novel*, Basingstoke: Palgrave Macmillan.

Tew, P. (2004), *The Contemporary British Novel*, London: Continuum.

Wallace, D. (2005), *The Woman's Historical Novel*, Basingstoke: Palgrave Macmillan.

Interviews

Aitkenhead, D. (2017), 'I've Revealed the Secrets I've Spent My Life Hiding', *Guardian*, 12 August. Available online: https://www.theguardian.com/books/2017/aug/12/maggie-o-farrell-secrets-spent-life-hiding-brushes-with-death

Allardice, L. (2021), 'Maggie O'Farrell: "Severe Illness Refigures You – It's Like Passing Through a Fire"', *Guardian*, 27 March. Available online: https://www.theguardian.com/books/2021/mar/27/maggie-ofarrell-severe-illness-refigures-you-its-like-passing-through-a-fire

Allfree, C. (2020), 'Maggie O'Farrell Interview: "You Should Never Second Guess What Your Reader Might Want"', *The Telegraph*, 10 September. Available online: https://www.telegraph.co.uk/books/authors/maggie-ofarrell-interview-could-write-novel-hamnet-mother/?WT.mc_id=tmgoff_psc_ppc_dsa_culture&gclid=CjwKCAiAjPyfBhBMEiwAB2CCIrNnqFZNw4pZaZ2dN59ukrfY3UzbRQD0boB7ZiKU4upL4EtQNRevzxoC_mIQAvD_BwE

Kellaway, K. (2020), 'Maggie O'Farrell: "Having to Bury a Child Must Be Unlike Anything Else"', *Guardian*, 22 March. Available online: https://www.theguardian.com/books/2020/mar/22/maggie-ofarrell-novel-hamnet-interview-the-agony-of-burying-your-child

Levy, E. (2022), 'Maggie O'Farrell on 'The Marriage Portrait': A Look at Scandal, History and the Future', *The Seattle Times*, 30 September. Available online: https://

www.seattletimes.com/entertainment/books/maggie-ofarrell-on-the-marriage
-portrait-a-look-at-scandal-history-and-the-future/

Naughtie, J. (2016), 'Maggie O'Farrell – *The Vanishing Act of Esme Lennox*', [Radio], BBC Radio 4 Book club, 3 July. Available online: https://www.bbc.co.uk/sounds/play /b07hwwjx

O'Farrell, M. (2010), 'An Interview with Maggie O'Farrell', *BookBrowse.com*. Available online: https://www.bookbrowse.com/author_interviews/full/index.cfm/author _number/1491/maggie-ofarrell

O'Farrell, M. (2018), 'Powells Q&A: Maggie O'Farrell, Author of *I Am, I Am, I Am*'. Available online: https://www.powells.com/post/qa/powells-qa-maggie-ofarrell -author-of-i-am-i-am-i-am

O'Farrell, M. (2020), 'Maggie O'Farrell: I Wrote at Least 17 Separate Drafts of *After You'd Gone*', *Guardian*, 17 October. Available online: https://www.theguardian.com/ books/2020/oct/17/cxxcx-maggie-ofarrell-on-after-youd-gone

O'Keeffe, A. (2020), 'Maggie O'Farrell Talks About Uncovering Lost Stories and Voices in her New Novel, *Hamnet*', *The Bookseller*, 17 January. Available online: https://www .thebookseller.com/author-interviews/maggie-ofarrell-talks-about-uncovering-lost -stories-and-voices-in-her-new-novel-hamnet

Robinson, D. (2022), 'Edinburgh International Book Festival Interview: *Hamnet* Author Maggie O'Farrell on Surviving Lockdown and the Italian Origins of her New Novel', *The Scotsman*, 27 August. Available online: https://www.scotsman.com/arts-and -culture/edinburgh-festivals/edinburgh-international-book-festival-interview -hamnet-author-maggie-ofarrell-on-surviving-lockdown-and-the-italian-origins-of -her-new-novel-3817667

Sooke, A. (2010), 'Maggie O'Farrell Interview', *The Telegraph*, 17 April. Available online: https://www.telegraph.co.uk/culture/books/7597512/Maggie-OFarrell-interview .html

Website

www.maggieofarrell.com/

Index

adaptation   2, 7, 128, 141
agency   8, 73, 109, 110, 122, 126, 128, 141
alienation   30, 82
art and artist   33, 35–7, 41–5, 56–7, 68, 71, 76, 78, 104, 122–4, 126–8
asylum and asylum records   9–16, 20
Auge, Marc   6, 23–6
awards   1–2, 7, 42, 47, 77, 89 n.1

Balaev, Michelle   75–6, *see also* trauma and trauma theory
Barker, Pat   79
   The Eye in the Door   79
Barry, Sebastian   19–21
   Secret Scripture, The   19–21
(be)longing   7, 20, 22, 23, 26, 27, 30, 112
Benjamin, Walter   62–3
Berthin, Christine   61, 66, 72–3
   Gothic Hauntings   72–3
blindness   25, 28
body   4, 5, 15, 48, 50, 63, 66, 86, 92, 94, 98–100, 102, 109, 111–12, 122–3, 126–7, 137
Branagh, Kenneth   107
   All is True   107
Browning, Robert   121, 126, 131
   My Last Duchess   121, 126
Burnett, Frances Hodgson   14
   Secret Garden, The   14

characterization   3, 8, 51–4, 56–8
city   5, 7, 22, 24, 28, 29, 31–3, 37–40, 43, 56, 58–9, 63, 67, 69, 70, 84, 100 n.4
communication   52, 61, 66–8, 74
confinement   10, 23, 26
Connolly, Cyril   42
contemporary fiction   1, 2, 8, 40
counter-narratives   21
Craps, Stef   75–7

Deakin, John   36, 38, 39, 79, 80
defamiliarization   8, 108
defiance   102, 122, 127
deinstitutionalization   6, 10, 11, 19
de' Medici, Lucrezia di Cosimo   8, 121
De Waal, Kit   7, 23, 29, 30
   The Trick to Time   7, 23, 27–30
Dillon, Sarah   7, 31, 34–5, 40–1, 44, 125
dislocation   7, 73
displacement   29, 61
doubleness, doubles, doubling   8, 24, 48, 53, 62, 63, 65, 71, 109, 112–16, 121, 126, 141
Drought Act   82

Edinburgh   15, 22, 24, 25, 28, 143
editorialization   48, 50
Elizabethan (world)   8, 107 n.2, 108–10, 114, 115, 116 n.14, 119, 140
England   12, 28, 29, 44, 49, 99, 110
escalation   7, 47, 56, 59, *see also* Saunders, George
estrangement   7, 70, 74, 83

falconry   90, 95, 98, 100, 105, 119, *see also* Turberville, George
fatherhood and father(s)   3, 14–16, 18–19, 24–9, 37, 46, 54–5, 57, 78, 81–2, 89, 91–2, 99, 108–10, 113, 115–18, 141, 143
feminism and feminist   90, 98, 99, 143
Finland   44
Fletcher, John   8, 90, 99, 101, 105
   Tamer Tamed; or, The Woman's Prize, The   90, 99
focal character   3, 46, 50–6
Forter, Greg   7, 76, 77
Foucault, Michel   35, 40
fourth wall   38, 51
fragmentation   7, 13, 75–7, 80, 86, 134

Freud, Sigmund   32–4, 40, 62, 75, 79
    'Studies on Hysteria'   33
    'Uncanny, The'   62
Freudian   65, 76

gender and gender roles   10, 57, 96, 98
ghost and ghostly   35–8, 42, 65, 69, 72,
    73, 75, 85, 89, 104, 116, 117
Gilman, Charlotte Perkins   12–13, 18, 21
    'Yellow Wallpaper, The'   12–13, 18, 21
gothic and domestic gothic   7, 60–1, 63,
    67, 69–70, 72–3, 138
Granta   60
grief   3, 23–5, 29, 47, 76, 80, 89, 106–9,
    114–15, 117–18, 132
Guardian   10, 42

hauntology and haunting   7, 61, 65, 83,
    see also Berthin, Christine, *Gothic
    Hauntings*
hawking   90, 94–6, 100, *see also*
    Turberville, George
history   6, 10, 12–13, 19–21, 25, 26,
    31–2, 34–5, 40–1, 72, 76, 96, 118,
    119, 140
Holmes, Sherlock   35
    'Adventure of the Golden Pince-Nez,
    The'   35
Hong Kong   22, 28, 29, 112
Horowitz, Gregg   76, 77
husbander, husbandry   89, 90, 95–101,
    103, 104
hysteria   10, 17, 33, 119

identity and identities   1, 7, 8, 23, 25, 26,
    32, 41–5, 65, 70, 71, 76, 94, 101,
    106, 108, 110–12, 115–16, 122–4,
    127, 129, 141
in-between spaces   6–7, 23, 25, 30
India   14–16, 48
infantilization   12
institutionalization   6, 9 n.1, 10, 12,
    19, 20
interpretation and interpreter   50, 61,
    64, 66
intertextuality   7
inversion   8, 108
Ireland   20, 29, 30, 47, 136
Irish Independent   4
Italy   1, 2, 4, 28, 87, 122, 142

journey   24–6, 117

Kirkus Reviews   2

layering   3, 8, 38, 39, 49, 67, 122
Lichtenstein, Rachel and Iain
    Sinclair   9 n.1
    Rodinsky's Room   9 n.1
literary fiction   59
Literary Review, The   4
literary studies   31, 40
London   3, 22–4, 28–9, 32–4, 38–40, 48,
    51–2, 65, 73, 77, 84, 102–4, 108,
    110, 112, 115, 118, 140
loss   3, 7, 22, 23, 25, 29, 33, 36, 76–8, 80,
    81, 94, 106, 107, 109, 116, 117, 120,
    130
love   3, 7, 14, 22–4, 26, 29, 48, 55–7, 60,
    75–7, 85, 87, 106, 111, 114 n.11,
    116, 120, 130, 137
Lunatics Act   10

McCann, Colum   7, 47, 54–9
    Let the Great World Spin   7, 47,
    54–9
madness   9 n.1, 10, 12, 13
Mantel, Hilary   85
Markham, Gervase   93, 96, 98
    English Housewife, The   93, 96, 98
marriage   1, 7, 8, 11, 16, 18, 20, 28, 46,
    50, 55, 57–9, 82–3, 91–4, 103,
    105–6, 111, 118, 121–3, 125–7, 141,
    see also O'Farrell, Maggie, *Marriage
    Portrait, The*; O'Farrell, Maggie,
    This Must Be the Place
masculinity   95, 122
Massey, Doreen   67
melancholia   7, 12, 75–8, 80–1, 88,
    see also Forter, Greg
memoir   1, 4, 7, 75, 77, 85–8, 135–7,
    139
memory and memories   3, 5, 7, 15, 17,
    18, 23–5, 29, 31–4, 36, 40, 41, 54,
    59, 65, 66, 75–80, 82, 83, 88, 89, 99,
    109, 115, 118, 129, 130
Meretoja, Hanna   76–7
misogyny   20, 42
mistranslation   61, 134
Mosse, Kate   4
motherhood   7, 32, 41, 44, 45

mourning 7, 75–8, 85, 109, *see also*
  Horowitz, Gregg
multiple viewpoints 7, 130

narrative perspective 1, 7, 23, 26, 129
narrative structure 1, 4, 8, 36, 51, 55,
  122, 129
narrator 12, 20, 31, 33, 38, 46, 52, 54, 55,
  63, 64, 79, 80, 86, 87
New York 55, 56, 58, 59, 67, 71, 84
New York Times 2
non-chronological storytelling 3, 4
nonconformity 10
non-place 6, 23–6

Observer 60
O'Farrell, Maggie
  After You'd Gone 1–3, 7, 22–8, 30,
    33, 106, 111, 115–17, 129, 133
  Boy Who Lost His Spark, The 5–6,
    143
  Distance Between Us, The 1, 4, 7, 22,
    23, 27–30, 33, 112, 113, 119
  Hamnet 2, 4, 7, 8, 60, 89–120, 131,
    136, 139–41
  Hand that First Held Mine, The 2,
    3, 7, 31–45, 75, 77–82, 84, 106–8,
    111, 114
  *I Am, I Am, I Am: Seventeen Brushes
    with Death* 1, 4, 7, 75, 85–8, 135
  Instructions for a Heatwave 2–4, 7,
    46, 75, 81–5, 106, 108, 111, 112,
    114, 119, 130
  Marriage Portrait, The 1, 2, 4, 8, 112,
    119, 121–8, 130, 139, 141, 143
  My Lover's Lover 7, 60–74, 106,
    107 n.1, 108, 112, 134
  This Must be the Place 2, 3, 7, 46–59,
    107, 112, 114, 133–4, 136, 139
  Vanishing Act of Esme Lennox, The 1,
    6, 9–21, 33, 106, 134
  Where Snow Angels Go 5, 137
onomancy 108
othering 14, 16
overpainting 8, 121–3, 126, 128, 141,
  143, *see also* underpainting

palimpsest and palimpsestuousness 7,
  31, 34–41, 43–5, 81
parenthood 107

Park, David 7, 23, 25, 27, 30
  Travelling in a Strange Land 7, 23,
    25–7, 30
patriarchy and patriarchal
  conventions 6, 100
phantom 63, 65, 68, 69
picture books 6, 134, 138, 139
playfulness 4, 37
playwright and playwrighting 107, 109,
  110, 116
point of view 33, 46, 47, 50–4, 58, 64, 65,
  71, 72, 79
Porter, Max 4
Powell, Enoch 11
prizes 1, 2, 8, 60, 89 n.1, 90, 99
psychoanalysis 31, 33

readership 2, 132
realism and realist fiction 75–7, 81,
  85, 86, 88, 92, *see also* Craps, Stef;
  Meretoja, Hanna
reception 9, 134–5
reflector 46, 52
reincarnation 141
reinterpretation and reiteration 7, 72
Renaissance (art) 1, 8, 94, 99, 121, 122,
  125, 143
reviewer(s) 3, 4
Rich, Adrienne 41
  Of Woman Born 41
Royal Shakespeare Company 2

Saunders, George 7, 47, 50, 53, 55, 56
Scotland 16, 28, 29, 135
Scotsman, The 4
secrets and secrecy 3, 9 n.1, 19, 21, 33,
  67, 69, 70, 75, 82, 86, 127, 130
self-consciousness 8, 132
self-fashioning 90, 94–6, 103
self-reflexivity 36
sexuality 15, 17, 18, 20
Shakespeare, William
  All's Well that Ends Well 90
  As You Like It 118
  Comedy of Errors 112
  Hamlet 89, 90, 104, 105, 108, 109,
    113, 115–19
  Macbeth 90, 97
  Midsummer Night's Dream 112
  Romeo and Juliet 90

Taming of the Shrew, The 8, 90
   (*see also* shrew)
Twelfth Night 112, 113
Showalter, Elaine 4, 10, 12
shrew 8, 89–93, 95, 97, 98, 101
Smith, Zadie 7, 47, 51, 53, 57
   NW 7, 47, 51–4, 57, 59
society and societal norms 1, 6, 10, 12,
   13, 16, 19, 41, 94, 100, 142
spectres 3, 26, 130
Stanzel, Franz Karl 46
Stern, Daniel 41
   Birth of a Mother, The 41
Storytelling 3, 4, 7, 8, 47, 81
Strehle, Susan 1, 2, 31, 77, 81, 84

Taylor, Barbara 11
temporal boundaries 39, 40
textual space 23, 60
Thatcher, Margaret 11
theatre 67, 69, 104, 109, 115, 116, 118
transatlantic dialogues 2
translator and translation 7, 60–4, 66,
   68, 70–4, 134

trauma and trauma theory 7, 15, 28, 33,
   50, 75–8, 80–3, 85, 86
Truong, Monique 41
   Bitter in the Mouth 41
Tuan, Yi-Fu 6, 23, 27–8
Turberville, George 95, 105
   Book of Falconry or Hawking, The 95
twins 8, 107, 109, 112, 114–16

underpainting 8, 121–3, 127, 128, 141,
   see also overpainting

vantage point(s) 14, 46, 47, 53, 56
Victorian (era) 10, 11, 15

Wales 27
Welfare State 11
Williams, Anne 69, 70
wiving 91, 96
Woolf, Virginia 7, 15, 32–4, 39, 42
   Mrs Dalloway 32, 39, 40
   'Sketch of the Past, A' 33
   To the Lighthouse 15
writing the self 4

www.ingramcontent.com/pod-product-compliance
Ingram Content Group UK Ltd.
Pitfield, Milton Keynes, MK11 3LW, UK
UKHW020847171025
463953UK00024B/100